THE DAILY STUDY BIBLE

(OLD TESTAMENT)

General Editor: John C.L. Gibson

EXODUS

THE RESOURCE ROOM
` CHURCH HOUSE
9 THE CLOSE
WINCHESTER
SO23 9LS

EXODUS

H. L. ELLISON

THE SAINT ANDREW PRESS
EDINBURGH

THE WESTMINSTER PRESS
PHILADELPHIA

Published by
The Saint Andrew Press
Edinburgh, Scotland
and
The Westminster Press®
Philadelphia, Pennsylvania

Printed and bound in Great Britain
by Thomson Litho Ltd., East Kilbride, Scotland

ISBN (Great Britain) 0 7152 0493 9

Reprinted 1985

Dedicated
to all who
share in
the greater EXODUS
from the world of
sin
brought about by
our Lord
Jesus Christ

GENERAL PREFACE

This series of commentaries on the Old Testament, of which Mr. Ellison's volume on *Exodus* is one of the first, has been planned as a companion series to the much-acclaimed New Testament series of the late Professor William Barclay. As with that series, each volume is arranged in successive headed portions suitable for daily study. The biblical text followed is that of the Revised Standard Version or Common Bible. Eleven contributors share the work, each being responsible for from one to three volumes. The series is issued in the hope that it will do for the Old Testament what Professor Barclay's series succeeded so splendidly in doing for the New Testament—make it come alive for the Christian believer in the twentieth century.

Its two-fold aim is the same as his. Firstly, it is intended to introduce the reader to some of the more important results and fascinating insights of modern Old Testament scholarship. Most of the contributors are already established experts in the field with many publications to their credit. Some are younger scholars who have yet to make their names but who in my judgment as General Editor are now ready to be tested. I can assure those who use these commentaries that they are in the hands of competent teachers who know what is of real consequence in their subject and are able to present it in a form that will appeal to the general public.

The primary purpose of the series, however, is *not* an academic one. Professor Barclay summed it up for his New Testament series in the words of Richard of Chichester's prayer—to enable men and women "to know Jesus Christ more clearly, to love Him more dearly, and to follow Him more nearly." In the case of the Old Testament we have to be a little more circumspect than that. The Old Testament was completed long before the time of Our Lord, and it was (as it still is) the sole Bible of the Jews, God's first people, before it became part of the Christian Bible. We must take this fact seriously.

Yet in its strangely compelling way, sometimes dimly and sometimes directly, sometimes charmingly and sometimes embarrassingly, it holds up before us the things of Christ. It should not be forgotten that Jesus Himself was raised on this Book, that He based His whole ministry on what it says, and that He approached His death with its words on His lips. Christian men and women have in this ancient collection of Jewish writings a uniquely illuminating avenue not only into the will and purposes of God the Father, but into the mind and heart of Him who is named God's Son, who was Himself born a Jew but went on through the Cross and Resurrection to become the Saviour of the world. Read reverently and imaginatively the Old Testament can become a living and relevant force in their everyday lives.

It is the prayer of myself and my colleagues that this series may be used by its readers and blessed by God to that end.

New College   JOHN C.L. GIBSON
Edinburgh   General Editor

CONTENTS

D. THE PASSOVER AND THE EXODUS FROM EGYPT
(12:1–15:21)

E. FROM THE SEA OF REEDS TO SINAI (15:22–18:27)

F. THE MAKING OF THE COVENANT (19:1–24:18)

INTRODUCTION

Exodus, in Hebrew *Shemot* (Names) after its first word, is in many ways one of the most important and spiritually interesting books in the Old Testament. It tells the story of how God freed his people from Egypt and bound them to himself by a covenant. We are given an insight into the way this link with God modified the people's traditional law, and how God's grace reacted to a broken covenant. Finally we are given through the symbolism of the Tabernacle, which finds its New Testament expression in the Epistle to the Hebrews, a picture of how man should approach God in worship.

This ancient book, which has influenced Judaism perhaps more deeply than any other, raises several problems of transmission and composition, though there are not many textual difficulties. There are further problems connected with chronology, numbers and miracles. Though much light has been thrown on these subjects by archaeology, it has been inadequate to create a consensus of opinion among scholars. Since, however, these problems do not usually have a direct bearing on the spiritual understanding and enjoyment of the book, there will be the minimum of passing reference to them, sufficient to indicate their existence, but no stress will be laid on my own solution to them. Those points for which the average reader will require some explanation have been relegated to the Appendices, where they are dealt with briefly.

The Old Testament revelation was an adequate revelation to those who received it, and it should, therefore, be primarily interpreted in the setting of those to whom it first came. On the other hand the whole Bible is the revelation of the one God (Heb. 1:1f.) and so references are made to the manner in which the revelation given in Exodus finds its counterpart in the perfect revelation in Jesus the Messiah.

For the sake of simplicity references to commentators and

other authorities use only the writers' names. Full details can be found in the list of books for Further Reading. Comments are based on the RSV, but where it seems of value, reference has been made to other modern translations. The commentary divisions are for the reader's convenience and have no ultimate authority.

EXODUS

A. THE HOUSE OF BONDAGE (1:1–2:22)

VANITY OF VANITIES

Exodus 1:1–14

1 These are the names of the sons of Israel who came to Egypt with
2 3 Jacob, each with his household: Reuben, Simeon, Levi, and Judah,
4 Issachar, Zebulun, and Benjamin, Dan and Naphtali, Gad and
5 Asher. All the offspring of Jacob were seventy persons; Joseph was
6 already in Egypt. Then Joseph died, and all his brothers, and all that
7 generation. But the descendants of Israel were fruitful and increased
greatly; they multiplied and grew exceedingly strong; so that the
land was filled with them.

8 Now there arose a new king over Egypt, who did not know
9 Joseph. And he said to his people, "Behold, the people of Israel are
10 too many and too mighty for us. Come, let us deal shrewdly with
them, lest they multiply, and, if war befall us, they join our enemies
11 and fight against us and escape from the land." Therefore they set
taskmasters over them to afflict them with heavy burdens; and they
12 built for Pharaoh store-cities, Pithom and Raamses. But the more
they were oppressed, the more they multiplied and the more they
spread abroad. And the Egyptians were in dread of the people of
13 14 Israel. So they made the people of Israel serve with rigour, and made
their lives bitter with hard service, in mortar and brick, and in all
kinds of work in the field; in all their work they made them serve
with rigour.

(i)

To the semi-nomadic Hebrews who entered Egypt with Jacob,
the land, even though it was passing through an exceptional
period of famine, must have seemed a Paradise after drought-
stricken Canaan and the Sinai desert which they had crossed. It

was true that they were only tolerated foreigners, but that had been their status also in Canaan. In Egypt it was easier to forget the fact, because they had been given exceptional privileges, thanks to Joseph's position at court. There the shepherd's life had been very hard (Gen. 31:38–40), but here it was relatively easy, for the land of Goshen was recognized as being particularly suited for pasture (Gen. 47:6). In addition, as will be stressed when dealing with the plagues on Egypt (chapters 7–9), there was and still is a remarkable regularity of climate, which would protect them from some of the major hazards of a shepherd's life in Canaan. Some of the contrasts with Canaan are brought out in Deut. 11:10–12.

The enumeration of Jacob's family (verses 1–6) is to stress that, though no clear chronological data are given, what follows is the direct continuation of the Genesis story. With the easing of their conditions of life, there was a rapid increase in their numbers, though no miraculous element is suggested. As the sequel suggests, there was an intermingling with their Egyptian neighbours; 3:22 even speaks of Egyptian lodgers. There may also have been some intermarriage with other Semitic groups.

The statement that "the land was filled with them" must be understood of Goshen. There is no vestige of evidence linking the Israelites with other parts of Egypt. The virtual lack of Egyptian elements in Israel's vocabulary, laws and religion shows that there was very little assimilation—something Egypt's rulers did not in any case desire, for they looked on Egypt as a race apart (Gen. 43:32). Jacob's descendants had lost the pilgrim vision (Heb. 11:8–10, 13–16), as has many a Christian, and had become satisfield with what the world had to offer.

(ii)

Then God touched the iridescent bubble of the Israelites' material complacency, as he so often has to with the Christian. Suddenly everything changed; overnight they became suspects instead of being privileged. A new dynasty brought a new king, who knew nothing of Joseph, or perhaps did not want to. In fact, since Joseph had been given an Egyptian name (Gen. 41:45) and had married into an Egyptian priestly family, and the records were kept by priests who had no interest in keeping the memory alive of one who had not worshipped Egypt's gods, with the passage of time it may well have been forgotten outside Israel that he had been a foreigner.

We are not told the new king's name, nor how long a period had elapsed since Joseph's death. This is deliberate, and it would be foolish to suggest that tradition had forgotten the details. We are being told the story of how *God* took his people out of Egypt; names, titles and numbers played no real part in his victorious action, and so they are ignored. Scholars, whose duty it is to be concerned with such matters, may deplore this, but it was not written for them, and we should gain nothing if, in a commentary like this, we were to air their disagreements.

In his estimate of the Israelite population the Pharaoh was doubtless making the same mistake so often made in Britain or other countries with foreign minorities today. Because they lived in a limited area, as is the tendency of such minorities, their absolute number was exaggerated. Their nearness to the eastern frontier gave some plausibility to his fear.

The 19th Dynasty of Egypt (*circa* 1300–1200 B.C.), in which the Exodus story must almost certainly be placed, did much building in north-eastern Egypt by the Pelusiac branch of the Nile delta, now silted up. Pi-Ramese or Raamses, the new capital, was not far from Goshen, in which Pithom is probably to be sought, so the Israelites were handy for any unskilled labour, especially the brick-making which was essential.

Between the end of harvest in April and the end of the Nile floods in November, the average farmer in Egypt, unless he was able to irrigate it, was unable to work his land—something that has been changed by the building of the Aswan dam—and so provided a reservoir for forced labour, which was used for the building of the great monuments of Egypt, and which cost the Pharaohs little more than the food for their workers. So it seemed absolutely natural to the new dynasty to treat the Israelites even as they did their natural subjects.

At a stroke all the Israelites' privileges vanished, but it was harder for them than for the mass of the Egyptians, for they had been accustomed to privilege for a couple of hundred years. For too long in many countries the Church has taken privilege for granted, and where it has disappeared, for example in Communist countries, the blow has often seemed serious. It is always harder for the one who loses privilege, rank and freedom than for the one who never had them. At first, however, the shock of loss and their resentment prevented the Israelites acquiescing in their new condition, which in their fellow-serfs had led to early physical collapse and death. It was probably this that gave the impression of rapid increase of population (verse 12).

It is hardly likely that the RSV is correct in rendering "the Egyptians were in dread of the people of Israel", for they could easily have exterminated them, or expelled them from the country. We should rather render with the NEB "came to loathe". They could not forget that they were Semites, and perhaps connected them with the Hyksos, who had subdued and dominated Egypt centuries earlier and had been mainly Semites. It was this trauma that caused the Pharaoh to turn to irrational action.

THE FOLLY OF HUMAN WISDOM I

Exodus 1:15–2:14

15 Then the king of Egypt said to the Hebrew midwives, one of
16 whom was named Shiphrah and the other Puah, "When you serve as midwife to the Hebrew women, and see them upon the birthstool, if
17 it is a son, you shall kill him; but if it is a daughter, she shall live." But the midwives feared God, and did not do as the king of Egypt
18 commanded them, but let the male children live. So the king of Egypt called the midwives, and said to them, "Why have you done
19 this, and let the male children live?" The midwives said to Pharaoh,

"Because the Hebrew women are not like the Egyptian women; for they are vigorous and are delivered before the midwife comes to 20 them." So God dealt well with the midwives; and the people 21 multiplied and grew very strong. And because the midwives feared 22 God he gave them families. Then Pharaoh commanded all his people, "Every son that is born to the Hebrews you shall cast into the Nile, but you shall let every daughter live."

1 Now a man from the house of Levi went and took to wife a daugh-
2 ter of Levi. The woman conceived and bore a son; and when she
3 saw that he was a goodly child, she hid him three months. And when she could hide him no longer she took for him a basket made of bulrushes, and daubed it with bitumen and pitch; and she put the
4 child in it and placed it among the reeds at the river's brink. And his
5 sister stood at a distance, to know what would be done to him. Now the daughter of Pharaoh came down to bathe at the river, and her maidens walked beside the river; she saw the basket among the reeds
6 and sent her maid to fetch it. When she opened it she saw the child; and lo, the babe was crying. She took pity on him and said, "This is
7 one of the Hebrews' children." Then his sister said to Pharaoh's daughter, "Shall I go and call you a nurse from the Hebrew women
8 to nurse the child for you?" And Pharaoh's daughter said to her,
9 "Go." So the girl went and called the child's mother. And Pharaoh's daughter said to her, "Take this child away, and nurse him for me, and I will give you your wages." So the woman took the child and
10 nursed him. And the child grew, and she brought him to Pharaoh's daughter, and he became her son; and she named him Moses, for she said, "Because I drew him out of the water."

11 One day, when Moses had grown up, he went out to his people and looked on their burdens; and he saw an Egyptian beating a
12 Hebrew, one of his people. He looked this way and that, and seeing
13 no one he killed the Egyptian and hid him in the sand. When he went out the next day, behold, two Hebrews were struggling together; and he said to the man that did the wrong, "Why do you strike your
14 fellow?" He answered, "Who made you a prince and a judge over us? Do you mean to kill me as you killed the Egyptian?" Then Moses was afraid, and thought, "Surely the thing is known."

The Pharaoh's obsession gave him no peace. As supreme head of the state and the fountain from which all justice flowed he did not want to set an example of downright injustice, so he called

the "Hebrew" midwives and suggested that they kill the baby
boys at birth—they could have claimed that they had been
stillborn. The fact that only two midwives are mentioned
presents a problem to be dealt with later, when we consider the
number of Israelites as a whole. The suggestion that these were
the only two names remembered by tradition is hardly adequate, for it runs counter to the whole impression created by the
story.

It is not clear whether the Pharaoh thought that his power
and majesty would terrorize these humble women into becoming accomplices in his evil plans and traitors to their own
people—something that has happened all too often in the
history of mankind—or whether, the term Hebrew being wider
than Israelite, they belonged to some other enslaved Semitic
group. It could even be as Josephus in his *Antiquities* main-
tains, that they were Egyptians, which is, however, most
improbable. In any case the king met a force greater than his:
"they feared God".

Their excuse for not obeying may possibly have been partly
true, but clearly they lied, and the king could not punish them,
for in so doing he would have exposed his plans. God's reward
was that he gave them "homes and families of their own"
(NEB), that is, within Israel.

When theologians have discussed the permissibility of lying,
this has been one of the passages commonly appealed to. There
is in fact far less condemnation of lying in the Old Testament
than we find in the Church today. That is because of its deep
understanding of the plight of the small man brought face to
face with those who have thrown aside all mercy and morality.
To be killed for the sake of the truth is a noble ideal, but all too
often the skilled interrogator knows how to frame his questions, so that silence can betray and condemn others to death.
If, in the face of modern totalitarianism, not a few Christians
have lied, those of us, who have never been in their position,
have no right to sit in judgment on them.

The Pharaoh then found himself compelled to come into the
open. The fact that the Israelites could not hide their new-born

babies from the Egyptians shows how closely they lived together. But why were the babies to be thrown into the Nile? A minute's pressure on their throats would have been enough. J.H. Hertz argued, "As most of the Israelites, however, lived away from the Nile, such a savage decree could not have been strictly carried out". This is hardly the impression we gain from the story. The Nile was one of Egypt's greatest gods. It is hardly unreasonable to read the suggestion into the decree that here was an abominable people, who would not worship the source of Egypt's life and prosperity. Let the god himself decide whether they were to live. It is not difficult to find ways and means by which one can wash one's hands and declare oneself innocent of wrongdoing and murder.

THE FOLLY OF HUMAN WISDOM II

Exodus 1:15–2:14 *(cont'd)*

But even this act of the Pharaoh led to the opposite of what he had expected. Amram and Jochebed (6:20)—we do not know how near to Levi they were, for we do not know how complete the genealogies are—obeyed the king, but entrusted their precious babe to the God who had created the Nile. As a result one whom the Pharaoh despised and would have wiped out found a secure place at the royal court.

There are no means of identifying Pharaoh's daughter—the suggestion that she was Hatshepsut, the only female Pharaoh, is based purely on romanticism—and we do not even know how she was able to adopt the child. We shall not, however, understand the story as it unrolls, unless we grasp that Moses had all the privileges of the blood royal. In addition, the compassion of the royal lady was probably shared by many other Egyptians, and, though we are not told so, the Pharaoh probably soon felt compelled to rescind his decree. It could even be that Moses' deliverance was interpreted as the Nile's rejection of such sacrifices.

There is a widespread tendency to question the truth of this story because, so it is said, a similar one was told of Sargon, king of Akkad, about a thousand years earlier, but the precise force of the Sargon legend is far from clear. In addition, if we deny the truth of the story, it is virtually impossible to understand how Moses could ever have reached his influential position.

We are not told how long Jochebed nursed her son, but in the society of the time a baby boy was not normally weaned until the age of three, and in exceptional cases five—this will almost certainly have been the case with Samuel—and it can be regarded as certain that Moses stayed long enough with his parents to have his people's identity and hopes ineradicably impressed upon him, as well as their faith in the God of the Patriarchs.

Of the years that followed we are told nothing. Stephen's statement, "Moses was instructed in all the wisdom of the Egyptians" (Acts 7:22) was an obvious deduction from the position he held. The story told by Josephus and others that he led an Egyptian army against Ethiopia, i.e. Nubia, captured their capital, and married the defeated king's daughter is not intrinsically impossible, but there is not likely to be any truth in it. The Bible passes over these years as irrelevant and balances the Pharaoh's folly with an example of equal folly on Moses' part.

No motivation is given for the killing of the Egyptian (2:11). For all we know he may have been doing his duty, and his victim may have deserved his punishment. There is always a temptation for many to help the underdog, whether or not he is in the right. This was specifically forbidden in the Law (23:3), for it can lead to much injustice, as has been clearly shown in some of our modern legislation in its laudable efforts to help the weak and poor. While Moses, owing to his position at court, could virtually ignore the law, where an Egyptian commoner, presumably an overseer of forced labour, was concerned, he could not even reasonably guarantee that the law would not catch up with the Israelite. In the long run it must be very rare to achieve justice by unjust means.

The statement that "he went out to see his people" is interpreted in Heb. 11:24 by "he refused to be known as the son of Pharaoh's daughter". He had evidently learnt enough from his parents to have been sickened by his anomalous position in court circles and by the gross idolatry that surrounded him at every step, an idolatry he was forced to accommodate himself to and which he could not openly reject. But he evidently thought, as we so often do, that he could both give up and retain; that he could become a leader in Israel and yet enjoy his Egyptian privileges. He did not realize, for all his education, that the very position he held would arouse the jealousy of the Israelites. Part of the price that God had to pay for the reconciling of the world to himself was the self-emptying of his Son; he had to become poor that we might be rich. This is something that church leaders are naturally very slow to learn, and the lower and poorer those we would lead, the more we have to serve them.

On the other hand Moses' self-identification with foreign and feared serfs was bound to awaken bitter hostility at court. It has been suggested that he hoped to lead Israel out of Egypt by an organized rebellion. If this is so, it was even more foolish, for the Pharaoh had his spies everywhere, and before anything could have been organized, it would have been nipped in the bud.

ALL HOPE GONE

Exodus 2:15–22

15 When Pharaoh heard of it, he sought to kill Moses. But Moses fled from Pharaoh, and stayed in the land of Midian; and he sat down by
16 a well. Now the priest of Midian had seven daughters; and they came and drew water, and filled the troughs to water their father's flock.
17 The shepherds came and drove them away; but Moses stood up and
18 helped them, and watered their flock. When they came to their

father Reuel, he said, "How is it that you have come so soon today?"
19 They said, "An Egyptian delivered us out of the hand of the
20 shepherds, and even drew water for us and watered the flock." He
said to his daughters, "And where is he? Why have you left the man?
21 Call him, that he may eat bread." And Moses was content to dwell
22 with the man, and he gave Moses his daughter Zipporah. She bore a
son, and he called his name Gershom; for he said, "I have been a
sojourner in a foreign land."

The statement that Pharaoh "sought to kill Moses" implies that
he had not abandoned or forfeited his position—something
that was later to give him the right to enter uninvited into the
Pharaoh's presence—and so a certain circumspection in arrest-
ing him was necessary. This enabled Moses to make a clean get-
away, for his position would have enabled him to pass the
frontier guards unchallenged.

The Midianites are associated with the area south of Moab
(Num. 22:4) and east of the Gulf of Aqabah, but since they were
a semi-nomadic people, we cannot be sure of the area here
indicated, nor use it with any confidence in our identification of
the site of Mount Sinai.

In such a setting Moses, in his Egyptian dress, must have
stood out like a sore thumb, while the air of authority it gave
him would have helped him to enforce his will. The whole
incident should be compared with Gen. 29:1–10, which explains the position. The shortage of water in many parts of the
Near East meant that it had to be shared out on a strict system.

To this day girls in this area are commonly used as shep-
herdesses, but only to the age of puberty. Moses would have
married Zipporah, Jethro's eldest daughter, when she reached
the accepted age for marriage. Presumably his arrangement
with his father-in-law would have been much the same as that of
his ancestor Jacob with Laban, though there is no suggestion of
sharp practice on either side.

During the long years that followed it seemed as though all
Moses' providential training had been for nothing. His first-
class education was apparently being wasted as he devoted all
his efforts to keeping a few sheep alive amid the sparse

vegetation of a semi-desert land. There is no evidence that Jethro's acceptance of Moses as son-in-law had given him any standing in the tribal councils of Midian.

It should be noted that there is no suggestion that there was spiritual growth, but it seems to have been a period in which the poison of Egypt was eliminated from his system, and he seems to have realized that his talents and wisdom had led him to a dead end. His naming of his eldest son Gershom (2:22) points to a new appreciation of true values. The word *ger,* generally translated as "sojourner" (less correctly by the AV as "stranger"), i.e. a resident alien, meant a legally tolerated person; compare Gen. 23:4, where the purchase of the cave of Machpelah was made so publicly and solemnly because it conferred on Abraham the right to live there. The name "Gershom" would have conveyed to those who heard it Moses' recognition that he was merely tolerated in Midian. In the Hebrew, however, "I have been" is emphatic and shows a repudiation of Egypt as his home as well. (For a note on Jethro's name see Appendix I.)

B. GOD'S INTERVENTION (2:23–6:27)

ISRAEL'S CRY TO GOD

Exodus 2:23–25

23 In the course of those many days the king of Egypt died. And the people of Israel groaned under their bondage, and cried out for help,
24 and their cry under bondage came up to God. And God heard their groaning, and God remembered his covenant with Abraham, with
25 Isaac, and with Jacob. And God saw the people of Israel, and God knew their condition.

The seemingly casual remark "the king of Egypt died" is generally passed over as a mere preparation for 4:19, but it is actually the turning-point in the story. Pope's famous aphorism, "Hope springs eternal in the human breast" is a classical example of the shallowness of cultured humanism. For the Israelites in Egypt their ill-treatment and forced labour could be looked on as an expression of the ruling Pharaoh's paranoia, and the hope was that things would improve once he was dead. In due course he died and nothing changed. So, all hope gone, the Israelites remembered God and discovered that he remembered them.

The turning to God in desperate prayer is all too often not a last hope but a confession of no hope. A story tells of a terrified lady saying to the passing captain as the ship was buffeted by a terrible storm, "Is there any hope, Captain?", to which he replied, "Our only hope is in God." Turning even paler, she gasped, "Are things really that bad?" The very fact that even Christians are apt to speak of marvellous answers to prayer indicates how often they are expecting very little.

But the Israelites, like so many others, discovered that when they remembered God, he remembered them; a classical example of the attribution of human terms and attributes to God, for he never in fact forgets.

THE STORY TO COME AND MODERN MAN

The days are long past, when probably many people in the Anglo-Saxon world were introduced in their childhood to the story of Israel's sufferings in Egypt and its glorious deliverance. They were then taught to regard it as being in some dim, half-understood way, part of their heritage.

Today, however, the name Israel invokes, first of all, thoughts of the Jewish state of that name, something that its leaders, especially in their dealings with Egypt, seek to foster. Apart from that, probably a majority regard the story as approaching the mythical, lost in the mists of early history. When they hear of the annual observance of the Passover, they are inclined to regard it as falling into very much the same category as Druidic ceremonies at Stonehenge on midsummer morn. They find it hard to understand that it is still observed by most Jewish families, even by those that show few vestiges of traditional religion. They find it harder still to understand, when they are told that the majority of the increasing number of

Jewish Christians observe it, and that there are not a few non-Jewish Christians, especially in Israel, who find a worthwhile meaning in it.

So far from commemorating a misty event in the far distant past, the Passover, followed by the Exodus, together with the Cross and empty tomb of Jesus Christ form the foci round which the revelation of God to man revolves.

Modern man has been brought up to regard the universe as a closed system, governed by immutable and unbreakable laws. The celebration of the Passover in the widest sense is the celebration of the sovereignty of God over and in history. The events it commemorates have no archaeological finds to confirm them, but they fit their background and setting.

The story is, however, much more than a liberating challenge to a modern world-view, which makes of man a slave to the world, over which he should have dominion. It speaks too to the weary soul, who has been enslaved by the "the daily round, the common task", to all those who have not heard Christ's invitation, "Come unto me, all who labour and are heavy laden, and I will give you rest" (Matt.11:28). It speaks of deliverance to those who labour not in brick and mortar, as did Israel, but who are caught up in the "rat race" of modern business life, to those who are driven to work not by the taskmaster's whip, but by the need to provide their daily bread and all those modern luxuries and gadgets which we have come to regard as essential, to keep up their standard of living, to compete in men's eyes with their neighbours, or as the popular expression has it "to keep up with the Jones's".

THE BURNING BUSH

Exodus 3:1–6

1 Now Moses was keeping the flock of his father-in-law, Jethro, the priest of Midian; and he led his flock to the west side of the
2 wilderness, and came to Horeb, the mountain of God. And the angel of the Lord appeared to him in a flame of fire out of the midst of a

bush; and he looked, and lo, the bush was burning, yet it was not
3 consumed. And Moses said, "I will turn aside and see this great
4 sight, why the bush is not burnt." When the Lord saw that he turned
aside to see, God called to him out of the bush, "Moses, Moses!"
5 And he said, "Here am I." Then he said, "Do not come near; put off
your shoes from your feet, for the place on which you are standing is
6 holy ground." And he said, "I am the God of your father, the God of
Abraham, the God of Isaac, and the God of Jacob." And Moses hid
his face, for he was afraid to look at God.

As Moses was carrying out his usual occupation of caring for
Jethro's sheep (for such is the force of the Hebrew), God
revealed himself to him. Far more than we commonly realize,
this is our normal experience, even though the full force and
meaning of that divine breaking into our lives may await a time
of quiet and withdrawal, as will have been the case with Paul
during his time in Arabia (Gal.1:17).

It came also through the commonplace, but the commonplace touched by God. In the intense heat of the dry desert
land—we can reckon from later details in the story that it was
early summer—the spontaneous ignition of some dry thorn
bush was nothing unusual, but what caught Moses' attention
was that the flame continued without the bush being consumed.

In itself we may doubt whether we are to see anything
miraculous intended here. The "flame of fire" is the glory of
God's presence, which transforms but does not consume; it
marked the presence of the angel of the Lord, "Yahweh present
in time and space". It was intended to make Moses realize that
nature in all its uniformity is not a barrier to exclude God, but
merely a veil to hide the working of God's power throughout
life around us.

It may well be that the burning bush later became a symbol to
Moses of himself or of Israel, of how inefficiency, weakness and
valuelessness can be transformed by God's glory and power and
yet not be consumed, even as the Presbyterian group of
churches has borrowed it to express this very fact. But any such
thought must be excluded, when Moses first realized that he
was facing God's presence. Even more must we reject the kind

of suggestion that Moses merely saw the shrub called the "burning bush" in brilliant flower, or the sunset light falling full on a thorn bush and producing the effect of flame. *We* might make such a mistake, but not a man who had tramped the desert as a shepherd for decades.

No one has yet satisfactorily analysed a prophet's call. So it is here. However it was done, Moses knew that God had appeared to him and had chosen him for a task, but . . . !

"Put off your shoes [i.e. sandals] from your feet, for the place where you are standing is holy ground." In the East the removal of the sandals was regarded as a mark of respect, and the removal of the head-covering as a mark of equality. This was probably because the slave went barefoot; cf. Isa. 20:2–4. It is the fact, not the form of respect that matters.

It was the universal belief of antiquity that the place in which a deity had revealed himself became in virtue of that fact holy, i.e. belonging to that deity. In one way this is a right and proper feeling, but if it is not kept in balance, it can distort and repel, as do many of the "holy places" in Palestine. God saw to it that his revelation to Moses was in an unidentifiable spot, and in spite of the traditionalist, as we shall see later, we cannot even identify Mount Sinai (Horeb) with certainty. The Christian's attitude should be that of Cowper's hymn:

> Jesus, where'er Thy people meet,
> They there behold Thy mercy-seat:
> Where'er they seek Thee, Thou art found,
> And every place is hallowed ground.
>
> For Thou, within no walls confined,
> Inhabitest the humble mind:
> Such ever bring Thee when they come,
> And going, take Thee to their home.

I WILL SEND YOU TO PHARAOH

Exodus 3:7–12

7 Then the Lord said, "I have seen the affliction of my people who are in Egypt, and have heard their cry because of their taskmasters; I
8 know their sufferings, and I have come down to deliver them out of the hand of the Egyptians, and to bring them up out of that land to a good and broad land, a land flowing with milk and honey, to the place of the Canaanites, the Hittites, the Amorites, the Perizzites,
9 the Hivites, and the Jebusites. And now, behold, the cry of the people of Israel has come to me, and I have seen the oppression with
10 which the Egyptians oppress them. Come, I will send you to Pharaoh that you may bring forth my people, the sons of Israel, out
11 of Egypt." But Moses said to God, "Who am I that I should go to
12 Pharaoh, and bring the sons of Israel out of Egypt?" He said, "But I will be with you; and this shall be the sign for you, that I have sent you: when you have brought forth the people out of Egypt, you shall serve God upon this mountain."

There are theories of the Atonement which seem to suggest that there is an insurmountable barrier separating God from man. Here we have perhaps the most striking Old Testament picture of God's outgoing to man: "I have seen . . . have heard . . . I know . . . I have come down to deliver them." There is but one step for the New Testament to add, "in the likeness of human flesh and as a sin-offering" (Rom. 8:3). But why then should he send Moses?

However we interpret Gen. 3, the cause of man's fall is clearly presented as his desire to stand on his own feet and manage by himself, a desire in which we have all shared. The trouble was that whereas man at first thought himself thwarted by God, he later discovered that he was hindered by his fellow-men. In the face of the threat of anarchy society has applied force in one way or another, except where love and devotion have been able to curb individual ambition. The direct intervention of God can command obedience and submission but not love. To win this he uses the human mediator, be it Moses or Jesus Christ. The difference was that Jesus "delighted to do the Father's will", but

Moses had to be reduced to the stage where he had virtually no will at all.

Moses' question, "Who am I?" was a mere recognition of fact. He had yet to learn the meaning of Paul's claim, "I will all the more gladly boast of my weaknesses, that the power of Christ may rest upon me" (2 Cor. 12:9). God's answer was, "I will be with you"; more was not needed; see Matt. 28:20.

At all times there have been those who were convinced that they were commissioned by God, but who destroyed both themselves and those who followed them. So great is the danger of our mistaking the voice of our own desires for the voice of God, that humble men at all times have asked for a sign, and when it has been reasonable and not merely a cloak for doubt, it has been given them. Here, however, the truest sign of all is given: go, and your success will show that you went aright. "When you have brought forth the people out of Egypt, you shall serve God upon this mountain." If it is asked whether there is not the danger of going astray, the answer must be "Of course there is, but the God you humbly obey will check you, when you go wrong." The biblical picture of this is given in Isa. 30:21, where the divine voice is heard only when there is a turning to the right or left.

THE DIVINE NAME

Exodus 3:13–22

13 Then Moses said to God, "If I come to the people of Israel and say to them, 'The God of your fathers has sent me to you,' and they ask me,
14 'What is his name?' what shall I say to them?" God said to Moses, "I AM WHO I AM." And he said, "Say this to the people of Israel, 'I AM
15 has sent me to you.'" God also said to Moses, "Say this to the people of Israel, 'The Lord, the God of your fathers, the God of Abraham, the God of Isaac, and the God of Jacob, has sent me to you': this is my name for ever, and thus I am to be remembered throughout all
16 generations. Go and gather the elders of Israel together, and say to them, 'The Lord, the God of your fathers, the God of Abraham, of Isaac, and of Jacob, has appeared to me, saying, "I have observed

17 you and what has been done to you in Egypt; and I promise that I
will bring you up out of the affliction of Egypt, to the land of the
Canaanites, the Hittites, the Amorites, the Perizzites, the Hivites
18 and the Jebusites, a land flowing with milk and honey." ' And they
will hearken to your voice; and you and the elders of Israel shall go
to the king of Egypt and say to him, 'The Lord, the God of the
Hebrews, has met with us; and now, we pray you, let us go a three
days' journey into the wilderness, that we may sacrifice to the Lord
19 our God.' I know that the king of Egypt will not let you go unless
20 compelled by a mighty hand. So I will stretch out my hand and smite
Egypt with all the wonders which I will do in it; after that he will let
21 you go. And I will give this people favour in the sight of the
22 Egyptians; and when you go, you shall not go empty, but each
woman shall ask of her neighbour, and of her who sojourns in her
house, jewelry of silver and of gold, and clothing, and you shall put
them on your sons and on your daughters; thus you shall despoil the
Egyptians."

(i)

Probably more has been written during the past two centuries
on this section than on any comparable portion of Exodus, and
it, together with 6:2ff., has been made the starting point for far-
reaching reconstructions of the religion of Israel as well as of
the identification of the sources underlying the Pentateuch. We
shall ignore these questions here, and also those interpretations
of the name, however attractive, which involve textual altera-
tions.

Why did Moses ask God's name? There is no suggestion that
the name used by the Patriarchs had been forgotten (3:6,16),
and a new name would have implied a new God—for the
implications of 6:2ff. see comments on the passage. It seems
probable that the widespread superstition that the knowledge
of a hidden name, whether of a person or a deity, could give
some magic power over him, lay behind Moses' request, and
that he was looking for some guarantee that would assure
himself, and Israel, of God's aid in the struggle to come.

To those, Jews or Christians, who forget that Moses was a
man of his time, who had been brought up in Egypt where
magic was a very potent factor in men's thinking, such a

suggestion will seem derogatory. But it seems more probable than J.H. Hertz's suggestion that Moses was asking about God's fame, record or power. If there were any evidence to support it, A. Cole's suggestion that Israel would have expected a new title for God, if Moses had really received a new revelation, would be attractive.

In fact there is little reason for taking Moses' mention of the people very seriously, for in 4:1 they are an obvious cloak for his own unwillingness and lack of faith, in spite of God's statement.

(ii)

Yahweh (for the name see Appendix II) replied by linking his name, or rather title, with the verb to be *(hayah)*. He said *ehyeh asher ehyeh,* generally translated "I Am Who (That, What) I Am", which was the understanding of the Septuagint, which took it as an affirmation, congenial to Greek thought, of the immutability of God. It could well be this, though we may question whether such an essentially philosophical concept suits the time of Moses. Others have seen it rather as an affirmation of God's inscrutability, into whose being man cannot penetrate, and possibly including a rebuke to Moses for his question.

Many leading commentators, from Rashi, a twelfth-century Jewish rabbi, on, have however pointed out that *ehyeh* is grammatically far better rendered "I shall (will) be", and so render "I will be That (What) I will be"; see margin of the RV, RSV, NEB, TEV, NIV. J.H. Hertz explained the title, "No words can sum up all that He will be to his people, but his everlasting faithfulness and unchanging mercy will more and more manifest themselves in the guidance of Israel." McNeile expressed it by saying, "The writer seems to have striven to express the thought that the Divine name revealed to Moses was a summing up of the entire Divine character and attributes. These could not be fully understood by any one generation of Israelites, and so God would continually manifest all that he would be to his people. The name contains infinite possibilities of adaptation." This is, of course, equally true for the Christian, and it is probably the way in which we should interpret, "Jesus

Christ is the same yesterday and today and for ever" (Heb. 13:8). No one can claim to know all that is to be known of God and his ways.

(iii)

In the remainder of this section God demonstrates his knowledge and purpose in contrast to Moses' imperfect understanding. In spite of his fears and previous failure (2:14) the leaders of the people would co-operate with him (verses 16-18); Pharaoh would be *forced* to accede to God's demands (verses 19-26), and the Egyptians would surprisingly reward the Israelites for their labours (verses 21-22). This last point will be dealt with in connection with 11:2,3; for the moment it is sufficient to note that the RSV, in company with probably all modern translations, drops the indefensible "borrow" of the AV.

In a land like Egypt with its many hundreds of gods, great and small, the mention of the god of the Hebrews would cause no surprise, except possibly because of the use of the singular. But Pharaoh would take for granted that the god of a foreign, enslaved people would be inferior to the mighty gods of Egypt. The sequel shows that there was no element of deceit in the request for "a three days' journey into the wilderness", i.e. right out of contact with the Egyptian frontier guards. Pharaoh knew perfectly well that this implied no return; indeed, since Israel was a tolerated alien people, he would have no claim on their return, once they had left his territory.

ANYONE BUT ME!

Exodus 4:1-17

1 Then Moses answered, "But behold, they will not believe me or listen to my voice, for they will say, 'The Lord did not appear to
2 you.'" The Lord said to him, "What is that in your hand?" He said,
3 "A rod." And he said, "Cast it on the ground." So he cast it on the
4 ground, and it became a serpent; and Moses fled from it. But the Lord said to Moses, "Put out your hand, and take it by the tail"—so

he put out his hand and caught it, and it became a rod in his hand—
5 "that they may believe that the Lord, the God of their fathers, the God of Abraham, the God of Isaac, and the God of Jacob, has
6 appeared to you." Again, the Lord said to him, "Put your hand into your bosom." And he put his hand into his bosom; and when he took
7 it out, behold, his hand was leprous, as white as snow. Then God said, "Put your hand back into your bosom." So he put his hand back into his bosom; and when he took it out, behold, it was restored
8 like the rest of his flesh. "If they will not believe you," God said, "or
9 heed the first sign, they may believe the latter sign. If they will not believe even these two signs or heed your voice, you shall take some water from the Nile and pour it upon the dry ground; and the water which you shall take from the Nile will become blood upon the dry ground."

10 But Moses said to the Lord, "Oh, my Lord, I am not eloquent, either heretofore or since thou hast spoken to thy servant; but I am
11 slow of speech and of tongue." Then the Lord said to him, "Who has made man's mouth? Who makes him dumb, or deaf, or seeing, or
12 blind? Is it not I, the Lord? Now therefore go, and I will be with your
13 mouth and teach you what you shall speak." But he said, "Oh, my
14 Lord, send, I pray, some other person." Then the anger of the Lord was kindled against Moses and he said, "Is there not Aaron, your brother, the Levite? I know that he can speak well; and behold, he is coming out to meet you, and when he sees you he will be glad in his
15 heart. And you shall speak to him and put the words in his mouth; and I will be with your mouth and with his mouth, and will teach you
16 what you shall do. He shall speak for you to the people; and he shall
17 be a mouth for you, and you shall be to him as God. And you shall take in your hand this rod, with which you shall do the signs."

(i)

Many and varied are the ways in which "the evil heart of unbelief" expresses itself. We might have expected Moses to have stressed the impossibility of influencing Pharaoh and his court, even as we today tacitly, though perhaps seldom openly, tend to accept that the Gospel will not overcome the powers of Mammon and secularism in our own time.

Moses, far more subtly, excused his refusal to go by laying the blame on the inadequacies of God's people. Even so we are often prepared to lay the blame for our present impotence on the Church and think that this absolves us from responsibility.

The signs given to Moses—they were really signs *for* him, for there is no evidence that the people would not have believed without them—were essentially irrational, i.e. unlike the plagues that fell on Egypt they have no scientific explanation, and unlike the supply of food and water in the wilderness they served no wider purpose.

In exactly the same way today we meet those who believe that the power and love of God are inadequately displayed in his providence and preservation and in his transformation of lives through the Gospel. So they demand that he show his favour and power by the gift of tongues and healing. Just as in the days of Moses God often grants them their desire, but we may question how much conviction this carries, especially when we discover that others can produce the same results without claiming that they come from God; cf.7:8–12.

(ii)

Since there is no scrap of evidence from other sources that Moses suffered from any form of speech defect, we should probably regard his claim to be "slow of speech and of tongue" as a last desperate effort to find some excuse for not going back to Egypt. At the best it is reasonable to suggest that Moses was conscious that the many years in Midian had made his Egyptian very rusty and had deprived him of skill in courtly speech. The one thing we may be sure of is that the rabbinic story which follows is pure invention. The story tells how as a child, having alarmed Pharaoh and his wise men by stretching out for the crown, he was saved by Gabriel's intervention, which made him choose a hot coal which burnt his lips, rather than gold.

The history of the Church and its missionary work is full of stories of men and women called by God to daunting tasks, who had to face genuine inhibitions—Gladys Aylward is a well-known modern example—but obeyed and triumphed by God's grace.

Driven into a corner, with no bolt-hole left, Moses desperately faced God, saying, "Oh, my Lord"—note "my Lord", not

Yahweh ("the Lord"), thereby recognizing God's right to command him—"send, I pray, some other person". This was a polite refusal to go, but a refusal for all that.

We are not told how God's anger showed itself, for true anger does not need words to make itself be felt. God simply said, "This is what you are going to do", and there was no gainsaying his command.

(iii)

It is often thought that the provision of Aaron as Moses' spokesman was a kind of punishment for his unwillingness. In fact it was probably intended from the first, for it served to enhance his dignity as God's representative. In the concepts of the time supreme greatness was shown by unwillingness to communicate with ordinary mortals, except through a spokesman (cf. Acts 14:12). Since God had apparently already told Aaron to go and meet his brother, he had probably already been chosen for this task. So often in matters of obedience we discover that God has started to work before we have said, "Yes".

Taken in conjunction with 7:1–2, verses 15 and 16 are of outstanding importance for our understanding of the commonest Hebrew word for a prophet *(nabi)*. Earlier works, basing themselves mainly on the apparent etymology of the word, interpreted *nabi* as meaning an ecstatic individual. Modern understanding, in which usage is recognized as more important than etymology, interprets it as "spokesman". This fits in with the New Testament usage, where the prophet is normally the giver of an authoritative message for a specific situation in contrast to the teacher, who expounds God's will and purpose in general.

I WILL HARDEN PHARAOH'S HEART

Exodus 4:18–23

18 Moses went back to Jethro his father-in-law and said to him, "Let

me go back, I pray, to my kinsmen in Egypt and see whether they are
19 still alive." And Jethro said to Moses, "Go in peace." And the Lord
said to Moses in Midian, "Go back to Egypt; for all the men who
20 were seeking your life are dead." So Moses took his wife and his sons
and set them on an ass, and went back to the land of Egypt; and in
his hand Moses took the rod of God.
21 And the Lord said to Moses, "When you go back to Egypt, see
that you do before Pharaoh all the miracles which I have put in your
power; but I will harden his heart, so that he will not let the people
22 go. And you shall say to Pharaoh, 'Thus says the Lord, Israel is my
23 first-born son, and I say to you, "Let my son go that he may serve
me"; if you refuse to let him go, behold, I will slay your first-born
son.'"

When Moses asked Jethro for permission to leave, it was more
than politeness. By marrying one of his daughters, he had
become a member of his family, and his whole standing in
Midian depended on this. He did not tell his father-in-law the
real purpose of his return to Egypt, lest he should oppose it.
There is no contradiction between verse 20 and 18:1–6. Once
Moses had realized how grim the struggle with Pharaoh would
be, he wisely sent his family back to Midian; cf. 1 Sam. 22:3–4.

Once Moses had shown his willingness to return and Jethro
had raised no objection, God made it clear (verse 19) that he
had removed the final obstacles from the way. In modern
terminology, we might say, he had come under the statute of
limitations, i.e. there was no one interested in pressing a court
case against him.

This is no rare experience. Repeatedly, when there has been
obedience Christians have found that difficulties, real or
imagined, have faded away.

Already earlier (3:19) God had warned Moses that only
force, God's force, would make Pharaoh let Israel go. Now he is
told that the stubbornness would be the result of God's action.
True enough, in 8:15,32; 9:34 Pharaoh is said to harden his own
heart (for details see Appendix III), and so some maintain that
God was only saying Amen to Pharaoh's own attitude. It seems
impossible, however, to reject the interpretation that though

the Egyptian king was not forced to act contrary to his nature, yet the initiative somehow came from God for the furtherance of his purposes of blessing (Rom. 9:14–18), though it seems impossible to deduce, as some have, a predestination to damnation included in this.

We are, however, not dealing with a blind fate. This is shown by the warning to be given to Pharaoh. Though he was regarded as a god, he is to be warned of the danger of defying Yahweh. Israel is called his "first-born son" to make it clear that with all his pre-eminence in God's purposes, God is not rejecting other peoples (cf. 19:5); God's choice, unlike man's, does not imply necessary rejection as a result. The call of Abram and the miraculous birth of Isaac are reason enough for the use of the title "son".

A BRIDEGROOM OF BLOOD

Exodus 4:24–31

24 At a lodging place on the way the Lord met him and sought to kill
25 him. Then Zipporah took a flint and cut off her son's foreskin, and touched Moses' feet with it, and said, "Surely you are a bridegroom
26 of blood to me!" So he let him alone. Then it was that she said, "You are a bridegroom of blood," because of the circumcision.
27 The Lord said to Aaron, "Go into the wilderness to meet Moses." So he went, and met him at the mountain of God and kissed him.
28 And Moses told Aaron all the words of the Lord with which he had
29 sent him, and all the signs which he had charged him to do. Then Moses and Aaron went and gathered together all the elders of the
30 people of Israel. And Aaron spoke all the words which the Lord had
31 spoken to Moses, and did the signs in the sight of the people. And
— the people believed; and when they heard that the Lord had visited the people of Israel and that he had seen their affliction, they bowed their heads and worshipped.

(i)

It matters little that this scene is as mysterious as the darkness in which it is set. Clearly Moses was circumcised, for this was the case with probably all upper-class Egyptians. That Zipporah circumcised only one of her sons—for the flint cf. Josh. 5:2— suggests that the older had already been circumcised. In all probability she acquiesced unwillingly where Gershom was concerned, but had refused with Eliezer.

The sudden illness that overtook Moses expressed the fact, valid at all times, that however worthy or unworthy the individual, no one has the right to claim to represent God and yet deliberately to disobey his revealed will.

There are circles in which it is maintained that the Pentateuch was later edited to eliminate material felt to be inappropriate. It is just an incident like this, as mysterious to the early rabbis as it is to us, which shows how carefully old material was preserved, even if it was no longer understood.

(ii)

There follows Moses' meeting with his brother. In the light of 4:14 we should render with the NEB and the TEV "the Lord had said". Since there is no suggestion of a divine revelation as to where it was to be, it seems probable that Moses had found means over the years to keep in touch with his family.

We should not take Aaron's actions for granted. He was the older brother (7:7), and as was pointed out in the comment on 4:14–16 his acceptance of the role of spokesman implied subordination to his brother. His willingness to do so may well have made the people's acceptance of Moses the easier. It is not clear why Aaron is called the Levite in verse 14. It could be that he already was a religious leader among the Israelites, and if so his ready acceptance of his younger brother does him the more credit.

BRICKS WITHOUT STRAW

Exodus 5:1–14

1 Afterward Moses and Aaron went to Pharaoh and said, "Thus says the Lord, the God of Israel, 'Let my people go, that they may hold a

2 feast to me in the wilderness.' " But Pharaoh said, "Who is the Lord, that I should heed his voice and let Israel go? I do not know the
3 Lord, and moreover I will not let Israel go." Then they said, "The God of the Hebrews has met with us; let us go, we pray, a three days' journey into the wilderness, and sacrifice to the Lord our God, lest
4 he fall upon us with pestilence or with the sword." But the king of Egypt said to them, "Moses and Aaron, why do you take the people
5 away from their work? Get to your burdens." And Pharaoh said, "Behold, the people of the land are now many and you make them
6 rest from their burdens!" The same day Pharaoh commanded the
7 taskmasters of the people and their foremen, "You shall no longer give the people straw to make bricks, as heretofore; let them go and
8 gather straw for themselves. But the number of bricks which they made heretofore you shall lay upon them, you shall by no means lessen it; for they are idle; therefore they cry, 'Let us go and offer
9 sacrifice to our God.' Let heavier work be laid upon the men that they may labour at it and pay no regard to lying words."
10   So the taskmasters and the foremen of the people went out and
11 said to the people, "Thus says Pharaoh, 'I will not give you straw. Go yourselves, get your straw wherever you can find it; but your work
12 will not be lessened in the least.' " So the people were scattered abroad throughout all the land of Egypt, to gather stubble for straw.
13 The taskmasters were urgent, saying, "Complete your work, your
14 daily task, as when there was straw." And the foremen of the people of Israel, whom Pharaoh's taskmasters had set over them, were beaten, and were asked, "Why have you not done all your task of making bricks today, as hitherto?"

(i)

From 5:15 we learn that access to Pharaoh, a god though he was reckoned to be, was far more easy than it was about a thousand years later at the Persian court (Esth. 4:11). For all that, the freedom Moses enjoyed is probably to be attributed to his having been adopted by Pharaoh's daughter.

His request was skilfully phrased. Pestilence and sword, i.e. war, would inevitably affect the Egyptians as well. In addition Egyptian labourers were accustomed to receiving time off for their religious duties. It is not very easy to understand Pharaoh's answer, for it is not over clear how we are to interpret "the people of the land". It could be a slighting reference to the foreign serf-population—Hebrew had a wider connotation than Israelite—or more probably the NEB is correct in following the Samaritan text and rendering "Your people already outnumber the native Egyptians". In either case it would seem to imply that the needs of the state took priority over the whim of some god outside the official pantheon. Had the expression been invented, he would doubtless have referred to religion's being the opium of the people. The Pharaoh's attitude is one we constantly meet where an individual or organization enjoys despotic power.

(ii)

Today we find it difficult to understand why Pharaoh should have so stoutly resisted the request to let Israel go. In spite of the fears expressed in 1:9, Israel would not have formed any major part of the population of Egypt, so Pharaoh was not faced with the problem that the East German government sought to solve, when they built the Berlin wall. Equally it is improbable that Israel represented outstanding intellects or talents, so he did not have the excuse of the Russian today, when he prevents the emigration of Jews.

However much Israel's sufferings and forced labour may be traced back to the irrational fears of an earlier Pharaoh, all that in a sense he was really doing was trying to bring this alien group into line with the vast majority of Egypt's underprivileged population. The work that Israel was now forced to do had been rendered by the bulk of Egypt's peasants ever since the time of Menes, the first Pharaoh to rule over the whole of the Nile valley from the Delta to the first cataract. This was the "system".

Christians are apt to blame individuals for the difficulties in which they find themselves, while all the time these difficulties are merely products of the unChristian system in which we have to live, whether we like it or not.

The churches have all too long acquiesced in a social system, which makes no claim to be Christian. We tacitly confess the fact, when we pray daily, "Thy kingdom come", though we have grown innured to the fact and have grown so accustomed to it, that apart from some small groups and fringe sects, we do not try to do much about it.

Pharaoh then was protecting the "system". Had he let Israel go, it might have been used as a precedent which could have shaken Egyptian society to the core; similarly the exercise of true Christian liberty in our convention-bound society might have most remarkable results, which would arouse bitter opposition.

(iii)

"A three days' journey" did not imply that Mount Sinai was only three days' distant from the Egyptian frontier. It is a vague term and since the wilderness began on the other side of the frontier posts, it implied completely clear of Egyptian influence. It is impossible to say whether Pharaoh immediately grasped the full implications of the request, but any doubts must soon have vanished. Any legal claims that he might have had over the people of Israel were based solely on their presence on Egyptian soil.

(iv)

The great stone monuments of ancient Egypt, which stand to this day in almost undiminished splendour, are, with the exception of statues of kings and gods, virtually confined to temples and tombs. Ordinary dwellings, even palaces, were normally made from sun-dried bricks. Unlike Mesopotamia these were not kiln-baked until a much later period. Chopped straw was not necessary, but experience had shown that it made the bricks stronger and easier to handle. The clay used was simply the soil near the building site; the straw had doubtless been collected at Pharaoh's command after the harvest, which explains the Israelites' difficulty in finding it, while lack of centuries of brick-making tradition left them ignorant of the fact that they could do without it. The statement that the people were scattered throughout all the land of Egypt (verse 12) is to be understood in terms of normal Hebrew usage as that part of Egypt in which they lived.

Pharaoh's command was a typical example of the irrational and spiteful behaviour that has constantly marred the actions of those that have been entrusted with absolute power. Those who claim to have received authority from God should behave with godly forbearance and love. Many a mother who desperately needs help in the home today cannot have it because an earlier generation abused its authority over its servants or others who worked for them.

Dictators have generally understood that the easiest way to enforce their will is to appoint little dictators under them, who for the sake of a little power would be willing to serve the sources of power. We are not told what privileges the Israelite foremen enjoyed, but they discovered, as all in their position are bound to, that their privilege lasts only as long as they can satisfy the dictator rather than God.

O LORD, WHY?

Exodus 5:15–6:1

15 Then the foremen of the people of Israel came and cried to Pharaoh,
16 "Why do you deal thus with your servants? No straw is given to your servants, yet they say to us, 'Make bricks!' And behold, your
17 servants are beaten; but the fault is in your own people." But he said, "You are idle, you are idle; therefore you say, 'Let us go and sacrifice
18 to the Lord.' Go now, and work; for no straw shall be given you, yet
19 you shall deliver the same number of bricks." The foremen of the people of Israel saw that they were in evil plight, when they said, "You
20 shall by no means lessen your daily number of bricks." They met Moses and Aaron, who were waiting for them, as they came forth
21 from Pharaoh; and they said to them, "The Lord look upon you and judge, because you have made us offensive in the sight of Pharaoh and his servants, and have put a sword in their hand to kill us."
22 Then Moses turned again to the Lord and said, "O Lord, why hast
23 thou done evil to this people? Why didst thou ever send me? For since I came to Pharaoh to speak in thy name, he has done evil to this people, and thou hast not delivered thy people at all."

1 But the Lord said to Moses, "Now you shall see what I will do to Pharaoh; for with a strong hand he will send them out, yea, with a strong hand he will drive them out of his land."

(i)

The Israelite foremen had no conception of the grandeur and far-reaching scope of God's plans—for that matter neither had Moses—and so they assumed that Moses had bungled matters. Let us not blame them. Christ's disciples were no better (Luke 24:21) and honesty should compel us to acknowledge that this has all too often been true of us. It is natural to expect God to intervene in human affairs for the sake of his people, but we are all too often unwilling to accept that this may cause their own suffering as well, as is well brought out in Hab. 3:16–19, where the prophet sees the result of his prayer for God's intervention. In the Apocalypse we have pictures of God's sovereignty and triumph, but this involves his granting the Beast power and authority for a strictly limited period of time, which includes the ability to "make war on the saints and to conquer them" (Rev. 13:7).

Here, however, the foremen seem entirely to fail to realize that had they resisted the temptation of a little man-given authority and privilege, they would not have been flogged. Bunyan's shepherd lad knew this when he sang

He that is down, needs fear no fall;
He that is low, no pride.
He that is humble ever shall
Have God to be his guide.

(ii)

The people of the Bible, just like the modern Christian, have their apparently unanswered prayers and questions. The outstanding example of the latter is Hab. 1:13, to which no answer is ever suggested—I omit Mark 15:34 because of the great variety of interpretations given to it. Here, however, we may suggest three answers to Moses' unanswered question. It would be unfair to Moses and Aaron to suggest that there was some truth in the implication that they had bungled matters, but they had to be faced with the fact that in their own strength they could achieve nothing. Then, if we ponder Jer. 2:2, we may realize better the tremendous adventure of the Exodus for a people that for at least four generations had led a fairly sedentary life. Without this sudden worsening of their position many might have felt it better to remain in Egypt. Finally the Israelite foremen might have resented the loss of their power and position and opposed the Exodus, if they had not felt the full effects of Pharaoh's despotism. Many Christians have had cause to bless adversity, as it has driven them to Christ for salvation or closer discipleship. The NIV removes all ambiguity in 6:1 by rendering "my strong hand"; compare the TEV "I will force him".

GOD THE SAVIOUR

Exodus 6:2–27

2 3 And God said to Moses, "I am the Lord. I appeared to Abraham, to Isaac, and to Jacob, as God Almighty, but by my name the Lord I
4 did not make myself known to them. I also established my covenant with them, to give them the land of Canaan, the land in which they
5 dwelt as sojourners. Moreover I have heard the groaning of the people of Israel whom the Egyptians hold in bondage and I have
6 remembered my covenant. Say therefore to the people of Israel, 'I am the Lord, and I will bring you out from under the burdens of the Egyptians, and I will deliver you from their bondage, and I will redeem you with an outstretched arm and with great acts of
7 judgment, and I will take you for my people, and I will be your God; and you shall know that I am the Lord your God, who has brought
8 you out from under the burdens of the Egyptians. And I will bring you into the land which I swore to give to Abraham, to Isaac, and to
9 Jacob; I will give it to you for a possession. I am the Lord.' " Moses spoke thus to the people of Israel; but they did not listen to Moses, because of their broken spirit and their cruel bondage.
10 11 And the Lord said to Moses, "Go in, tell Pharaoh king of Egypt to
12 let the people of Israel go out of his land." But Moses said to the Lord, "Behold, the people of Israel have not listened to me; how

then shall Pharaoh listen to me, who am a man of uncircumcised
13 lips?" But the Lord spoke to Moses and Aaron, and gave them a
charge to the people of Israel and to Pharaoh king of Egypt to bring
the people of Israel out of the land of Egypt.

14   These are the heads of their fathers' houses: the sons of Reuben,
the first-born of Israel: Hanoch, Pallu, Hezron, and Carmi; these
15 are the families of Reuben. The sons of Simeon: Jemuel, Jamin,
Ohad, Jachin, Zohar, and Shaul, the son of a Canaanite woman;
16 these are the families of Simeon. These are the names of the sons of
Levi according to their generations: Gershon, Kohath, and Merari,
the years of the life of Levi being a hundred and thirty-seven years.
17 18 The sons of Gershon: Libni and Shime-i, by their families. The sons
of Kohath; Amram, Izhar, Hebron, and Uzziel, the years of the life
19 of Kohath being a hundred and thirty-three years. The sons of
Merari: Mahli and Mushi. These are the families of the Levites
20 according to their generations. Amram took to wife Jochebed his
father's sister and she bore him Aaron and Moses, the years of the
21 life of Amram being one hundred and thirty-seven years. The sons of
22 Izhar: Korah, Nepheg, and Zichri. And the sons of Uzziel: Misha-el,
23 Elzaphan, and Sithri. Aaron took to wife Elisheba, the daughter of
Amminadab and the sister of Nahshon; and she bore him Nadab,
24 Abihu, Eleazar, and Ithamar. The sons of Korah: Assir, Elkanah,
25 and Abiasaph; these are the families of the Korahites. Eleazar,
Aaron's son, took to wife one of the daughters of Puti-el; and she
bore him Phinehas. These are the heads of the fathers' houses of the
Levites by their families.

26   These are the Aaron and Moses to whom the Lord said: "Bring
27 out the people of Israel from the land of Egypt by their hosts." It was
they who spoke to Pharaoh king of Egypt about bringing out the
people of Israel from Egypt, this Moses and this Aaron.

(i)

In connection with 3:13–22 it was mentioned that 6:2ff. was one
of the keystones in the very widely-accepted documentary
theory of the Pentateuch. This theory will not be pursued here,
but we shall try to grasp the implications of the passage for
ourselves in the form in which the final editors have handed it
down to us.

God answers Moses' question by reminding him, "I am
Yahweh". This is not the revelation of a name, but a call to

realize its implications, "I shall be that (what) I shall be". Moses would have his answer in the development of events in the future.

The Patriarchs had experienced him as God Almighty *(El Shaddai)*. Strangely enough this title is found only six times in Genesis, three times in connection with a theophany, a vision of God; the other three times (once only as the Almighty) in the context of aid needed. More strangely still no completely satisfying explanation of *Shaddai* has been offered, but there are no good grounds for quarrelling with the Septuagint renderings "all sovereign" (which is preferable to "almighty") or "self-sufficient", i.e. needing no aid from others.

The Patriarchs had experienced his keeping and preserving power, but though he had made a covenant with them, they had not experienced its fulfilment. Now their descendants were to enjoy it. By this time, however, the Israelites were feeling too crushed to respond to mere words.

If we think a bit, we shall realize that this situation has repeated itself frequently in the history of Christianity. The very acceptance of the name of Christian, the very fact of believing in one God made acceptance of his omnipotence almost unavoidable and belief in miracle, until recently, obvious. But to many it seemed as though God were not concerned with salvation in this world. So repeatedly the enslaved and wronged resorted to the use of force, only to find that victory turned to dust and ashes. Perhaps the outstanding example of this in British history was the triumph of the "saints" in the great Civil War, where the death of Cromwell was followed by greater despotism and laxness of living under Charles II than what they had apparently triumphed over under Charles I. It was not until Israel had lost all hope, that God freed his people, and it was the message of a crucified Messiah that overcame the Roman empire, until the victors then turned to force to make others bow the knee. Today atheistic Communism has been discovering that the more it has been depriving the Church of position, privilege and power, the more it has shown that the powers of death cannot prevail against it (Matt. 16:18; 2 Cor. 4:7–12).

(ii)

The paragraph about the sub-divisions of Israel is not without its importance. We live in an age in which there is renewed interest in family trees and a searching after one's roots. For many, threatened with being overwhelmed by the crushing anonymity of modern society, this seems to bring a new feeling of individuality. If we try to picture the great historic movement of the two millennia from Abraham to Jesus, we can gain some idea of the unnamed millions who were swept away by the onward march of time (Ps. 90:5–10), leaving not even their names as a memorial. Equally we know that, so far as future generations are concerned, we are not likely to be more than names in registers of births, deaths and marriages, unless, indeed, these are wiped out in some nuclear explosion.

The genealogies which meet us from time to time in the pages of Scripture are a divine reminder that though we have been forgotten by man, we have never been forgotten by God, and even though man has not recorded any details of our lives, we have played our predetermined part in the working out of God's purposes.

In this particular context the purpose of the genealogies is to show where Moses and Aaron fitted into the scheme of things. So they are not carried beyond the tribe of Levi. Remarkably enough Moses' sons are not mentioned, and only one of Aaron's grandsons. But the mention of Levi's two elder brothers implies the existence of the other sons of Jacob, and privilege in God's service never implies rejection of others (see comment on 19:5).

C. WITH A MIGHTY HAND AND AN OUTSTRETCHED ARM (6:28–11:10)

GOD'S MESSENGERS

Exodus 6:28–7:7

28 29 On the day when the Lord spoke to Moses in the land of Egypt, the Lord said to Moses, "I am the Lord; tell Pharaoh king of Egypt all

30 that I say to you." But Moses said to the Lord, "Behold, I am of uncircumcised lips; how then shall Pharaoh listen to me?"

1   And the Lord said to Moses, "See, I make you as God to Pharaoh;
2 and Aaron your brother shall be your prophet. You shall speak all that I command you; and Aaron your brother shall tell Pharaoh to
3 let the people of Israel go out of his land. But I will harden Pharaoh's heart, and though I multiply my signs and wonders in the land of
4 Egypt, Pharaoh will not listen to you; then I will lay my hand upon Egypt and bring forth my hosts, my people the sons of Israel, out of
5 the land of Egypt by great acts of judgment. And the Egyptians shall know that I am the Lord, when I stretch forth my hand upon Egypt
6 and bring out the people of Israel from among them." And Moses
7 and Aaron did so; they did as the Lord commanded them. Now Moses was eighty years old, and Aaron eighty-three years old, when they spoke to Pharaoh.

(i)

The repetition in 6:28–30 is not so much, as some would have it, an indication of the beginning of a new source, but a sign that the storyteller is entering on a new section of the story. He is about to tell of the mighty acts of God, so he reminds his hearers of the inadequacy of the instrument used. When we tell the story of the mighty movements of the Spirit, we are generally tempted to depict their leaders as larger than life—though today with our vogue of the anti-hero, they may well be "debunked" and cut down to far less than their true size. This undervaluation might be all right, if it were intended to stress the truth of 2 Cor. 12:9, but the usual purpose is to belittle God by belittling his instruments.

The underlying purpose of the passage is stressed by God's calling "my people, the sons of Israel," my hosts, i.e. armies. Israel is probably the only nation in history to boast of its humble origin. Its ancestor was "Abram the Hebrew" (Gen. 14:13), i.e. a landless man, a second-class citizen, and the real beginning of the nation was in a mob of serfs. This stress on divine activity is underlined once again by the mention of the ages of Moses and Aaron, ages at which men normally sought rest from their labours; cf. Ps. 90:10.

God's purpose was that the Egyptians "shall know that I am Yahweh". This expression, particularly common in Ezekiel, where it occurs over sixty times in slightly varying forms, is not the revelation of a name but of the character of the one who owns it, as shown especially in his power, displayed in punishment, in protection and in grace.

(ii)

Taken in conjunction with 4:15–16 (see the commentary), 7:1–2 make the Old Testament concept of prophet clear. Just as Aaron was the middleman between Moses and Pharaoh, so the prophet was the middleman between God and the people, i.e. God's mouthpiece. Unlike the word "seer", which stressed the way the message came, at least to some prophets, it stressed his function.

While it is obvious that "I make you as God to Pharaoh" refers to his God-given authority, we may well ask ourselves whether more is not involved. Superstition is always likely to recoil on the superstitious. Pharaoh had been brought up to believe that he was a god, however much his experiences might contradict it. He may very well have come to think that Moses was in some sense a god incarnate, which helps to explain why he did not adopt drastic measures against the two brothers. This was one way in which God would harden Pharaoh's heart. A humble request *might* have received a gracious answer; a demand which implicitly denied his deity was more than he could stomach.

It is worth remembering that the New Testament phrase to ask something *in* the name of Jesus does not simply mean the repetition of a formula but implies that we are acting as Jesus' representatives. Of course, when it has become a mere formula, there is neither authority nor power in it. Through the power of the indwelling Spirit all Christians should be in one way or another Christ's spokesmen.

WHAT MAN CAN DO GOD CAN DO BETTER

Exodus 7:8–13

8 9 And the Lord said to Moses and Aaron, "When Pharaoh says to you, 'Prove yourselves by working a miracle,' then you shall say to Aaron, 'Take your rod and cast it down before Pharaoh, that it may
10 become a serpent.'" So Moses and Aaron went to Pharaoh and did as the Lord commanded; Aaron cast down his rod before Pharaoh
11 and his servants, and it became a serpent. Then Pharaoh summoned the wise men and the sorcerers; and they also, the magicians of
12 Egypt, did the same by their secret arts. For every man cast down his rod, and they became serpents. But Aaron's rod swallowed up their
13 rods. Still Pharaoh's heart was hardened, and he would not listen to them; as the Lord had said.

Egypt was a land in which magic flourished. For the ordinary man magic has changed its meaning and normally means no more than the conjurer's art. Basically, however, it is the belief that one can manipulate God, the gods or spirits by some form of words or actions and so make them do one's will. Though it was no essential part of magic, the magician, very often a priest, sought to impress the simple man by performing what we normally understand by magic today. Since the gods of Egypt were nature gods, their worshippers assumed that one who could do the apparently supernatural, would, therefore, also be able to influence, and in some degree control, the gods behind nature.

Just as Scripture gives no suggestion how Moses was able to do his signs (4:1–9), so there is no suggestion how the Egyptian magicians—Jannes and Jambres in later Jewish tradition (2 Tim. 3:8)—were able to do theirs. The how is immaterial: Yahweh challenged them on their own ground and defeated them.

We should notice specially that, apart from the last, there is nothing supernatural in the plagues on Egypt. They are intensifications of natural troubles, which have plagued Egypt down the centuries, though some have disappeared since the heightening of the Aswan dam and the resultant end of the annual inundation. Like most biblical miracles they point to God's control of nature rather than to power to do that which is apparently contrary to nature; cf. Rom. 8:28. This should warn us against paying too much attention to those who claim to have more than normal powers, whether they are used for good or evil. Quite apart from the possibility that they may be derived from evil spirits—a possibility that modern man rejects all too easily—there is no doubt that many men and women possess in their own right "paranormal" powers, which the simple man all too often thinks are supernatural.

The genuine fairy tale, that revealer of ordinary man's deepest desires, shows us clearly enough how man longs to break the trammels of nature by magic art and more than normal powers. Man, made in the image of God, has in our time, by accepting the trammels of nature achieved results his ancestors would have called miraculous. Even so, God's so-called miracles, so far as we can understand them, are based on his knowledge of nature, which he called into being, and on his use of its latent powers.

The elders of Israel did not ask for signs, but when they saw them, they believed (4:30-31). Pharaoh asked for one (7:9), but did not believe, even though the final outcome was one he could not have foreseen. "Pharaoh's heart became hard" (NIV), i.e. his whole reaction was one of rejection—the RSV "Pharaoh's heart was hardened" is ambiguous and misleading, for he himself did the hardening.

The result was what might have been expected. Pharaoh had asked for a sign, but what sign does one give to unwillingness and unbelief?

THE PLAGUES AND THEIR MEANING

The story of the plagues is so dramatic and to some so well known that we are apt to overlook some of the underlying concepts. They are often seen as a straight contest between Yahweh, represented by Moses and Aaron, and the Pharaoh. Closer reading should convince us that Pharaoh is far more than an individual. In the tradition-bound, monolithic society that had developed in Egypt over the centuries, he was the living symbol of Egyptian society as a whole, supported equally by the priesthood, for the "magicians" were all priests, and the high court officials, who were the instruments that made the centralized government effective. The people are mentioned only incidentally, for they were little more than serfs. So Moses was facing not merely the stubbornness of one man, but the whole weight of a civilization that had persisted for over two thousand years. For Pharaoh and his advisers to give way was equivalent to denying the whole basis of Egyptian society, though we must not rule out a special element provided by the Pharaoh's personal character.

Then, all too often, we do not ask ourselves why God should have acted as he did, for, after all, other methods were open to him. The answer is suggested by the subsequent history of Israel right down to the return from the Babylonian Exile. The outstanding charge brought against the people of Israel both in the historical and prophetic Scriptures is that they worshipped Yahweh as though he were a nature god, sharing his authority with the other deities controlling natural phenomena. Though there are few if any traces of Egyptian religion in the popular religion of Israel, Ezek. 23:8,19 show that it had had a corrupting influence. We must not think that this is merely a memory of the past. There are not a few Christians who quite readily confess their acceptance of popular superstitions. Though they claim to be children of God, they are perturbed by the breaking of a mirror, the spilling of salt, the sitting of thirteen at a table, and many such more. They are prepared to worship Lady Luck, and they lend a ready ear to the advocates of astrology, who claim that the position of sun, moon and planets, to say nothing of the signs of the Zodiac at the time of birth, exercise a determining power, which can be only God's prerogative.

There is nothing particularly surprising when we find age-old superstitions living on in remote rural areas, but what are we to say when we find them observed and revived even among university graduates?

It is true that as the anthropologist has thrown the net of his studies ever wider and wider, and others have turned their attention to what is best called the "paranormal"—the terms supernatural and occult are question-begging—we discover how true Shakespeare's words were, when he wrote,

> There are more things in heaven and earth, Horatio,
> than are dreamt of in your philosophy.

But this can never justify the Christian in believing that he or any other mortal can force the Lord of heaven and earth to do his will by some rigmarole or form of mumbo-jumbo, or that the sons and daughters of the living God, made and being remade in the likeness of God, can be dominated or even influenced by God's inanimate creation. Worst of all, perhaps, is the growing preoccupation with evil spirits. It is one thing to believe that they exist, a belief for which there is Scriptural warrant, and quite another to believe that they are able to usurp power over those who have come under Christ's lordship.

For those who experienced them the real victims of the plagues were Egypt's nature gods, who were increasingly shown to be powerless to protect their worshippers. At this distance in time it is impossible to be sure in every case which of the myriad gods of Egypt were affected, but it is quite clear that the first and ninth of the plagues showed the inability of Egypt's chief gods, the Nile and the sun, to stand against Yahweh.

Some think that it was unfair of Yahweh to make the Egyptians suffer in this way, but there was no other method of showing up the basic falsity of nature worship, which in one form or another was universal at the time. Israel could not fulfil the purpose of its election until it gained a true concept of God and of his power.

THE FIRST THREE PLAGUES

Exodus 7:14–8:19

14 Then the Lord said to Moses, "Pharaoh's heart is hardened, he

15 refuses to let the people go. Go to Pharaoh in the morning, as he is going out to the water; wait for him by the river's brink, and take in
16 your hand the rod which was turned into a serpent. And you shall say to him, 'The Lord, the God of the Hebrews, sent me to you, saying, "Let my people go, that they may serve me in the wilderness;
17 and behold, you have not yet obeyed." Thus says the Lord, "By this you shall know that I am the Lord; behold, I will strike the water that is in the Nile with the rod that is in my hand, and it shall be
18 turned to blood, and the fish in the Nile shall die, and the Nile shall become foul, and the Egyptians will loathe to drink water from the
19 Nile." ' " And the Lord said to Moses, "Say to Aaron, 'Take your rod and stretch out your hand over the waters of Egypt, over their rivers, their canals, and their ponds, and all their pools of water, that they may become blood; and there shall be blood throughout all the land of Egypt, both in vessels of wood and in vessels of stone.' "

20 Moses and Aaron did as the Lord commanded; in the sight of Pharaoh and in the sight of his servants, he lifted up the rod and struck the water that was in the Nile, and all the water that was in the
21 Nile turned to blood. And the fish in the Nile died; and the Nile became foul, so that the Egyptians could not drink water from the
22 Nile; and there was blood throughout all the land of Egypt. But the magicians of Egypt did the same by their secret arts; so Pharaoh's heart remained hardened, and he would not listen to them; as the
23 Lord had said. Pharaoh turned and went into his house, and he did
24 not lay even this to heart. And all the Egyptians dug round about the Nile for water to drink, for they could not drink the water of the Nile.

25 Seven days passed after the Lord had struck the Nile.

1 Then the Lord said to Moses, "Go in to Pharaoh and say to him,
2 'Thus says the Lord, "Let my people go, that they may serve me. But if you refuse to let them go, behold, I will plague all your country
3 with frogs; the Nile shall swarm with frogs which shall come up into your house, and into your bedchamber and on your bed, and into the houses of your servants and of your people, and into your ovens
4 and your kneading bowls; the frogs shall come up on you and on your people and on all your servants." ' "

5 And the Lord said to Moses, "Say to Aaron, 'Stretch out your hand with your rod over the rivers, over the canals, and over the
6 pools, and cause frogs to come upon the land of Egypt!' " So Aaron stretched out his hand over the waters of Egypt; and the frogs came

7 up and covered the land of Egypt. But the magicians did the same by their secret arts, and brought frogs upon the land of Egypt.

8 Then Pharaoh called Moses and Aaron, and said, "Entreat the Lord to take away the frogs from me and from my people; and I will

9 let the people go to sacrifice to the Lord." Moses said to Pharaoh, "Be pleased to command me when I am to entreat, for you and for your servants and for your people, that the frogs be destroyed from

10 you and your houses and be left only in the Nile." And he said, "Tomorrow." Moses said, "Be it as you say, that you may know that

11 there is no one like the Lord our God. The frogs shall depart from you and your houses and your servants and your people; they shall

12 be left only in the Nile." So Moses and Aaron went out from Pharaoh; and Moses cried to the Lord concerning the frogs, as he

13 had agreed with Pharaoh. And the Lord did according to the word of Moses; the frogs died out of the houses and courtyards and out of

14 the fields. And they gathered them together in heaps, and the land

15 stank. But when Pharaoh saw that there was a respite, he hardened his heart, and would not listen to them; as the Lord had said.

16 Then the Lord said to Moses, "Say to Aaron, 'Stretch out your rod and strike the dust of the earth, that it may become gnats

17 throughout all the land of Egypt.' " And they did so; Aaron stretched out his hand with his rod, and struck the dust of the earth, and there came gnats on man and beast; all the dust of the earth

18 became gnats throughout all the land of Egypt. The magicians tried by their secret arts to bring forth gnats, but they could not. So there

19 were gnats on man and beast. And the magicians said to Pharaoh, "This is the finger of God." But Pharaoh's heart was hardened, and he would not listen to them; as the Lord had said.

THE NILE TURNS TO BLOOD (7:14–24)

The first three plagues were little more than a softening-up process, a major nuisance but little more. The first was linked with the annual inundation of the Nile, on which the continuing fertility of Egypt always depended until the building of the Aswan dam in our day. Pharaoh's going down to the river (7:15) was probably for a religious ceremony to greet the inundation, but as Aaron struck the water it grew steadily redder. In itself there was probably nothing unusual in this, for much red earth is brought down from the Abyssinian highlands. This time the effect will have been heightened by various organisms *(flagelates)* and bacteria, which poisoned the fish. Obviously the Nile water was not turned into literal blood any more than Joel 2:31 was meant to be taken literally; cf. Rev. 6:12.

That this is the correct interpretation is suggested by the fact that the plague was allowed to run its course, i.e. it passed with the inundation. Also, by digging near the river, the people were able to filter out enough of the impurities to make the water drinkable.

Before the judgment began, God said, "Pharaoh's heart is unyielding" (verse 14, NIV), and at the end of it the verdict is, "Pharaoh's heart became hard" (verse 22, NIV); see comment on 7:13. Presumably for Pharaoh the visitation was little more than a major nuisance, though the death of the fish will have hit the common people hard (see Num. 11:5); since it was an intensification of a common phenomenon, however serious, it could be shrugged off as a coincidence.

The apocryphal *Wisdom of Solomon,* probably composed in Egypt about 100 B.C., states, "At the sight of the bloody Nile, the Egyptians with horror were reminded of Pharaoh's murderous command against the Hebrew children" (11:6–7), but since that particular form of barbarism had apparently long since ceased, it is not likely that many remembered it.

FROGS (7:25–8:15)

Frogs were associated with the goddess Heqt, who helped women in childbirth, but they were unclean for the Egyptians. They teemed in the Nile, especially after the inundation. Basically the miraculous element was that the frogs came and died at the times stated. Their leaving of the river was probably due to the pollution of the water; their death may have been due to dehydration or infection.

Pharaoh evidently cared little for the inconvenience caused to his people by the pollution of the Nile, but when the swarming frogs overcame all the efforts of his slaves to keep them out of the palace, the one who could summon all the luxuries of Egypt could not, like so many today born with a silver spoon in their mouths, endure the discomfort. He was willing to promise anything to get rid of the frogs and equally ready to forget the promise once they were gone. So we meet again the ominous words, he "hardened his heart". He dug his heels in and refused to be forced to do what he did not want to.

TICKS (8:16–19)

Retribution came swiftly. Though it is not expressly stated, we are clearly intended to see Aaron striking the ground in Pharaoh's sight immediately after his refusal to let Israel go. It is not clear what the third affliction was, for the meaning of *kinnim* is uncertain. It can equally well mean lice (AV, RV), gnats or mosquitoes, but the most likely seems to be ticks, as suggested by Cansdale. Their eggs are laid in the ground, where the minute young wait for suitable hosts to pass. It matters little what they were, for as Hyatt remarks, "In any event a country like Egypt, with its dry, hot climate, has always been troubled by numerous small insects."

They were probably too small to be manipulated by the magicians, who could not, in any case, reproduce the apparently spontaneous appearance of the vermin. The use of the capital with "God" (8:19, RSV, NIV) is misleading. It is not a confession that it was the work of Yahweh, but that the plague was supernatural and caused by some deity. Had they acknowledged the power of Yahweh, it might conceivably have weighed with the Pharaoh, but their half-hearted concession simply discredited them, and "Pharaoh's heart was hard" (NIV). Today also men are far too ready to say "supernatural", when they should say "God", and so spare themselves the trouble and duty of taking events seriously.

THE SECOND THREE PLAGUES

Exodus 8:20–9:12

20 Then the Lord said to Moses, "Rise up early in the morning and wait

for Pharaoh, as he goes out to the water, and say to him, 'Thus says
21 the Lord, "Let my people go, that they may serve me. Else, if you will
not let my people go, behold, I will send swarms of flies on you and
your servants and your people, and into your houses; and the houses
of the Egyptians shall be filled with swarms of flies, and also the
22 ground on which they stand. But on that day I will set apart the land
of Goshen, where my people dwell, so that no swarms of flies shall be
there; that you may know that I am the Lord in the midst of the
23 earth. Thus I will put a division between my people and your people.
24 By tomorrow shall this sign be."'" And the Lord did so; there came
great swarms of flies into the house of Pharaoh and into his servants'
houses, and in all the land of Egypt the land was ruined by reason of
the flies.

25   Then Pharaoh called to Moses and Aaron, and said, "Go,
26 sacrifice to your God within the land." But Moses said, "It would
not be right to do so; for we shall sacrifice to the Lord our God
offerings abominable to the Egyptians. If we sacrifice offerings
abominable to the Egyptians before their eyes, will they not stone
27 us? We must go three days' journey into the wilderness and sacrifice
28 to the Lord our God as he will command us." So Pharaoh said, "I
will let you go, to sacrifice to the Lord your God in the wilderness;
29 only you shall not go very far away. Make entreaty for me." Then
Moses said, "Behold, I am going out from you and I will pray to the
Lord that the swarms of flies may depart from Pharaoh, from his
servants, and from his people, tomorrow; only let not Pharaoh deal
30 falsely again by not letting the people go to sacrifice to the Lord." So
31 Moses went out from Pharaoh and prayed to the Lord. And the
Lord did as Moses asked, and removed the swarms of flies from
Pharaoh, from his servants, and from his people; not one remained.
32 But Pharaoh hardened his heart this time also, and did not let the
people go.

1   Then the Lord said to Moses, "Go in to Pharaoh, and say to him,
'Thus says the Lord, the God of the Hebrews, "Let my people go,
2 that they may serve me. For if you refuse to let them go and still hold
3 them, behold, the hand of the Lord will fall with a very severe plague
upon your cattle which are in the field, the horses, the asses, the
4 camels, the herds, and the flocks. But the Lord will make a
distinction between the cattle of Israel and the cattle of Egypt, so
that nothing shall die of all that belongs to the people of Israel."'"
5 And the Lord set a time, saying, "Tomorrow the Lord will do this

6 thing in the land." And on the morrow the Lord did this thing; all the cattle of the Egyptians died, but of the cattle of the people of Israel
7 not one died. And Pharaoh sent, and behold, not one of the cattle of the Israelites was dead. But the heart of Pharaoh was hardened, and he did not let the people go.
8   And the Lord said to Moses and Aaron, "Take handfuls of ashes from the kiln, and let Moses throw them toward heaven in the sight
9 of Pharaoh. And it shall become fine dust over all the land of Egypt, and become boils breaking out in sores on man and beast through-
10 out all the land of Egypt." So they took ashes from the kiln, and stood before Pharaoh, and Moses threw them toward heaven, and it
11 became boils breaking out in sores on man and beast. And the magicians could not stand before Moses because of the boils, for the
12 boils were upon the magicians and upon all the Egyptians. But the ·Lord hardened the heart of Pharaoh, and he did not listen to them; as the Lord had spoken to Moses.

Just as many commentators have seen an organic link between the first three plagues, the second and third being connected with the disastrous inundation of the Nile, so there seems to be a link between the next three.

   The first three were bound up with serious inconvenience, the next three brought actual loss and physical suffering. In addition they differed from the first three by the land of Goshen being spared from them. Then Pharaoh's determination shows signs of cracking, while the magicians, the supporters of the religious establishment, give up the struggle.

FLIES (8:20–32)

As in 7:15 the divine Pharaoh goes down to the divine Nile (probably flowing normally by this time) for ritual purposes, only to be challenged by the representatives of Yahweh. If he would not let Yahweh's people go, he would loose his swarms of flies, his lower creation, on him, but Pharaoh would know that this was no ordinary, natural visitation, for there would be an invisible barrier keeping them out of Goshen. Various natural-istic explanations as to how Goshen was spared have been offered, but since none carry conviction, they can be ignored.

   Though the flies are not identified, it is generally assumed that they were biting ones, like the dog-fly. In any case they so upset daily life that 8:24 says "the land was ruined by them", presumably by stopping all work out of doors.

Pharaoh had turned down Moses' first request for a break for sacrifice (5:4–5,17) as being based on sheer laziness. Now that there was a general stoppage of work, he graciously permitted it, providing it could be supervised by his police (8:25).

We need not analyse Moses' answer and ask what element in Israel's sacrifices or ritual would have awakened Egyptian wrath, or even for that matter why ceremonies performed in Goshen should awaken popular fury.

Moses knew that Pharaoh was cracking, and he was not going to be satisfied with anything less than full surrender. Pharaoh knew Moses' intention and so did not enter into an argument about his answer. One of Pharaoh's main supports had collapsed, but we hear the ominous words, "the Lord hardened the heart of Pharaoh". Even if the priests gave up the struggle, the incarnate god would not do so—to have been brought up from childhood to believe that one is more than a man is a terrible burden. For the time being he was still encouraged in his stand by the state officials, for though many of them probably did not believe his claim to deity, they saw in it the best guarantee of their own authority.

CATTLE PLAGUE (9:1–7)

The sequel to Pharaoh's failure to keep his promise was a plague affecting all the Egyptians' livestock: it is not likely that the Israelites had either horses or camels. The former were used exclusively for the war chariots, while the latter were still luxury animals, and neither feature in the story of the wilderness wanderings.

The very rapid death of the animals supports the idea that it was due to anthrax carried by the flies, but this cannot be proved. Since the flies did not trouble the land of Goshen, there was no reason for the livestock there suffering.

It has frequently been pointed out that in contrast with the statement that all the livestock of the Egyptians died (9:6), we have a further mention of them in 9:19, and of the chariot horses of Egypt in chapters 14–15. The usual explanation is careless editing of different sources, but since the same source is involved in the latter case, this is improbable. It is far more likely that we should stress "in the field" (9:3), i.e. the livestock under shelter was not affected. Grazing land in Egypt was strictly limited. While this plague meant ruin for many smaller Egyptians, Pharaoh remained unmoved by the calamity and his heart remained obstinate.

BOILS (9:8–12)

The earlier plagues had been an inconvenience, which grew steadily more serious. The death of the livestock had threatened the Egyptians' livelihood, but now it became clear that their lives were in jeopardy. Presumably the scattering of ashes from the kiln ("soot from a furnace", NIV) was a symbolic action to show that what followed was not mere chance. Boils, whatever their cause, were a commonplace in Egypt (Deut. 28:27); these may well have been caused by the bite of the flies, but it seems somewhat far-fetched to suggest that the priests "could not stand before Moses", because the boils were on their feet. Far rather it implies that they withdrew from the struggle, for they felt unable to resist further.

HAIL

Exodus 9:13–35

13 Then the Lord said to Moses, "Rise up early in the morning and stand before Pharaoh, and say to him, 'Thus says the Lord, the God
14 of the Hebrews, "Let my people go, that they may serve me. For this time I will send all my plagues upon your heart, and upon your servants and your people, that you may know that there is none like
15 me in all the earth. For by now I could have put forth my hand and struck you and your people with pestilence, and you would have
16 been cut off from the earth; but for this purpose have I let you live, to

show you my power, so that my name may be declared throughout
17 all the earth. You are still exalting yourself against my people, and
18 will not let them go. Behold, tomorrow about this time I will cause
very heavy hail to fall, such as never has been in Egypt from the day
19 it was founded until now. Now therefore send, get your cattle and all
that you have in the field into safe shelter; for the hail shall come
down upon every man and beast that is in the field and is not
20 brought home, and they shall die." ' " Then he who feared the word
of the Lord among the servants of Pharaoh made his slaves and his
21 cattle flee into the houses; but he who did not regard the word of the
Lord left his slaves and his cattle in the field.

22   And the Lord said to Moses, "Stretch forth your hand toward
heaven, that there may be hail in all the land of Egypt, upon man and
beast and every plant of the field, throughout the land of Egypt."
23 Then Moses stretched forth his rod toward heaven; and the Lord
sent thunder and hail, and fire ran down to the earth. And the Lord
24 rained hail upon the land of Egypt; there was hail, and fire flashing
continually in the midst of the hail, very heavy hail, such as had
25 never been in all the land of Egypt since it became a nation. The hail
struck down everything that was in the field throughout all the land
of Egypt, both man and beast; and the hail struck down every plant
26 of the field, and shattered every tree of the field. Only in the land of
Goshen, where the people of Israel were, there was no hail.

27   Then Pharaoh sent, and called Moses and Aaron, and said to
them, "I have sinned this time; the Lord is in the right, and I and my
28 people are in the wrong. Entreat the Lord; for there has been enough
of this thunder and hail; I will let you go, and you shall stay no
29 longer." Moses said to him, "As soon as I have gone out of the city, I
will stretch out my hands to the Lord; the thunder will cease, and
there will be no more hail, that you may know that the earth is the
30 Lord's. But as for you and your servants, I know that you do not yet
31 fear the Lord God." (The flax and the barley were ruined, for the
32 barley was in the ear and the flax was in bud. But the wheat and the
33 spelt were not ruined, for they are late in coming up.) So Moses went
out of the city from Pharaoh, and stretched out his hands to the
Lord; and the thunder and the hail ceased, and the rain no longer
34 poured upon the earth. But when Pharaoh saw that the rain and the
hail and the thunder had ceased, he sinned yet again, and hardened
35 his heart, he and his servants. So the heart of Pharaoh was
hardened, and he did not let the people of Israel go; as the Lord had
spoken through Moses.

The battle-lines were now clearly drawn. The god-man, who knew his impotence to influence nature was now prepared to take on the all-Creator, even though his priests had confessed their impotence. God in his mercy warned Pharaoh of what was involved (verses 14–17). This was no example of a non-moral nature god throwing his weight about, but a deity of might incomprehensible—this was not the time to teach mono-theism!—who was manipulating all the powers of nature to accomplish his purposes.

Pharaoh was not an accidental obstacle, but a God-willed means to demonstrate Yahweh's power (verses 15–16). Egypt would not be eliminated (verse 19), for God's purpose was to show his power in deliverance, not in destruction. This is an ever-recurring theme in Scripture. It recurs in a strikingly different form in Isaiah chapters 40–49, where God declares that he has raised up Cyrus, who does not know him, to be his instrument for Israel's second Exodus. We find it also in the Apocalypse, where even the powers of evil are called forth by the Lamb to accomplish his purposes for the Church and Israel.

Those who foresaw that Hitler could not win in his effort to annihilate the Jews were not fanatics, but rather those who understood Scripture sanely. In the same way those who know that Marxism can never finally prevail against the Church are clearer-eyed than those who proclaim that the Church has had its day.

Some may not like its martial tune, but the hymn is true when it affirms:

> Crowns and thrones may perish,
>   Kingdoms rise and wane,
> But the Church of Jesus
>   Constant will remain
>
> Gates of hell can never
>   'gainst that church prevail;
> We have Christ's own promise
>   And that must prevail.

Now as the threat to life and limb increased, so did the miraculous element. True enough, the hailstorm was, like what had gone before, an intensification of the natural, but earlier plagues had greatly intensified natural troubles that were relatively common in Egypt. However in a virtually rainless land (annual average eight inches on the Mediterranean coast, less than an inch at Cairo, and virtually nil at Aswan) hail was a rarity.

The thunderstorm, of a ferocity seldom experienced in more temperate latitudes, must in itself have been terrifying; the "fire" (verse 24) was, of course, lightning. When we remember how much damage can be done by small hailstones, we can imagine their effect, when they were big enough to kill man and beast. They must, in addition, have broken down the huts of many of the poorer people.

We must be careful how we criticize Pharaoh for once more breaking his word. The plagues were mitigated up till then. Now the warning was, "This time I will strike home with all my plagues against you" (verse 14, NEB). God has given men free will. He can crush it, but then man ceases to be fully man. It is a law of God's creation that to fall below what we should be brings suffering and death, but these will not recreate the image and likeness of God in us. This we find only as we find God. As Elijah discovered, when God spoke to him at Sinai (Horeb), it was with a still, small voice, not in wind, earthquake or fire (1 Kgs. 19:11–12). It is one of the paradoxes of religious experience that while it is ultimately in the stillness that we meet with God, yet we need the storm and earthquake to prepare us for the stillness. Pharaoh thought himself a god, and there was no hope of his bowing before the God of gods, until all the storms of life had broken about his head.

LOCUSTS

Exodus 10:1–20

1 Then the Lord said to Moses, "Go in to Pharaoh; for I have hardened his heart and the heart of his servants, that I may show

2 these signs of mine among them, and that you may tell in the hearing of your son and your son's son how I have made sport of the Egyptians and what signs I have done among them; that you may know that I am the Lord."

3 So Moses and Aaron went in to Pharaoh, and said to him, "Thus says the Lord, the God of the Hebrews, 'How long will you refuse to humble yourself before me? Let my people go, that they may serve 4 me. For if you refuse to let my people go, behold, tomorrow I will 5 bring locusts into your country, and they shall cover the face of the land, so that no one can see the land; and they shall eat what is left to you after the hail, and they shall eat every tree of yours which grows 6 in the field, and they shall fill your houses, and the houses of all your servants and of all the Egyptians; as neither your fathers nor your grandfathers have seen, from the day they came on earth to this day.' " Then he turned and went out from Pharaoh.

7 And Pharaoh's servants said to him, "How long shall this man be a snare to us? Let the men go, that they may serve the Lord their 8 God; do you not yet understand that Egypt is ruined?" So Moses and Aaron were brought back to Pharaoh; and he said to them, "Go, 9 serve the Lord your God; but who are to go?" And Moses said, "We will go with our young and our old; we will go with our sons and daughters and with our flocks and herds, for we must hold a feast to 10 the Lord." And he said to them, "The Lord be with you, if ever I let you and your little ones go! Look, you have some evil purpose in 11 mind. No! Go, the men among you, and serve the Lord, for that is what you desire." And they were driven out from Pharaoh's presence.

12 Then the Lord said to Moses, "Stretch out your hand over the land of Egypt for the locusts, that they may come upon the land of 13 Egypt, and eat every plant in the land, all that the hail has left." So Moses stretched forth his rod over the land of Egypt, and the Lord brought an east wind upon the land all that day and all that night; 14 and when it was morning the east wind had brought the locusts. And the locusts came up over all the land of Egypt, and settled on the whole country of Egypt, such a dense swarm of locusts as had never 15 been before, nor ever shall be again. For they covered the face of the whole land, so that the land was darkened, and they ate all the plants in the land and all the fruit of the trees which the hail had left; not a green thing remained, neither tree nor plant of the field, through all 16 the land of Egypt. Then Pharaoh called Moses and Aaron in haste.

and said, "I have sinned against the Lord your God, and against you.
17 Now therefore, forgive my sin, I pray you, only this once, and
18 entreat the Lord your God only to remove this death from me." So
19 he went out from Pharaoh, and entreated the Lord. And the Lord
turned a very strong west wind, which lifted the locusts and drove
them into the Red Sea; not a single locust was left in all the country
20 of Egypt. But the Lord hardened Pharaoh's heart, and he did not let
the children of Israel go.

The locust is an apparently harmless insect, somewhat larger
than our grasshopper and cricket. Normally it presents no
threat to man, and it can even offer an acceptable addition to
his diet (Lev. 11:21–22; Matt. 3:4). But like many other insects
and small animals, once circumstances are favourable (compare the rabbit in Australia) it can threaten man's existence by
devouring the crops on which he depends. For the lands
bordering on the deserts of the Near and Middle East the locust
was a name of terror, and still is, in spite of man's modern
technology of destruction, which seem to be inadequate to stem
the locust swarms, once they have reached full strength. Joel
chapter 2, if we allow for some slight poetic licence, shows the
impression created by a locust swarm.

The gardener and farmer in the West, in spite of all its
science, may well think of some other pest that may threaten
ruin, but it should also make us think of how the power of God
is shown by his use of the very small in destruction.

Even the proud lords of Egypt turned pale when they heard
of the threat of the locusts. The hail had already crippled them,
and they turned on Pharaoh demanding positive action, but
then put their heads together discussing how the impact of
concession could be minimized.

Since they will have judged Yahweh by their own nature
gods, they probably believed that all he really wanted was
worship and sacrifice; see 5:1–3 and 8:25–28. The idea that he
wanted such a rabble as this people was too absurd to contem-
plate. Even today we find it hard to accept; see 1 Cor. 1:26–29.
Except in certain fertility cults in nature religions the woman
normally had little or no part to play, and so the concession

suggested, that only the men be allowed to go, was a genuine one. But then it became clear, as Pharaoh had doubtless known all along, that freedom and not merely worship was the goal, "the evil purpose" he speaks of in verse 10.

Since the locusts were carried by a strong wind from the east, they had presumably been building up their numbers in the Arabian desert, one of their normal breeding grounds. The reality caused the braggart on the throne of Egypt to collapse with a sob of "only this once", and, like millions before and after him, with the relief came forgetfulness. It could be that a more dramatic way of getting rid of the locusts would have impressed him more deeply. We remember how Naaman rebelled against the simplicity of the cure for his leprosy (2 Kgs. 5:11–12). In the very simplicity of God's methods we often fail to see the best evidence for his almightiness.

DARKNESS

Exodus 10:21–29

21 Then the Lord said to Moses, "Stretch out your hand toward heaven that there may be darkness over the land of Egypt, a darkness to be
22 felt." So Moses stretched out his hand toward heaven, and there was
23 thick darkness in all the land of Egypt three days; they did not see one another, nor did any rise from his place for three days; but all the
24 people of Israel had light where they dwelt. Then Pharaoh called Moses, and said, "Go, serve the Lord; your children also may go
25 with you; only let your flocks and your herds remain behind." But Moses said, "You must also let us have sacrifices and burnt
26 offerings, that we may sacrifice to the Lord our God. Our cattle also must go with us; not a hoof shall be left behind, for we must take of them to serve the Lord our God, and we do not know with what we
27 must serve the Lord until we arrive there." But the Lord hardened
28 Pharaoh's heart, and he would not let them go. Then Pharaoh said to him, "Get away from me; take heed to yourself; never see my face
29 again; for in the day you see my face you shall die." Moses said, "As you say! I will not see your face again."

Before God broke the heart and the resistance of the Egyptians he gave one last warning. Though it is not expressly stated, it should be clear that when Moses stretched out his hand heavenward, it was done, if not in the sight of Pharaoh, at least in the presence of some high member of the court.

There is general agreement as to the nature of this plague. It was caused by the strong wind that had blown the locusts away, but it had also brought a severe sandstorm with it, which not only shut out the light of the sun, but also shut in and nearly smothered the individual. Under such circumstances even sophisticated means of artificial lighting, beyond anything available at that time, have little or no value.

The plagues had started with a blow at the prestige of the Nile, one of Egypt's two leading deities. Now it was the other, the sun, which was shown to be powerless to withstand the power of Yahweh and his representatives. It was also the crowning insult for Pharaoh, who was held to be in some sense the incarnation of Amun-Ra, the sun god.

As with the first visitation, this was allowed to run its course. At the end of the three days Pharaoh was ready to surrender. It is unlikely that he attributed much value to the retaining of the cattle of the Hebrews. Rather it was his last desperate effort to "save face", something that is so important to the Oriental, and, if we were willing to acknowledge it, very often to us.

Had Moses been waging a political battle, he might well have accepted some such compromise, but from God's enemy he demanded unconditional surrender. Man would always like to bargain with God, as Jacob did at Bethel (Gen. 28:20–22); but when he returned from Paddan-aram, God having done far more for him than he ever expected, he found that the need for complete surrender was awaiting him (Gen. 32:22–29).

There is no more reason for taking Moses' answer to Pharaoh's angry rejection of any more negotiation (verse 19) as being any more inspired than Pharaoh's words. They were to meet again briefly (12:31).

THE LAST PLAGUE

Exodus 11:1-10

1 The Lord said to Moses, "Yet one plague more I will bring upon Pharaoh and upon Egypt; afterwards he will let you go hence; when 2 he lets you go, he will drive you away completely. Speak now in the hearing of the people, that they ask, every man of his neighbour and 3 every woman of her neighbour, jewelry of silver and of gold." And the Lord gave the people favour in the sight of the Egyptians. Moreover, the man Moses was very great in the land of Egypt, in the sight of Pharaoh's servants and in the sight of the people.

4 And Moses said, "Thus says the Lord: About midnight I will go 5 forth in the midst of Egypt; and all the first-born in the land of Egypt shall die, from the first-born of Pharaoh who sits upon his throne, even to the first-born of the maidservant who is behind the mill; and 6 all the first-born of the cattle. And there shall be a great cry throughout all the land of Egypt, such as there has never been, nor 7 ever shall be again. But against any of the people of Israel, either man or beast, not a dog shall growl; that you may know that the 8 Lord makes a distinction between the Egyptians and Israel. And all these your servants shall come down to me, and bow down to me, saying, 'Get you out, and all the people who follow you.' And after that I will go out." And he went out from Pharaoh in hot anger. 9 Then the Lord said to Moses, "Pharaoh will not listen to you; that my wonders may be multiplied in the land of Egypt."

10 Moses and Aaron did all these wonders before Pharaoh; and the Lord hardened Pharaoh's heart, and he did not let the people of Israel go out of his land.

We, with our greater feeling for logic and order, which we have inherited from the Greeks, link the last plague closely with the nine that went before it. But here, as is shown by the various repetitions in this chapter, e.g. verses 3, 10, it is clear that the story of the plagues is being wound up, the last being reserved for the next section on the Passover. But it seems advisable to bow to our conventions and consider here some of the more general aspects of the last blow to Egypt, though much could be said for the Hebraic manner of seeing things. Tradition is such, that we seldom stop to think of what was involved in the death of the first-born. But terrible as it was, it is doubtful whether it was as terrible as we normally assume.

In 13:2, 11–15 we have instructions as to how the first-born among humans and domestic animals are to be treated, *if they are males,* and this is repeated in 34:19–20. It seems clear that females are completely excluded for reasons that are not even hinted at, so there seems to be no valid reason for assuming that first-born daughters were in jeopardy. There is no suggestion either that fathers were in danger because they happened to be first-born sons. They may have been, but we must not take it for granted. We forget that "there was not a house, where one was not dead" (12:30) is a typical piece of oriental writing, for there must have been homes, especially in the light of Egypt's high infantile mortality, where there was no first-born to die.

In addition, we cannot exclude the probability, that some Egyptians, especially among the humbler classes, imitated the ritual the Israelites were carrying through. So while we must think of the judgment as a terrible blow to the Egyptians, especially to the wealthier, where the proportion of first-born dying in infancy will have been far lower than among the poor peasants, we are hardly called on to imagine the immense mortality often thought of.

Possibly no land in antiquity was more obsessed with death than Egypt. The real power of the priesthood lay in its alleged ability to guarantee the dead a safe passage to the "Western World" under the benign rule of Osiris. This terrible visitation which defied and defies all rational explanation, showed that Yahweh was not only lord of the forces of nature, but also of life and death.

It is more than likely that we should render "the Lord had said to Moses" in verse 1, for verse 4 is obviously the continuation of 10:29, which introduced Moses' parting words to Pharaoh. Verse 8 suggests that even as the priesthood had collapsed, so now the high court officials were prepared too late to defy their master.

D. THE PASSOVER AND THE EXODUS FROM EGYPT (12:1-15:21)

THE EGYPTIAN PASSOVER I

Exodus 12:1-28

1 2 The Lord said to Moses and Aaron in the land of Egypt, "This month shall be for you the beginning of months; it shall be the first 3 month of the year for you. Tell all the congregation of Israel that on the tenth day of this month they shall take every man a lamb 4 according to their fathers' houses, a lamb for a household; and if the household is too small for a lamb, then a man and his neighbour next to his house shall take according to the number of persons; according to what each can eat you shall make your count for the 5 lamb. Your lamb shall be without blemish, a male a year old; you 6 shall take it from the sheep or from the goats; and you shall keep it until the fourteenth day of this month, when the whole assembly of 7 the congregation of Israel shall kill their lambs in the evening. Then they shall take some of the blood, and put it on the two doorposts 8 and the lintel of the houses in which they eat them. They shall eat the flesh that night, roasted; with unleavened bread and bitter herbs 9 they shall eat it. Do not eat any of it raw or boiled with water, but 10 roasted, its head with its legs and its inner parts. And you shall let none of it remain until the morning, anything that remains until the 11 morning you shall burn. In this manner you shall eat it: your loins girded, your sandals on your feet, and your staff in your hand; and 12 you shall eat it in haste. It is the Lord's passover. For I will pass through the land of Egypt that night, and I will smite all the first-born in the land of Egypt, both man and beast; and on all the gods of 13 Egypt I will execute judgments: I am the Lord. The blood shall be a sign for you, upon the houses where you are; and when I see the blood, I will pass over you, and no plague shall fall upon you to destroy you, when I smite the land of Egypt.

14 "This day shall be for you a memorial day, and you shall keep it as a feast to the Lord; throughout your generations you shall observe it 15 as an ordinance for ever. Seven days you shall eat unleavened bread; on the first day you shall put away leaven out of your houses, for if

any one eats what is leavened, from the first day until the seventh
16 day, that person shall be cut off from Israel. On the first day you shall hold a holy assembly, and on the seventh day a holy assembly; no work shall be done on those days; but what every one must eat,
17 that only may be prepared by you. And you shall observe the feast of unleavened bread, for on this very day I brought your hosts out of the land of Egypt: therefore you shall observe this day, throughout
18 your generations, as an ordinance for ever. In the first month, on the fourteenth day of the month at evening, you shall eat unleavened
19 bread, and so until the twenty-first day of the month at evening. For seven days no leaven shall be found in your houses; for if any one eats what is leavened, that person shall be cut off from the congrega-
20 tion of Israel, whether he is a sojourner or a native of the land. You shall eat nothing leavened; in all your dwellings you shall eat unleavened bread."

21 Then Moses called all the elders of Israel, and said to them, "Select lambs for yourselves according to your families, and kill the
22 passover lamb. Take a bunch of hyssop and dip it in the blood which is in the basin, and touch the lintel and the two doorposts with the blood which is in the basin; and none of you shall go out of the door
23 of his house until the morning. For the Lord will pass through to slay the Egyptians; and when he sees the blood on the lintel and on the two doorposts, the Lord will pass over the door, and will not
24 allow the destroyer to enter your houses to slay you. You shall observe this rite as an ordinance for you and for your sons for ever.
25 And when you come to the land which the Lord will give you, as he
26 has promised, you shall keep this service. And when your children
27 say to you, 'What do you mean by this service?' you shall say, 'It is the sacrifice of the Lord's passover, for he passed over the houses of the people of Israel in Egypt, when he slew the Egyptians but spared our houses.'" And the people bowed their heads and worshipped.
28 Then the people of Israel went and did so; as the Lord had commanded Moses and Aaron, so they did.

Both ignorance of Jewish practice and natural unwillingness to devote time to ritual details in the Bible have meant that many Christians do not realize that there were marked differences between the original celebration of the Passover and its repetitions down the centuries until the destruction of the Temple in A.D. 70, and also in its modern form among Jews.

THE TIME OF YEAR

Israel was accustomed to begin its year in Tishri, the seventh month, approximately our September-October. Then the agricultural year both in Canaan and Babylonia is at an end; the hard-baked soil longs for life-bringing rain, which has not fallen for five months or more. Nature itself seems to point to this time as marking a renewal of life. But now God fixed Abib, later called by its Babylonian name Nisan, approximately our March-April, as the beginning of the year. Abib (13:4; Deut. 16:1) means "green ears" (of corn). In the colder north and west of Europe spring seems to mark the renewal of life, and so we sing at Easter:

Earth with joy confesses, clothing her with green,
All good things return with her returning king;
Green in ev'ry meadow, leaves on ev'ry tree,
Speak Thy sorrows ended, life returns with Thee.

But in the Near and Middle East, the cereal crops have been growing steadily all winter, and by Passover it was possible to bring a sheaf of first fruits (barley) as an offering (Lev. 23:10–11). So, while links with the soil continued, the New Year was to begin with the celebration of the birthday of the nation, when God freed it.

THE PROBLEM OF THE FEAST OF UNLEAVENED BREAD

It is held by many that originally there was no connection between the Passover ritual and the feast of Unleavened Bread which followed it; the former being a spring festival of the shepherds, the latter of the agriculturists. This may well be so, though it is unprovable. But for our purposes here what matters is not origins, but God's use of them. How many who celebrate Easter think of the fact that the name comes from Eostre, a Germanic fertility goddess?

THE EGYPTIAN PASSOVER II

Exodus 12:1–28 *(cont'd)*

THE PASSOVER RITUAL (12:1–13)

The Egyptian Passover differed from its annual memorial repetitions in the smearing of the blood on the lintels and doorposts, and in the signs of haste and preparedness. Since its repetitions were pilgrim feasts, not held in one's own home, the blood ritual would have largely lost its significance, even as a reminder. The original feast was for those about to be delivered, the memorial repetition for those who had been delivered. The stress on speed and preparedness, reinforced by the use of unleavened bread, struck a note that is constantly heard in Scripture, and that may be summed up in the call, "*Today,* if you hear his voice . . ." (Ps. 95:7).

The Passover sacrifice was of a sheep or goat a year old—the traditional rendering "lamb" is misleading. Later rulings fixed the number of adults participating at at least ten. As a sacrifice it was unique, for it did not fit into the framework of any of the sacrifices detailed in the early chapters of Leviticus. This may be due to the fact that the latter were all intended in various ways to maintain the Covenant once Israel had come into it, while the Passover made the Covenant possible. It is not chance, that while the death of Christ is seen in the New Testament as in various ways providing the reality behind the Levitical sacrifices, it is especially with the Passover that it is linked, for his death was to bring men into the New Covenant.

Since the Passover "lamb" was a sacrifice, it has been symbolically represented in the modern Jewish Passover only by a shank bone ever since the destruction of the Temple in A.D. 70. The Samaritans, however, still offer sacrifices and roast and eat the "lambs" on Mount Gerizim, where their temple used to stand.

The leavening of bread was normally carried out, not by the use of yeast, or of some other special product, but by the keeping over of part of the dough from one batch of baking to the next. It is widely, and probably correctly, believed that this chain of leavening was broken once a year. This was indubitably so for the Israelite, thanks to the Passover and the week of Unleavened Bread. So it stood, not merely for the speed involved in the deliverance, but also for the new beginning.

Later, partly because the Levitical legislation prohibited the use of leavened bread in sacrifices on the altar, leaven was seen as a picture of those human drives and impulses, which can transform life in the individual and in society. Since their results are generally for the worse, leaven in later Judaism as well as in the New Testament, has very often a bad significance, but reference to Lev. 7:14; 23:17 shows that this need not be the case. The implications of a new beginning and of evil are united in 1 Cor. 5:6–8.

The sacrificial animal was to be chosen on the 10th of the month and kept till the 14th. This was presumably to prevent a last moment hitch and to offer it to public scrutiny, so that a blemished animal should not be used. Later, when the sacrificing was done by priests this requirement was not observed. It was killed "between the two evenings" (RV, mg., JB); cf. 29:39; 30:8. The Samaritans still interpret this as the time between the sun's touching the horizon and dark; this is followed by the NEB "between dusk and dark", and the NIV "twilight". The custom in the time of Christ was between three and five, but the extreme haste indicated and the two other passages where the term is used suggest the correctness of the Samaritan tradition. The crowd of worshippers in Jerusalem in New Testament times would explain the lengthening of the time.

There is no necessary contradiction between "boil" in verse 9 and Deut. 16:7, for the verb rendered "boil" in the latter passage was used of cooking generally. Whatever their original purpose, the bitter herbs have traditionally been regarded as representing the bitterness of Egyptian bondage. The modern Jew uses horseradish.

THE RITUAL OF THE FEAST OF UNLEAVENED BREAD (12:14–20)

So important was the removal of leaven that it had to be removed completely before the feast began. That seems to be the force of verse 15; compare Mark 14:12 and parallels in Matt. and Luke, where the 14th Nisan, on which the "lamb" was sacrificed, is called the first day of "unleavened bread". This law applied equally to the sojourner, the foreigner allowed to live in their land, even though he was not allowed to eat the Passover meal itself (verse 45). The principle was that while no compulsion was placed on the outsider to accept the people's religion, yet he was expected to conform to its more public expression (see the discussion on 20:8–11, the Sabbath law). This law was easy to carry out in a primitive society, but as life grew more urbanized and complex, and more modern methods of baking were introduced, it became necessary to sell all the leaven in Jewish shops to a Gentile. Even today in Israel all the leaven in the country is sold to a high Christian cleric, who sells it back once the feast is over.

FINAL INSTRUCTIONS (12:21–28)

While the word rendered "house" can be applied to a tent, 3:22 clearly suggests that the Israelites had become settled, living in the same type of small hut as the ordinary Egyptian. The feast of booths *(Sukkoth,* Tabernacles) presupposes that Israel after the Exodus had to live in booths, not tents, at least at first. The requirement that people should not leave the house till morning applied only to the Egyptian Passover; compare Christ's going to Gethsemane with his disciples after the meal.

We may compare "the destroyer" (verse 23) with 2 Sam. 24:16–17. We find it difficult to appreciate such language and would feel much happier if we could identify the particular germ or virus responsible for the death of the first-born, though that would not explain the selectivity of their deaths. But in so doing, we normally forget that the disease germ is, for all that, the active agent in God's hands. We are apt so to magnify God, that we cease to think of him as using the almost infinitely small.

To this day, at the Passover meal, the youngest child present capable of doing so asks questions about the peculiarities of the celebration. Our outward ritual of worship should be calculated to arouse our children's curiosity; they should be capable of receiving an intelligible answer. It is encouraging that it is becoming commoner for children to be present at the Lord's Supper, even if they do not participate.

OUT OF EGYPT

Exodus 12:29–42

29 At midnight the Lord smote all the first-born in the land of Egypt, from the first-born of Pharaoh who sat on his throne to the first-born of the captive who was in the dungeon, and all the first-born of
30 the cattle. And Pharaoh rose up in the night, he, and all his servants, and all the Egyptians; and there was a great cry in Egypt, for there
31 was not a house where one was not dead. And he summoned Moses and Aaron by night, and said, "Rise up, go forth from among my people, both you and the people of Israel; and go, serve the Lord, as
32 you have said. Take your flocks and your herds, as you have said, and be gone; and bless me also!"
33 And the Egyptians were urgent with the people, to send them out
34 of the land in haste; for they said, "We are all dead men." So the people took their dough before it was leavened, their kneading
35 bowls being bound up in their mantles on their shoulders. The people of Israel had also done as Moses told them, for they had asked of the Egyptians jewelry of silver and of gold, and clothing;
36 and the Lord had given the people favour in the sight of the Egyptians, so that they let them have what they asked. Thus they despoiled the Egyptians.
37 And the people of Israel journeyed from Rameses to Succoth, about six hundred thousand men on foot, besides women and
38 children. A mixed multitude also went up with them, and very many
39 cattle, both flocks and herds. And they baked unleavened cakes of the dough which they had brought out of Egypt, for it was not leavened, because they were thrust out of Egypt and could not tarry, neither had they prepared for themselves any provisions.

40   The time that the people of Israel dwelt in Egypt was four hundred
41 and thirty years. And at the end of four hundred and thirty years, on
     that very day, all the hosts of the Lord went out from the land of
42 Egypt. It was a night of watching by the Lord, to bring them out of
     the land of Egypt; so this same night is a night of watching kept to
     the Lord by all the people of Israel throughout their generations.

When it is a question of yielding to God's will, man has an
almost boundless power for self-deception. God seldom forces
men to yield, but when he does, it can be an aweful thing.

Because Pharaoh summoned Moses and Aaron by night,
some have envisaged Israel on the move by night, in contraven-
tion of verse 22. But however near Moses may have been to
Pharaoh's palace in Pi-Ramese, it will have been broad daylight
before the messengers reached him and he made the double
journey to Pharaoh and back to his people.

Even in the moment of his humiliation, Pharaoh could not
bring himself fully to acknowledge that he had been in the
wrong. He asked for a blessing, which presumably meant that
Moses should lift the curse which, as Pharaoh saw it, he had put
on Egypt and its king. The RSV, with the NEB, and the TEV, is
correct in having pluperfects in verses 35–36. The asking for
gold and silver was hardly something that would have been left
to the last moment, when they were desperately being urged to
leave. In addition, however, it is made clear that the giving by
the Egyptians was not a desperate, last moment bribe to get rid
of the threat to their existence; Yahweh had given them favour,
i.e. grace, in the sight of the Egyptians. No explanation is given,
and we are clearly intended to understand that the willingness
to give was the result of God's action; cf. 3:21; 11:3. Since the
Israelites were not dispersed throughout the land, the amount
involved was not so great. In addition 3:22 and 11:2 suggest that
the donors were mainly those living in closest proximity to the
Israelites, so they had cause for gratitude that they had been
spared the worst effects of the plagues.

The journey from Rameses to Succoth was from the centre to
the western extremity of Goshen, obviously picking up groups
of families as they went. The latter name, an adaptation of the

Egyptian name and meaning "booths", has given its name to the Feast of Tabernacles (Sukkoth); see comment on 12:22.

The number of Israelites leaving Egypt is given as approximately 600,000 men who could march. This agrees with the census total in Num. 1 and presupposes a total of two to three million, when women, old men and children are included. Then we have to allow for the unspecified number in "the mixed multitude", who were probably mainly Semitic slaves, for the term Hebrew was not restricted to Israel. Lovers of the miraculous have made valiant efforts to defend these high numbers, but it is not a question whether their arguments are possible, which they generally are, but the archaeologically proven fact that these high numbers simply do not fit into the population figures of both Egypt and Canaan, where the normal city population did not exceed five thousand, as has been revealed by inscriptions and excavations. To this we should add the repeated stress on their fewness in Deut. 4:38; 7:7, 17, 22.

The most probable explanation of the exaggerated numbers lies in the development over the centuries of the meaning of *eleph,* normally translated as "thousand". It seems to have developed from "tent group" through "tribal division" to "thousand"; compare Mic. 5:2 in the AV with the RSV, NEB, NIV. Since, however, this realization does not enable us to fix the total number of Israelites with any certainty, it is best to leave the matter open. The magnitude of God's deliverance does not depend on the number involved in it.

Equally we need spend no time on the 430 years, with its variants in the ancient Greek and Samaritan versions, beyond noting that Israel had remained a coherent people in Egypt, in full possession of its traditions and customs. At the Exodus they were far from being a mere rabble of slaves. This bears out the suggestions made earlier that the refusal to give names to the Pharaohs involved in the Exodus was quite deliberate, and did not come from ignorance. Beyond this, there is no spiritual significance in the 430 years; see Gen. 15:13, 16.

In verse 42 the NIV renders very well, "Because the Lord kept vigil that night to bring them out of Egypt, on this night all the

Israelites are to keep vigil to honour the Lord for the generations to come". To this day the religious Jew tries to spin out the
Passover celebration to last till as late an hour as family
circumstances permit. The various songs with which it ends are
intended to keep the children awake and interested for as long
as possible.

FURTHER RULES FOR THE PASSOVER

Exodus 12:43–51

43 And the Lord said to Moses and Aaron, "This is the ordinance of the
44 passover: no foreigner shall eat of it; but every slave that is bought
45 for money may eat of it after you have circumcised him. No
46 sojourner or hired servant may eat of it. In one house shall it be
eaten; you shall not carry forth any of the flesh outside the house;
47 and you shall not break a bone of it. All the congregation of Israel
48 shall keep it. And when a stranger shall sojourn with you and would
keep the passover to the Lord, let all his males be circumcised, then
he may come near and keep it; he shall be as a native of the land. But
49 no uncircumcised person shall eat of it. There shall be one law for
the native and for the stranger who sojourns among you."
50 Thus did all the people of Israel; as the Lord commanded Moses
51 and Aaron, so they did. And on that very day the Lord brought the
people of Israel out of the land of Egypt by their hosts.

There is too great a tendency on the part of some to look for
separate sources, when reading a book like this. Though we,
with the more orderly thinking of the modern West, would have
placed this section earlier in the chapter, its present position is
significant. There can be no reasonable doubt that many of the
"mixed multitude" (verse 38) will have followed Israel's example and sacrificed a "lamb", and why not? The Church has
always understood that in the moment of crisis finer points of
church order are forgotten. Those who wished to shelter under
the blood were welcome. But once law and order prevailed, the
foreigner (verse 43), the sojourner and the hired servant (verse
45), were to be excluded. The foreigner made no claim to be an

Israelite, the uncircumcised sojourner showed no desire to be an Israelite. Clearly the hired servant is also considered as not being an Israelite; see commentary on 21:1-6 (on slaves). In New Testament times social conditions had changed, especially in Galilee; see Matt. 20:1-16. Today the average Jew will welcome a Gentile friend at his Passover celebration, but that is because there is no sacrificial lamb. It was the partaking of the sacrifice that ruled out the non-Israelite.

This section introduces us to a number of important features in Israelite life. Though it was not compulsory, it was regarded as natural that a slave would be circumcised, i.e. brought into the community of Israel. He was then regarded as a member of the wider family group—for the female slave see comments on 21:7-11. This meant that slavery was normally more humane in Israel than in the Graeco-Roman world; it had in fact largely died out by the time of the New Testament.

Then the principle is laid down of one law for both the native and the stranger. In the context it means that by the very fact of joining Israel by circumcision all physical origin was ignored. Presumably the sojourner in Num. 15:15-16 is also a proselyte. But in Lev. 24:22 the principle is widened to embrace all permitted to live in Israel, whether they adopted the worship of Israel's God or not. Although in New Testament times there was a ceremony for the reception of proselytes, at first a mere declaration of intent, sealed by circumcision, was sufficient. It is typical of the whole biblical attitude, where act and life are more important than words, that to this day the Jew assumes that he who lives correctly believes correctly. The stress on verbal orthodoxy, which has brought so much suffering and division to the Church is part of the early Church's legacy from the Greeks.

THE CONSECRATION OF THE FIRST-BORN

Exodus 13:1-16

1 2 The Lord said to Moses, "Consecrate to me all the first-born;

whatever is the first to open the womb among the people of Israel, both of man and of beast, is mine."

3   And Moses said to the people, "Remember this day, in which you came out from Egypt, out of the house of bondage, for by strength of hand the Lord brought you out from this place; no leavened bread
4   shall be eaten. This day you are to go forth, in the month of Abib.
5   And when the Lord brings you into the land of the Canaanites, the Hittites, the Amorites, the Hivites, and the Jebusites, which he swore to your fathers to give you, a land flowing with milk and
6   honey, you shall keep this service in this month. Seven days you shall eat unleavened bread, and on the seventh day there shall be a
7   feast to the Lord. Unleavened bread shall be eaten for seven days; no leavened bread shall be seen with you, and no leaven shall be seen
8   with you in all your territory. And you shall tell your son on that day, 'It is because of what the Lord did for me when I came out of
9   Egypt.' And it shall be to you as a sign on your hand and as a memorial between your eyes, that the law of the Lord may be in your mouth; for with a strong hand the Lord has brought you out of
10   Egypt. You shall therefore keep this ordinance at its appointed time from year to year.

11   "And when the Lord brings you into the land of the Canaanites, as
12   he swore to you and your fathers, and shall give it to you, you shall set apart to the Lord all that first opens the womb. All the firstlings
13   of your cattle that are males shall be the Lord's. Every firstling of an ass you shall redeem with a lamb, or if you will not redeem it you shall break its neck. Every first-born of man among your sons you
14   shall redeem. And when in time to come your son asks you, 'What does this mean?' you shall say to him, 'By strength of hand the Lord
15   brought us out of Egypt, from the house of bondage. For when Pharaoh stubbornly refused to let us go, the Lord slew all the first-born in the land of Egypt, both the first-born of man and the first-born of cattle. Therefore I sacrifice to the Lord all the males that first
16   open the womb; but all the first-born of my sons I redeem.' It shall be as a mark on your hand or frontlets between your eyes; for by a strong hand the Lord brought us out of Egypt."

In the New Testament Rom. 6:13 and 12:1 express the claims of God to control a man completely, even as Heb. 4:9–10 does for his time and actions. In the Old we have foreshadowings of such an attitude. Here we have the claim that the first-born sons are

God's, because he had spared them in Egypt (a further support for the suggestion that girls were not involved in the death of the first-born). It used to be widely suggested that this marked a transition from the actual sacrifice of the first-born, but de Vaux has shown that human sacrifice was a rarity in the Bible lands, and that there is no evidence for such a general practice in Israel.

Why there should be a further mention of the feast of Unleavened Bread here is not clear. The most probable reason is that a change of diet—far from welcome to many modern Jews—would make a far stronger impact on the memory than the one night's celebration of the Passover. What is well known, however, is that in the Inter-Testamental period the more pious began to interpret the words "sign" and "mark" in verses 9 and 16 literally. Whatever may be said of Deut. 6:8;11:18, a literal understanding seems most unlikely here. The very fact that *tephilim* (phylacteries) are normally worn only at morning prayers, not on Sabbaths and festivals, suggests strongly the artificial nature of the literal interpretation of the command.

That the first-born of cattle, if they are female, are exempted from belonging to God is probably simply a parallelism with the exemption of girls. The suggestion that it was because male animals were generally offered has no validity; see Lev. 3:1,6; 4:28,32; 5:6. A better reason might be that God had no wish to make the sacrificial ritual too heavy on the people. Meat-eating was not as common as with us, and the eating of an immature animal was deprecated (Amos 6:4), so the sacrifice of an ox was less burdensome that that of a heifer.

The special mention of the ass is because it was the one "unclean" animal likely to be found in an Israelite household. Even at a later date the camel was rare, and the horse came in first in the time of Solomon, and then only for use in war-chariots.

The custom of redeeming the first-born is still practiced by religious Jews. At the age of 30 days the equivalent of five shekels is paid to one thought to be descended from Aaron.

FROM SUCCOTH TO THE SEA OF REEDS

Exodus 13:17–14:9

17 When Pharaoh let the people go, God did not lead them by way of the land of the Philistines, although that was near; for God said,
18 "Lest the people repent when they see war, and return to Egypt." But God led the people round by the way of the wilderness toward the Red Sea. And the people of Israel went up out of the land of Egypt
19 equipped for battle. And Moses took the bones of Joseph with him; for Joseph had solemnly sworn the people of Israel, saying, "God will visit you; then you must carry my bones with you from here."
20 And they moved on from Succoth, and encamped at Etham, on the
21 edge of the wilderness. And the Lord went before them by day in a pillar of cloud to lead them along the way, and by night in a pillar of
22 fire to give them light, that they might travel by day and by night; the pillar of cloud by day and the pillar of fire by night did not depart from before the people.

1 2 Then the Lord said to Moses, "Tell the people of Israel to turn back and encamp in front of Pi-ha-hiroth, between Migdol and the sea, in front of Baal-zephon; you shall encamp over against it, by the
3 sea. For Pharaoh will say of the people of Israel, 'They are entangled
4 in the land; the wilderness has shut them in.' And I will harden Pharaoh's heart, and he will pursue them and I will get glory over Pharaoh and all his host; and the Egyptians shall know that I am the Lord." And they did so.
5 When the king of Egypt was told that the people had fled, the mind of Pharaoh and his servants was changed toward the people, and they said, "What is this we have done, that we have let Israel go
6 from serving us?" So he made ready his chariot and took his army
7 with him, and took six hundred picked chariots and all the other
8 chariots of Egypt with officers over all of them. And the Lord hardened the heart of Pharaoh king of Egypt and he pursued the
9 people of Israel as they went forth defiantly. The Egyptians pursued them, all Pharaoh's horses and chariots and his horsemen and his army, and overtook them encamped at the sea, by Pi-ha-hiroth, in front of Baal-zephon.

The silting up of the Pelusiac (easternmost) branch of the Nile and the cutting of the Suez Canal, and it may be the silting up of the northern edge of the Gulf of Suez, have made it difficult to reconstruct the geography of the Exodus. At the time there was less land, in contrast to water, to defend on Egypt's eastern frontier, so there were only strong frontier posts guarding the main routes across the desert. One of these was "the way of the land of the Philistines" (the name here is due to a later editor), the short route along the Mediterranean coast to Canaan. Since it was the route used by the majority of invaders, it was heavily guarded. The other, "the way of Shur" (Gen. 16:7), lay further south and linked with the caravan-route running via Beer-sheba up the centre of Canaan. This too will have been strongly guarded.

The fighting that might have been expected on the former would have come not merely from the Egyptian frontier forces but also from the inhabitants of the strongly-fortified towns in the southern coastal plain of Canaan.

Instead of bringing Israel out of Egypt by a recognized route, God directed the people towards the *Yam Suph,* the Sea of (papyrus) Reeds—Red Sea represents the Greek of the Septuagint. The name is also used for the Gulf of Aqaba (Num. 21:4; Deut. 2:1). So it was presumably used for the Gulf of Suez, including possible northern extensions and perhaps also for papyrus swamps in the north or centre of the isthmus. Since conflicting identifications are offered for the place-names in 14:1, and there is no certainty as to the location of Mount Sinai, and hence for the later wilderness route, there is no point in trying to fix the place of crossing. We need only to visualize water in front, Pharaoh's army behind (14:9) and empty steppe-land to right and left.

The mention that Israel marched "in battle array" is meant to stress that here was no disorganized rabble fleeing for its life. The same applies to the mention of Joseph's mummified body in Gen. 50:25–6—the use of "bones" does not imply that his body had decayed—showing that, in spite of the haste of their leaving, everything was done in order. Where God is in charge, speed does not degenerate into panic.

We have already seen that however much there is a naturalistic explanation underlying the plagues, there is an element of the supernatural in the story. The same principle confronts us now even more forcibly. The pillar of cloud may well have been the result of a desert whirlwind, but no desert whirlwind ever behaved as this one did. Some see links between the pillar of fire and volcanic activity, which is suggested by some elements of the story, but once again this fails to explain how it acted. The use of "the angel of God" (14:19) implies a personal, divine direction of cloud and fire.

The sudden change of direction (14:2) must have made Pharaoh think that the people had lost their way, "wandering around the land in confusion hemmed in by the desert" (NIV). One may reasonably ask why God put this obvious temptation in Egypt's way. He could have led Israel through the sea without involving the Egyptians. Here we touch on the outstanding weakness in all "natural" and nature religions. The power of God, or gods, is not denied, but to a very great extent it is assumed that he allows the principle of "might is right" to triumph among men. The Egyptians had to learn that Yahweh was no desert God but the controller of human destiny.

In every period, professional armies tend to have some weapon which smites terror into the untrained man's heart, however brave and strong he may be. With the Egyptians at that time it was their chariot force. Horses were not used for riding—the horsemen of the story are charioteers—but they were used in chariots, in which there would be a driver and a fighter, normally armed with bow and arrows. The infantry, though well-trained, served on such occasions mainly to defend the chariots, if they got into trouble on difficult ground.

THE CROSSING OF THE SEA OF REEDS

Exodus 14:10–31

10 When Pharaoh drew near, the people of Israel lifted up their eyes, and behold, the Egyptians were marching after them; and they were

11 in great fear. And the people of Israel cried out to the Lord; and they said to Moses, "Is it because there are no graves in Egypt that you have taken us away to die in the wilderness? What have you done to

12 us, in bringing us out of Egypt? Is not this what we said to you in Egypt, 'Let us alone and let us serve the Egyptians'? For it would have been better for us to serve the Egyptians than to die in the

13 wilderness." And Moses said to the people, "Fear not, stand firm, and see the salvation of the Lord, which he will work for you today; for the Egyptians whom you see today, you shall never see again.

14 15 The Lord will fight for you, and you have only to be still." The Lord said to Moses, "Why do you cry to me? Tell the people of Israel to go

16 forward. Lift up your rod, and stretch out your hand over the sea and divide it, that the people of Israel may go on dry ground through

17 the sea. And I will harden the hearts of the Egyptians so that they shall go in after them, and I will get glory over Pharaoh and all his

18 host, his chariots, and his horsemen. And the Egyptians shall know that I am the Lord, when I have gotten glory over Pharaoh, his chariots, and his horsemen."

19 Then the angel of God who went before the host of Israel moved and went behind them; and the pillar of cloud moved from before

20 them and stood behind them, coming between the host of Egypt and the host of Israel. And there was the cloud and the darkness; and the night passed without one coming near the other all night.

21 Then Moses stretched out his hand over the sea; and the Lord drove the sea back by a strong east wind all night, and made the sea

22 dry land, and the waters were divided. And the people of Israel went into the midst of the sea on dry ground, the waters being a wall to

23 them on their right hand and on their left. The Egyptians pursued, and went in after them into the midst of the sea, all Pharaoh's horses,

24 his chariots, and his horsemen. And in the morning watch the Lord in the pillar of fire and of cloud looked down upon the host of the

25 Egyptians, and discomfited the host of the Egyptians, clogging their chariot wheels so that they drove heavily; and the Egyptians said, "Let us flee from before Israel; for the Lord fights for them against the Egyptians."

26 Then the Lord said to Moses, "Stretch out your hand over the sea, that the water may come back upon the Egyptians, upon their

27 chariots, and upon their horsemen." So Moses stretched forth his hand over the sea, and the sea returned to its wonted flow when the morning appeared; and the Egyptians fled into it, and the Lord

28 routed the Egyptians in the midst of the sea. The waters returned

and covered the chariots and the horsemen and all the host of Pharaoh that had followed them into the sea; not so much as one of
29 them remained. But the people of Israel walked on dry ground through the sea, the waters being a wall to them on their right hand and on their left.
30   Thus the Lord saved Israel that day from the hand of the Egyptians; and Israel saw the Egyptians dead upon the seashore.
31 And Israel saw the great work which the Lord did against the Egyptians, and the people feared the Lord; and they believed in the Lord and in his servant Moses.

We can easily understand the terror of the Israelites. They must have felt like so many modern "freedom fighters", when suddenly faced by ranks of crack troops and a battalion of tanks. Nor should we be surprised that they turned on Moses. It was he who had been, as they saw it, the originator, sustainer and organizer of the whole enterprise. Surely he should have foreseen such an outcome!

In addition we know from experience, that, however much we have experienced God's power and care for us, an entirely new experience leaves us with the uncomfortable feeling, "Can God really cope with this situation?"

Moses realized, as the people did not, that the situation was one of God's creating, and so he met the people's fear with strong words of comfort and confidence, "Fear not ... the Lord will fight for you"; but in spite of that, he was quaking inside, so God asked him why he was crying out for help. He had brought Israel there, and so the onward path was forward. Both Moses and Israel had to learn that God was as much controller of chaos, as symbolized by the waters of the sea, as he was of the ordinary course of nature. It is always a temptation for the preacher and religious teacher to use strong words of assurance from Scripture, while secretly wondering how on earth they would be fulfilled.

There is no suggestion that Moses' stretching out of his rod had any direct connection with the miracle that followed it. It indicated to Israel that what followed was no mere natural phenomenon. The same applies to the return of the water after the Israelites had crossed. The explanation of the divided waters is a strong east wind. There may, however, have been another contributing factor. Other references to the Exodus, all poetical in their nature, e.g. Judg. 5:4-5; Pss. 77:16-19; 114:3-6; Hab. 3:3-6, suggest earthquake shock. If this were so, the sea-bed may have been temporarily lifted, only to sink again, when Israel was safely across. This would help to explain the very rapid return of the water and the clogging of the chariot wheels.

One of the reasons why so many do not take this entirely credible story seriously is the pictures they saw in Sunday school showing a wall of water standing up on either side of the Israelites, as though held up by sheets of glass. The idea is based on the poetry of 15:8. The prose account in 14:29 means no more than that the Egyptians had no opportunity of outflanking them due to the water. The Egyptian's terror and confusion will have been the greater because it all happened under the light of the moon a few days past full. There is no suggestion that Pharaoh himself accompanied his chariots. Indeed the very fact that his death is neither mentioned nor implied is reason enough to conclude that he did not—there is no evidence that any Pharaoh of that period met his death by drowning. He will probably have been told, or have decided, that it was beneath his dignity to pursue fugitive slaves any further.

The day is summed up in the simple phrase, "Thus the Lord saved Israel". The Jew has shown his understanding of this fact by omitting the name of Moses, with one unimportant exception, from the *Haggadah,* the traditional liturgy of the Jewish Passover.

Once or twice in a lifetime the average Christian finds himself in a position like Israel's. When he knows that it is God who has brought him into it, he will find that God's command is to go forward.

THE SONG OF THANKSGIVING

— Exodus 15:1–21

1 Then Moses and the people of Israel sang this song to the Lord, saying,
    "I will sing to the Lord, for he has triumphed gloriously;
      the horse and his rider he has thrown into the sea.
2 The Lord is my strength and my song,
    and he has become my salvation;
  this is my God, and I will praise him,
    my father's God, and I will exalt him.
3 The Lord is a man of war;
    the Lord is his name.

4 "Pharaoh's chariots and his host he cast into the sea;
    and his picked officers are sunk in the Red Sea.
5 The floods cover them;
    they went down into the depths like a stone.
6 Thy right hand, O Lord, glorious in power,
    thy right hand, O Lord, shatters the enemy.
7 In the greatness of thy majesty thou overthrowest thy
      adversaries;
    thou sendest forth thy fury, it consumes them like stubble.
8 At the blast of thy nostrils the waters piled up,
    the floods stood up in a heap;
    the deeps congealed in the heart of the sea.
9 The enemy said, 'I will pursue, I will overtake,
    I will divide the spoil, my desire shall have its fill of them.
    I will draw my sword, my hand shall destroy them.'
10 Thou didst blow with thy wind, the sea covered them;
    they sank as lead in the mighty waters.

11 "Who is like thee, O Lord, among the gods?
    Who is like thee, majestic in holiness,
    terrible in glorious deeds, doing wonders?
12 Thou didst stretch out thy right hand,
    the earth swallowed them.

13 "Thou hast led in thy steadfast love the people whom thou has
      redeemed,
    thou hast guided them by thy strength to thy holy abode.
14 The peoples have heard, they tremble;
    pangs have seized on the inhabitants of Philistia.
15 Now are the chiefs of Edom dismayed;
    the leaders of Moab, trembling seizes them;
    all the inhabitants of Canaan have melted away.
16 Terror and dread fall upon them;
    because of the greatness of thy arm, they are as still as a
      stone,
  till thy people, O Lord, pass by,
    till the people pass by whom thou hast purchased.
17 Thou wilt bring them in, and plant them on thy own mountain,
    the place, O Lord, which thou hast made for thy abode,
    the sanctuary, O Lord, which thy hands have established.
18 The Lord will reign for ever and ever."
19   For when the horses of Pharaoh with his chariots and his horsemen
    went into the sea, the Lord brought back the waters of the sea upon
    them; but the people of Israel walked on dry ground in the midst of the
20 sea. Then Miriam, the prophetess, the sister of Aaron, took a timbrel
    in her hand; and all the women went out after her with timbrels and
21 dancing. And Miriam sang to them:
    "Sing to the Lord, for he has triumphed gloriously;
    the horse and his rider he has thrown into the sea."

The outburst of thanksgiving is only natural, but we are apt to
overlook the suffering our deliverance may have caused to
others. It was true spiritual insight that caused Rabbi Johanan
to say, "When the Egyptians were drowning in the Red Sea, the
angels in heaven were about to break into songs of jubilation.
But the Holy One silenced them with the words, 'My creatures
are perishing, and you are ready to sing!' "

This points us to that spiritual mystery, which finds its Old
Testament expression in "I form the light and create darkness, I
bring prosperity and create disaster" (Isa. 45:7, NIV), but
whose supreme expression and interpretation is the Cross of
Christ.

The history of the song is disputed. Some consider it to be an expansion of Miriam's song (verse 21), but it is more likely that this was used as the title for the whole song. The "timbrels" (tambourines), or hand drums, and dances accompanied a victory celebration (1 Sam. 18:6). Modern study has shown the archaic nature of the song as a whole, though many would regard some parts of it as later additions.

The traditional translation has sometimes missed the force of the archaic language. In verses 1 and 21 follow the margin "the horse and its chariot". In verse 2 follow the NEB, "The Lord is my refuge and my defence, he has shown himself my deliverer." "Man of war" (verse 3) simply means warrior (JB, NIV). There are certain standard metaphors that run through the Bible, one of them being the right hand or arm (verse 6) used as a picture of strength and power. Modern man, brought up in a tradition of science and the laws of nature, tends to find some of the Old Testament anthropomorphisms and related concepts, especially in its poetry, impossibly naive. This applies to calling the strong east wind (14:21) "the blast of thy nostrils" (verse 8). Without denying the reality of the laws of nature we must learn to appreciate more deeply that our God is not controlled by his creation but controls it. The scientist is always loathe to give full weight to the scientifically inexplicable and to feel that "coincidence" is an adequate explanation for facts that seem to contradict his theories, but mankind's history and personal experience contain too much to be thus airily dismissed. Neither Queen Elizabeth's verdict on the destruction of the Spanish Armada, "He blew and they were scattered", nor the widespread recognition that the unexpected stilling of the Channel waters on the eve of D-day in 1944 was God's action, was the expression of pious sentiment, but a genuine recognition of divine providence.

The triumphant question, "Who is like thee, O Lord, among the gods?" expresses the first stage of Israel's long road to a complete monotheism, which ruled out the possibility of the existence of other gods. Whether we call this first stage monolatry, or ethical monotheism, it was the recognition that no other power in heaven or on earth needed to be considered.

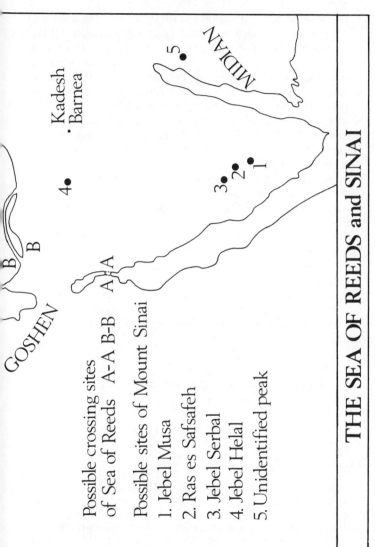

Possible crossing sites
of Sea of Reeds   A–A B–B

Possible sites of Mount Sinai

1. Jebel Musa
2. Ras es Safsafeh
3. Jebel Serbal
4. Jebel Helal
5. Unidentified peak

THE SEA OF REEDS and SINAI

Our interpretation of verses 13–18 (RSV "Thou hast led . . .)
will depend mainly on how we interpret the tenses used in them.
They begin in Hebrew with "perfects", but in itself this means
nothing, for in prophetic verse we frequently meet what the
grammarians call "the prophetic perfect", i.e. though the future
is intended, the perfect is used in the certainty that it will come
to pass—the most familiar example of this is in Isa. 9:2–7. This
is how the NIV understands the verbs here, and the fact that in
verses 16–18 (" . . . fall . . . wilt bring . . .") we pass over to
"imperfects", i.e. future tenses, seems to justify its interpretation. There is nothing in verse 17 to demand a later date for "thy
own mountain", which probably refers to Canaan as a whole.
The plains and valleys of Palestine give the impression of being
mere extensions of the hills rather than having an independent
existence.

No incident is elsewhere recounted to justify calling Miriam
"the prophetess"; though in Num. 12:2 she clearly claims to
have so acted. As we saw earlier a prophet is a person who
proclaims God's will and word, i.e. his spokesman. Because this
is generally concerned with the circumstances of a specific
situation, most prophetic messages in both Testaments have
not been preserved for later generations. Few books date so
quickly as a volume of sermons.

E. FROM THE SEA OF REEDS TO SINAI
(15:22–18:27)

MARAH AND ELIM

Exodus 15:22–27

22 Then Moses led Israel onward from the Red Sea, and they went into
   the wilderness of Shur; they went three days in the wilderness and
23 found no water. When they came to Marah, they could not drink the
   water of Marah because it was bitter; therefore it was named Marah.
24 And the people murmured against Moses, saying, "What shall we

25 drink?" And he cried to the Lord; and the Lord showed him a tree, and he threw it into the water, and the water became sweet.

There the Lord made for them a statute and an ordinance and
26 there he proved them, saying, "If you will diligently hearken to the voice of the Lord your God, and do that which is right in his eyes, and give heed to his commandments and keep all his statutes, I will put none of the diseases upon you which I put upon the Egyptians; for I am the Lord, your healer."
27 Then they came to Elim, where there were twelve springs of water and seventy palm trees; and they encamped there by the water.

Most Bible maps covering the Exodus give suggested sites for the various places at which Israel stopped. Since, however, we are uncertain where the Sea of Reeds was crossed and even of the site of Mount Sinai, it is well that we ignore them, as their identification adds nothing to our understanding of the story. The statement that Israel went into "the wilderness of Shur" means no more than that they moved into the steppe land east of Egypt. "Marah" means bitter; cf. Ruth 1:20. Wells and pools in the steppe are often brackish.

The term "murmured" is a very common one in Exodus and Numbers; see and compare Exod. 14:10–12; 16:2–3; 17:1–3; Num. 11:4–5; 14:2–3; 16:11; 20:2–5; 21:4–5. We should be careful how we criticize the Israelites. It is a very common experience that the joy of conversion, of a living contact with Christ, often turns to deep disappointment as unexpected difficulties are encountered. We do not find it easy to grasp that difficulties are part of God's loving training (Heb. 12:3–11), and it is all too easy for preachers to depict the Christian life in a way that leaves little room for suffering with Christ (Rom. 8:17). This helps to explain why God was so long-suffering with Israel in the wilderness.

No indication is given by which we can identify the tree. The Hebrew can equally be rendered "piece of wood" (NIV) or "bush" (Hyatt). It is apparently an Arab belief that a desert bush can be used in this way, and it is quite probable that nothing miraculous is intended. This would explain verse 26. God had tested Israel by deflating the euphoria caused by the crossing of the sea, but then showed how ridiculously easy it was for him to meet the sudden crisis. Obedience to his will, which implied trust, would be met by God's protecting hand over them.

We may ignore the mediaeval spiritualizing of the tree as the Cross, which brings sweetness to life's bitterest moments. If we want to spiritualize, we should rather stress that, if we have to experience Marah, we may well expect that the rest and consolation of Elim will follow.

QUAILS AND MANNA I

Exodus 16:1-36

1 They set out from Elim, and all the congregation of the people of Israel came to the wilderness of Sin, which is between Elim and Sinai, on the fifteenth day of the second month after they had
2 departed from the land of Egypt. And the whole congregation of the people of Israel murmured against Moses and Aaron in the wilder-
3 ness, and said to them, "Would that we had died by the hand of the Lord in the land of Egypt, when we sat by the fleshpots and ate bread to the full; for you have brought us out into this wilderness to kill this whole assembly with hunger."
4   Then the Lord said to Moses, "Behold, I will rain bread from heaven for you; and the people shall go out and gather a day's portion every day, that I may prove them, whether they will walk in
5 my law or not. On the sixth day, when they prepare what they bring
6 in, it will be twice as much as they gather daily." So Moses and Aaron said to all the people of Israel, "At evening you shall know
7 that it was the Lord who brought you out of the land of Egypt, and in the morning you shall see the glory of the Lord, because he has heard your murmurings against the Lord. For what are we, that you
8 murmur against us?" And Moses said, "When the Lord gives you in the evening flesh to eat and in the morning bread to the full, because the Lord has heard your murmurings which you murmur against him—what are we? Your murmurings are not against us but against the Lord."
9   And Moses said to Aaron, "Say to the whole congregation of the

people of Israel, 'Come near before the Lord, for he has heard your
10 murmurings.' " And as Aaron spoke to the whole congregation of
the people of Israel, they looked toward the wilderness, and behold,
11 the glory of the Lord appeared in the cloud. And the Lord said to
12 Moses, "I have heard the murmurings of the people of Israel; say to
them, 'At twilight you shall eat flesh, and in the morning you shall be
filled with bread; then you shall know that I am the Lord your
God.'"

13 In the evening quails came up and covered the camp; and in the
14 morning dew lay round about the camp. And when the dew had
gone up, there was on the face of the wilderness a fine, flake-like
15 thing, fine as hoarfrost on the ground. When the people of Israel saw
it, they said to one another, "What is it?" For they did not know
what it was. And Moses said to them, "It is the bread which the Lord
16 has given you to eat. This is what the Lord has commanded: 'Gather
of it, every man of you, as much as he can eat; you shall take an omer
apiece, according to the number of the persons whom each of you
17 has in his tent.' " And the people of Israel did so; they gathered, some
18 more, some less. But when they measured it with an omer, he that
gathered much had nothing over, and he that gathered little had no
19 lack; each gathered according to what he could eat. And Moses said
20 to them, "Let no man leave any of it till the morning." But they did
not listen to Moses; some left part of it till the morning, and it bred
21 worms and became foul; and Moses was angry with them. Morning
by morning they gathered it, each as much as he could eat; but when
the sun grew hot, it melted.

22 On the sixth day they gathered twice as much bread, two omers
apiece; and when all the leaders of the congregation came and told
23 Moses, he said to them, "This is what the Lord has commanded:
'Tomorrow is a day of solemn rest, a holy sabbath to the Lord; bake
what you will bake and boil what you will boil, and all that is left
24 over lay by to be kept till the morning.' " So they laid it by till the
morning, as Moses bade them; and it did not become foul, and there
25 were no worms in it. Moses said, "Eat it today, for today is a sabbath
26 to the Lord; today you will not find it in the field. Six days you shall
gather it; but on the seventh day, which is a sabbath, there will be
27 none." On the seventh day some of the people went out to gather,
28 and they found none. And the Lord said to Moses, "How long do
29 you refuse to keep my commandments and my laws? See! The Lord
has given you the sabbath, therefore on the sixth day he gives you

bread for two days; remain every man of you in his place, let no man
30 go out of his place on the seventh day." So the people rested on the
seventh day.

31   Now the house of Israel called its name manna; it was like
coriander seed, white, and the taste of it was like wafers, made with
32 honey. And Moses said, "This is what the Lord has commanded:
'Let an omer of it be kept throughout your generations, that they
may see the bread with which I fed you in the wilderness, when I
33 brought you out of the land of Egypt.'" And Moses said to Aaron,
"Take a jar, and put an omer of manna in it, and place it before the
34 Lord, to be kept throughout your generations." As the Lord
commanded Moses, so Aaron placed it before the testimony, to be
35 kept. And the people of Israel ate the manna forty years, till they
came to a habitable land; they ate the manna, till they came to the
36 border of the land of Canaan. (An omer is the tenth part of an
ephah.)

Many a young Christian, when he has committed himself to
Christ, finds himself faced with a number of restrictions, some
of which are clearly the demands of Scripture, though many
may well rest on church tradition. His feelings of irritation,
even of rebellion, may be increased by the apparent lack of
understanding of those older church members who have so
adapted themselves to these restrictions, that they take them for
granted.

This was in large measure the position of the Israelites, once
they had been swallowed up by the unaccustomed wilderness
life, though here the restrictions were material rather than
ethical and spiritual. It is probable that they felt that Moses,
with his long experience as shepherd in Midian had little
understanding for their plight.

QUAILS AND MANNA II

Exodus 16:1–36 *(cont'd)*

The complaints at Marah were excusable. Where water is
essential to life, to be faced by a virtually undrinkable source is
a disappointment, exceeded only by that created by a mirage.

During the rest at Elim, however, hopes of an easier existence will have grown up, only to be dashed by the realities of the wilderness of Sin. The name has, of course, no connection with evil in Hebrew.

Though it is not stated that they were in danger of starvation, a month after they had left Egypt, they must have been reduced to iron rations. It was quite natural that they should look back to Egypt, where, if inscriptions are to be trusted, forced labourers were reasonably fed, though in all probability they had complained there too. We can, however, absolve them of unreasonable exaggeration. They are not likely to have been given meat often in Egypt, but the parallel passage, Num. 11:4–5, makes special mention of fish, which was readily available. The Hebrew word *basar* is wide enough to include all food from living animals. There was no divine rebuke, for while the form of the request was wrong, its substance was reasonable.

There was a double giving, quails and manna. The former was exceptional and is mentioned again only in Num. 11:31–33. Beyond their arrival at the stated time, there was nothing miraculous about them, for the peninsula of Sinai lies on their annual migration path. It is a common Christian experience that God's special giving is very often linked with the natural, marked out only by the timing of the gift.

The position with regard to the manna is very different. Today it is a commonplace that a substance is found in Sinai, which closely resembles the biblical description of manna. It is the honeydew excretion of two scale insects, which live on the branches of the tamarisk, a common desert shrub. It was already known to Josephus in his *Antiquities*. It is called *mann* by the Beduin. Other similar phenomena have also been recorded.

Seeing that so many of the apparently miraculous happenings in Exodus have an essentially natural basis as their cause, it would be presumptuous to deny that there is any link here with the modern phenomenon. But there are such striking differences that any purely naturalistic explanation of manna must be ruled out. It is also quite inadequate to suggest that the Bible has simply exaggerated a much simpler event.

The modern "manna" is found only in early summer, and only in limited areas of Sinai. In some years it is not found at all. It does not melt as the temperature rises (verse 21), nor does it breed maggots (verse 20, NEB, NIV) if kept. Quite apart from the regularity and quantity of the biblical manna, it had an inexplicable ability to adapt itself to the individual's needs (verses 17–18). In addition it adapted itself to the Sabbath (verses 22–27). The double portion (verse 22) was not due to the people's deliberate gathering, but to the already mentioned adaptation. It is not unlikely that the petition in the Lord's Prayer, "Give us this day our daily bread" looks back to this, for its meaning is probably, "Give us this day our ration of bread".

There is no middle ground here between rejection and acceptance of the story. Analogy with other miraculous incidents in Exodus suggests that God used the modern *mann,* but his recorded use of it transcends any explanation we can offer. But before we mutter "sheer invention", let us remember that it links with the miracle of the feeding of the Five Thousand, the only miracle recorded in all four Gospels, and the turning of the water into wine at Cana.

Spiritually it has encouraged every generation of Christians to take Christ's words seriously, "Seek first God's kingdom and his righteousness, and all these things [food, clothing] will be yours as well" (Matt. 6:33), and they have not been disappointed.

Obviously the command in verses 32 and 33 that it be kept "throughout your generations" came after the making of the Tabernacle, but in the usual way of Hebrew historical writing it is used to round off the account of the manna. By the time of Solomon the jar of manna had disappeared, we are not told how or when (1 Kgs. 8:9). The word Sabbath may possibly be also the adaptation of a term first used a little later; see the treatment of 20:8–11.

If the question is asked why the provision of manna should have been hedged in, in the way it was, it is answered in verse 4, where the RSV is misleading. Render, "In this way I will test them and see whether they will follow my instructions" (NIV, NEB).

WATER FROM THE ROCK

Exodus 17:1–7

1 All the congregation of the people of Israel moved on from the wilderness of Sin by stages, according to the commandment of the Lord, and camped at Rephidim; but there was no water for the
2 people to drink. Therefore the people found fault with Moses, and said, "Give us water to drink." And Moses said to them, "Why do
3 you find fault with me? Why do you put the Lord to the proof?" But the people thirsted there for water, and the people murmured against Moses, and said, "Why did you bring us up out of Egypt, to
4 kill us and our children and our cattle with thirst?" So Moses cried to the Lord, "What shall I do with this people? They are almost ready
5 to stone me." And the Lord said to Moses, "Pass on before the people, taking with you some of the elders of Israel; and take in your
6 hand the rod with which you struck the Nile, and go. Behold, I will stand before you there on the rock at Horeb; and you shall strike the rock, and water shall come out of it, that the people may drink."
7 And Moses did so, in the sight of the elders of Israel. And he called the name of the place Massah and Meribah, because of the faultfinding of the children of Israel, and because they put the Lord to the proof by saying, "Is the Lord among us or not?"

There is a popular saying in the north of England, "There's nowt so queer as folks", to which we might reverently add, "Except God". We constantly think that we can tie God down to our formulations and expectations. Since God had just shown his power by giving them food, they assumed that Moses must be to blame for the lack of water; "a dispute arose between them and Moses" (verse 2, NEB)—the verb used implies virtually a formal impeachment.

Moses pointed out that they were really challenging God, putting him to the test—"tempt" (AV) had the same meaning in

Jacobean English—for the giving of the manna should have convinced them that God would supply this need as well. Their very despair, shown in their readiness to stone Moses, proved that they did not believe that God could meet their need.

God's answer was that Moses should go forward ahead of the people—a sign that they had been on the right road—taking with him some of the elders as witnesses, and when he came to a rock, where he would realize God's presence (there is no suggestion of a visible appearance of God) he should hit it with his rod.

Werner Keller, after quoting Major C.S. Jarvis' account of how one of his sergeants brought water from a rock in Sinai by an accidental blow with a spade, adds: Moses "had obviously got to know this highly unusual method of finding water during his exile among the Midianites". This is an example of how the miraculous should not be approached. Jarvis' account points to the natural means behind the miracle, but Keller brings no evidence that the natives of Sinai ever used this method to obtain water, or that there was any outward sign of the right rock to hit. Had the divine hand not been in it, it would have been a million to one chance against success.

We are told that the rock was in Horeb. As Israel had not yet reached Mount Sinai this is support for the widely-held view that Horeb represents the whole area or mountain range, while Sinai is the name of a peak.

A similar means of obtaining water is mentioned in Num. 20:2–13, where once again the name Meribah is used. This is regarded by some as a doublet of the story in Exodus, and the inference is drawn that Sinai must have been near Kadesh in the north of the peninsula. For what it is worth it may be noted that in Hebrew different words for rock are used in the two accounts.

Jewish legend assumed that the same rock was involved in both incidents, but in widely separated places, and this lies behind Paul's mention of "the supernatural rock which followed them" (1 Cor. 10:4).

THE BATTLE WITH AMALEK

Exodus 17:8–16

8 9 Then came Amalek and fought with Israel at Rephidim. And Moses said to Joshua, "Choose for us men, and go out, fight with Amalek; tomorrow I will stand on the top of the hill with the rod of God in my
10 hand." So Joshua did as Moses told him, and fought with Amalek;
11 and Moses, Aaron, and Hur went up to the top of the hill. Whenever Moses held up his hand, Israel prevailed; and whenever he lowered
12 his hand, Amalek prevailed. But Moses' hands grew weary; so they took a stone and put it under him, and he sat upon it, and Aaron and Hur held up his hands, one on one side, and the other on the other
13 side; so his hands were steady until the going down of the sun. And Joshua mowed down Amalek and his people with the edge of the sword.
14 And the Lord said to Moses, "Write this as a memorial in a book and recite it in the ears of Joshua, that I will utterly blot out the
15 remembrance of Amalek from under heaven." And Moses built an
16 altar and called the name of it, The Lord is my banner, saying, "A hand upon the banner of the Lord! The Lord will have war with Amalek from generation to generation."

The Amalekites were a Beduin tribe located in the arid area between Canaan and Egypt. As always with such nomads we cannot pinpoint their main centre. The reasons for their attack on Israel are not made clear. From Deut. 25:17 we might infer that it was just a quest for plunder, though it could have been a reaction to Israel's entry into what they considered to be their tribal area, or their desire to control the new water supply. The sequel, however, shows that it was considered to be a breach of basic desert morality.

Moses' action has puzzled many. It was probably to impress on Israel what they were so slow to learn, that God was in command and in control of all details of their desert march. While Rom. 8:28 may have seemed obvious to Paul, it is one of the most difficult truths for many a Christian to grasp.

Hur was obviously an older man of importance, but apart from 24:14 there is no other mention of him. It is casual references like this which show how firmly based the Pentateuch is on ancient knowledge, whenever it may have received its present written form. The fluctuating nature of the battle until final victory was won is one of the indications that the Israelites were not as numerous as the figure in 12:37 suggests.

Neither the attack by Amalek nor its defeat is surprising, but the statement that Yahweh desired their ultimate annihilation is; cf. Deut. 25:17–19; 1 Sam. 15:2–3. This is unique in the Old Testament, for the command to annihilate the Canaanites had another motivation. Israel was to suffer from other nomadic raiders, but that did not call for any such drastic revenge. It would appear that either the way in which Amalek treated the stragglers, or its attempt to grab the new water supply, offended against basic standards of behaviour; "he feared not God" (Deut. 25:18). Compare Amos 1:3–2:3, where sentence is passed on Israel's neighbours for similar breaches of basic standards of morality.

The erection of an altar was Moses' recognition of God's presence and of him as giver of victory and uniter of the tribesmen of Israel against their enemy. The explanation of the name of the altar is difficult, because of the brevity of the Hebrew; Childs understands "A hand upon the banner of Yahweh" as a war cry.

The sooner the mediaeval, allegorical interpretation, sometimes still met today, that Amalek is a type of the flesh, is forgotten the better. There is no valid support for it.

This victory by the freed serfs over the war-hardened desert nomads must have been a tremendous encouragement to the Israelites.

JETHRO'S VISIT

Exodus 18:1–27

1 Jethro, the priest of Midian, Moses' father-in-law, heard of all that

God had done for Moses and for Israel his people, how the Lord had
2 brought Israel out of Egypt. Now Jethro, Moses' father-in-law, had
3 taken Zipporah, Moses' wife, after he had sent her away, and her
two sons, of whom the name of the one was Gershom (for he said, "I
4 have been a sojourner in a foreign land"), and the name of the other,
Eliezer (for he said, "The God of my father was my help, and
5 delivered me from the sword of Pharaoh"). And Jethro, Moses'
father-in-law, came with his sons and his wife to Moses in the
6 wilderness where he was encamped at the mountain of God. And
when one told Moses, "Lo, your father-in-law Jethro is coming to
7 you with your wife and her two sons with her," Moses went out to
meet his father-in-law, and did obeisance and kissed him; and they
8 asked each other of their welfare, and went into the tent. Then
Moses told his father-in-law all that the Lord had done to Pharaoh
and to the Egyptians for Israel's sake, all the hardship that had come
9 upon them in the way, and how the Lord had delivered them. And
Jethro rejoiced for all the good which the Lord had done to Israel, in
that he had delivered them out of the hand of the Egyptians.
10 And Jethro said, "Blessed be the Lord, who has delivered you out
11 of the hand of the Egyptians and out of the hand of Pharaoh. Now I
know that the Lord is greater than all gods, because he delivered the
people from under the hand of the Egyptians, when they dealt
12 arrogantly with them." And Jethro, Moses' father-in-law, offered a
burnt offering and sacrifices to God; and Aaron came with all the
elders of Israel to eat bread with Moses' father-in-law before God.
13 On the morrow Moses sat to judge the people, and the people
14 stood about Moses from morning till evening. When Moses' father-
in-law saw all that he was doing for the people, he said, "What is this
that you are doing for the people? Why do you sit alone, and all the
15 people stand about you from morning till evening?" And Moses said
to his father-in-law, "Because the people come to me to inquire of
16 God; when they have a dispute, they come to me and I decide
between a man and his neighbour, and I make them know the
17 statutes of God and his decisions." Moses' father-in-law said to him,
18 "What you are doing is not good. You and the people with you will
wear yourselves out, for the thing is too heavy for you; you are not
19 able to perform it alone. Listen now to my voice; I will give you
counsel, and God be with you! You shall represent the people before
20 God, and bring their cases to God; and you shall teach them the
statutes and the decisions, and make them know the way in which

21 they must walk and what they must do. Moreover choose able men
    from all the people, such as fear God, men who are trustworthy and
    who hate a bribe; and place such men over the people as rulers of
22 thousands, of hundreds, of fifties, and of tens. And let them judge
    the people at all times; every great matter they shall bring to you, but
    any small matter they shall decide themselves; so it will be easier for
23 you, and they will bear the burden with you. If you do this, and God
    so commands you, then you will be able to endure, and all this
    people also will go to their place in peace."
24   So Moses gave heed to the voice of his father-in-law and did all
25 that he had said. Moses chose able men out of all Israel, and made
    them heads over the people, rulers of thousands, of hundreds, of
26 fifties, and of tens. And they judged the people at all times; hard
    cases they brought to Moses, but any small matter they decided
27 themselves. Then Moses let his father-in-law depart, and he went his
    way to his own country.

Deut. 1:9-18 strongly suggests that the incident of Moses
choosing able men as leaders (verses 13-26) should be placed
shortly before Israel left Sinai, and there are a number of minor
indications that this was so. This is confirmed by 19:1-2, where
the definitive arrival at Sinai is recorded.

As mentioned in the comment on 16:33-34 a common
feature of Hebrew historical writing is that chronological order
takes second place to the flow of the story. From Israel's arrival
at Mount Sinai until its departure is one compact story, and the
editor did not want to interrupt it by bringing Jethro in at the
correct chronological point. He had the choice of putting him at
the beginning or end, and chose the former.

There is another example of this at the start of the chapter,
for there is no earlier mention of Moses' having sent his wife
and sons back to Jethro from Egypt. That was, of course, a very
sensible precaution, in case Pharaoh vented his wrath on Moses
by killing his wife and family. The unpleasant modern practice
of taking people hostage to use them to exert pressure on the
unwilling had not yet become normal practice in those "bad old
days".

Far-reaching theories have been built on the discussion

between Moses and Jethro in verses 8-12. It has been suggested that Moses learnt the worship of Yahweh from Jethro. In fact this passage suggests rather that Jethro may have learnt of Yahweh through Moses, and now acknowledged that his son-in-law's God was in fact all that he had claimed him to be. This seems to be the meaning, for Jethro sacrificed to "God", not Yahweh, even though the context suggests that he was bowing to the superiority of Israel's God. Moses is not mentioned in the ceremony, because the sacrificial meal was presumably held in his tent.

Jethro soon discovered that Moses had fallen into the trap that "charismatic" leaders so often fall victim to. Though, as the mention of "the elders of Israel" (verse 12) shows, tribal organization already existed, Moses allowed himself to be regarded as omnicompetent and responsible for all the problems that might arise among the people.

There were three bad results. Moses himself was overworked and could not cope with all he had to do. The people were deprived of the swift justice that was needed. Finally the elders and other competent individuals were deprived of the opportunity of using their talents. Jethro realized, however, that there were situations which only Moses was capable of dealing with.

Many a church would be happier, if this lesson were learnt by its members, and above all that the most "charismatic" is not always the wisest.

F. THE MAKING OF THE COVENANT
(19:1-24:18)
THE ARRIVAL AT MOUNT SINAI

Exodus 19:1-2

1 On the third new moon after the people of Israel had gone forth out of the land of Egypt, on that day they came into the wilderness of
2 Sinai. And when they set out from Rephidim and came into the wilderness of Sinai, they encamped in the wilderness; and there Israel encamped before the mountain.

Strangely enough we have no certain knowledge of the site of Sinai-Horeb. Elijah still knew it (1 Kgs. 19:8), unless we assume that he was divinely guided there, but there is no evidence that any tradition of it remained after the Babylonian Exile. The rabbis were and are completely indifferent about it. None of the protests against the handing back of the Sinaitic peninsula to Egypt under the Camp David agreement were based on the sacredness of the mountain.

The earliest known identification of the site was made by Christian monks in the fourth century A.D., but they chose Jebel Serbal. By the time of the Emperor Justinian the site had been moved to Jebel Musa, which is the traditional site today. There are, however, biblical indications which do not suit the south of the Sinai peninsula—the name was applied to the peninsula only after the identification of the mountain. Other suggestions are Jebel Helal in the north of the peninsula, or even a peak east of the Gulf of Akaba. Fortunately the nature of this commentary does not demand the expression of a personal opinion. For further details see the Commentaries of Driver and Hyatt and the various Bible dictionaries.

All this uncertainty underlines that God had no wish that Sinai should become a sacred place of pilgrimage. The rabbis showed spiritual insight, when they taught that the Law was given in the wilderness, which belonged to no nation exclusively.

THE OFFER OF THE COVENANT

Exodus 19:3–9

3 And Moses went up to God, and the Lord called to him out of the mountain, saying, "Thus you shall say to the house of Jacob, and tell
4 the people of Israel: You have seen what I did to the Egyptians, and
5 how I bore you on eagles' wings and brought you to myself. Now therefore, if you will obey my voice and keep my covenant, you shall be my own possession among all peoples; for all the earth is mine,
6 and you shall be to me a kingdom of priests and a holy nation. These are the words which you shall speak to the children of Israel."

7 So Moses came and called the elders of the people, and set before
8 them all these words which the Lord had commanded him. And all
   the people answered together and said, "All that the Lord has
   spoken we will do." And Moses reported the words of the people to
9 the Lord. And the Lord said to Moses, "Lo, I am coming to you in a
   thick cloud, that the people may hear when I speak with you, and
   may also believe you for ever." Then Moses told the words of the
   people to the Lord.

(i)

Except in some theological systems and financial transactions
the concept of covenant has largely disappeared from modern
thought, but Old Testament society, and indeed the Ancient
Near East, was largely dominated by it. Though the term
covenant *(berit)* might not be used, it was presupposed in the
mutual obligations within the family, tribe and nation, between
the nation and its gods, and between nations or groups which
had treaties with each other. These obligations were summed
up in the word *chesed,* basically loyalty, but acquiring a much
richer meaning in Israel's religion; see the commentary on 34:6.

When God made a covenant with Abraham—later confirmed with Isaac and Jacob—he used a ceremony in common
use, then and much later; cf. Gen. 15:9–17; Jer. 34:18–19.
Similarly he chose circumcision as the covenant mark (Gen.
17:9–10), a custom almost universal, though with other significance, in the West-Semitic world and widespread in Egypt. So
now he used an approximation to the suzerainty treaties of the
time, by which the relationship between conquerors and their
new subjects were fixed.

Many find it strange that God should act like this. While it is
true, "My ways are higher than your ways and my thoughts
than your thoughts" (Isa. 55:9), the Bible, the record of God's
self-revelation, shows that he has always used human language
and customs. But in using the familiar he has filled it with
meaning beyond what man dreamt was in it.

(ii)

So we are told, "Moses went up to God", to acclaim him as

victor, not over them, but on their behalf, and to acknowledge the fulfilment of the "sign" (3:12) given at the burning bush, probably a full year earlier. Then God demanded, as was the custom in suzerainty treaties, that the people accept whatever terms he might put, even before their formulation, basing his demand on his victory. To this was added a promise of what he would do, if the covenant were accepted.

This has always been God's way with men. We are exhorted in the light of God's mercies to present ourselves as a living sacrifice, without any hint being given as to how the sacrifice will be used, except that it will involve our transformation (Rom. 12:2). God's love shown in the giving of his Son should be sufficient to give us confidence that what is entrusted to him will be treated with the deepest love. Much of the disappointment in many a Christian life goes back to an unwillingness to rest unconditionally in his love.

What he does promise us is that we shall be *"his own possession"* (Deut. 7:6; 1 Pet. 2:9). The concept here is taken from the old idea that all the riches of a land belonged to its ruler, but there was a section of it which only he controlled. But to this is added a rider, "for all the earth is mine". When we make a choice, it of necessity means that we have also rejected something else. It is not so with God. To his choice of Israel he added his appreciation of the worth of others, "all the earth is mine". The implication is that God's choice is for the sake of others. It was his failure to give adequate value to the difference between divine and human choice that gave Calvin's teaching on predestination that element of hardness that has made it so repulsive to so many today.

(iii)

In addition Israel would be a "kingdom of priests". In both Testaments the word rendered "kingdom" has a somewhat different connotation to what it usually has in English, where we think of an area over which a king rules. Both in Hebrew and Greek the stress is on the fact of sovereignty, i.e. the phrase means priests over whom God has complete sway.

It is remarkable that the Hebrew for priest *(kohen)* is not the common Semitic word *(chomer)* which is, in the Bible, used only for the priests of the "high places" (2 Kgs. 23:5; Zeph. 1:4). No convincing explanation of this has been offered, though Martin Buber has suggested that *kohen* means one who has the right of entrée either to the king or God. If this is correct, it would go far in explaining the unexpected use of the word in 2 Sam. 8:18; 20:26 and also its use in the New Testament for the people of God as a whole.

"And a holy nation" *(goi)*. We should expect this to be the climax of the promise, and so it is. Hebrew has two words for nation or people *'am*, Greek *laos*, and *goi*, Greek *ethnos*, which differ little in their meaning, except that the former is applied consistently to Israel and to the Church in the New Testament, the latter to other peoples, "the Gentiles", the heathen. Here, where one expects this usage to be followed, *goi* is used for Israel, *ethnos* of the Church in 1 Pet. 2:9. The election of Israel, of the Church, is not due to their being different from the non-elect. They are made different by the fact that they become "holy", i.e. set apart for God's use.

Whenever Israel or the Church cease to be holy, set apart from the world for God, they revert to the level of mankind around them.

(iv)

Following the pattern of suzerainty treaties the people accepted Yahweh's terms (verse 8), although these had not yet been given. We can find a New Testament analogy in Acts 9:16, where the revelation to Saul (Paul) of what he had to suffer was to follow his reception of baptism, the covenant sign. It belongs to the essence of faith that a man accepts God's will *before* its implications have been made clear to him.

Just as the suzerainty treaty was confirmed in a major public ceremony, so was God's covenant with Israel. It was fitting that it should be so, for it was one of the turning points in man's ethical and spiritual history.

THE SETTING OF THE COVENANT

Exodus 19:10–25

10 And the Lord said to Moses, "Go to the people and consecrate them
11 today and tomorrow, and let them wash their garments, and be
ready by the third day; for on the third day the Lord will come down
12 upon Mount Sinai in the sight of all the people. And you shall set
bounds for the people round about, saying, 'Take heed that you do
not go up into the mountain or touch the border of it; whoever
13 touches the mountain shall be put to death; no hand shall touch him,
but he shall be stoned or shot; whether beast or man, he shall not
live.' When the trumpet sounds a long blast, they shall come up to
14 the mountain." So Moses went down from the mountain to the
people, and consecrated the people; and they washed their gar-
15 ments. And he said to the people, "Be ready by the third day; do not
go near a woman."

16 On the morning of the third day there were thunders and
lightnings, and a thick cloud upon the mountain, and a very loud
trumpet blast, so that all the people who were in the camp trembled.
17 Then Moses brought the people out of the camp to meet God; and
18 they took their stand at the foot of the mountain. And Mount Sinai
was wrapped in smoke, because the Lord descended upon it in fire;
and the smoke of it went up like the smoke of a kiln, and the whole
19 mountain quaked greatly. And as the sound of the trumpet grew
louder and louder, Moses spoke, and God answered him in thunder.
20 And the Lord came down upon Mount Sinai, to the top of the
mountain; and the Lord called Moses to the top of the mountain,
21 and Moses went up. And the Lord said to Moses, "Go down and
warn the people, lest they break through to the Lord to gaze and
22 many of them perish. And also let the priests who come near to the
Lord consecrate themselves, lest the Lord break out upon them."
23 And Moses said to the Lord, "The people cannot come up to Mount
Sinai; for thou thyself didst charge us, saying, 'Set bounds about the
24 mountain, and consecrate it.'" And the Lord said to him, "Go down,
and come up bringing Aaron with you; but do not let the priests and
the people break through to come up to the Lord, lest he break out
25 against them." So Moses went down to the people and told them.

Probably nothing would have shocked the kings of old more than if they could have seen the modern royal "walkabout" made familiar to millions by T.V. Royal pomp and splendour seldom surpassed the absurdity of Ahasuerus (Esth. 4:11), and it was taken for granted that God should robe himself in even greater majesty, when he deigned to reveal himself to the eyes of mortal man.

One of the features of the biblical revelation of God is that, generally speaking, it conformed very largely to the expected pattern; there is seldom significance in the details. So it is here. The cloud and smoke and fire, though we have them again in 40:34 and in e.g. 1 Kgs. 8:12(RSV), Isa. 6:4 and Nah. 1:3, were not necessary for a theophany; compare God's appearances in Genesis, where this kind of thing occurs only in 15:12. In fact, in the life of Jesus of Nazareth we have the perfect example of the divine "walkabout". One of the very few Christian kings, who seems to have learnt the lesson was Godfrey, the first Crusader king of Jerusalem, who refused coronation saying that he would not wear a crown of gold in the city where his Saviour had been crowned with thorns.

On the human side, however, while Jesus can at any time be met in one's working clothes, with hands and feet dirtied from daily toil, the increasing neglect of the Saturday night bath, and the clean Sunday shirt, and the best Sunday suit does mark the loss of a very real respect for the King of kings.

The forbidding of sexual relationships for a time (cf. 1 Sam. 21:4–5) is not intended as a depreciation of them, but rather a suggestion, that in the light of what was involved, their thoughts should be turned to the highest.

We have a very primitive concept of the "holy" in the "setting of bounds" in verse 12. By God's presence on the mountain it was made "holy", i.e. excluded from ordinary use, and hence could not be touched by man or beast. If the ban was broken, the man or animal acquired something of the holiness; since that made him dangerous to others, he had to be killed. It took Israel a long time to learn that holiness was not something primarily physical.

THE TEN COMMANDMENTS

Exodus 20:1–17

1 2 And God spoke all these words, saying, "I am the Lord your God, who brought you out of the land of Egypt, out of the house of bondage.

3 "You shall have no other gods before me.

4 "You shall not make for yourself a graven image, or any likeness of anything that is in heaven above, or that is in the earth beneath, or

5 that is the water under the earth; you shall not bow down to them or serve them; for I the Lord your God am a jealous God, visiting the iniquity of the fathers upon the children to the third and the fourth

6 generation of those who hate me, but showing steadfast love to thousands of those who love me and keep my commandments.

7 "You shall not take the name of the Lord your God in vain; for the Lord will not hold him guiltless who takes his name in vain.

8 9 "Remember the sabbath day, to keep it holy. Six days you shall

10 labour, and do all your work; but the seventh day is a sabbath to the Lord your God; in it you shall not do any work, you, or your son, or your daughter, your manservant, or your maidservant, or your

11 cattle, or the sojourner who is within your gates; for in six days the Lord made heaven and earth, the sea, and all that is in them, and rested the seventh day; therefore the Lord blessed the sabbath day and hallowed it.

12 "Honour your father and your mother, that your days may be long in the land which the Lord your God gives you.

13 "You shall not kill.

14 "You shall not commit adultery.

15 "You shall not steal.

16 "You shall not bear false witness against your neighbour.

17 "You shall not covet your neighbour's house; you shall not covet your neighbour's wife, or his manservant, or his maidservant, or his ox, or his ass, or anything that is your neighbour's."

INTRODUCTORY

Christian thinkers have always felt that the Ten Commandments (Heb. Ten Words) occupy a peculiar position in the Law.

In contrast, after the destruction of the Jewish state in A.D. 70, they tended to be played down by the rabbis, who wanted to counter any idea that any one part of the Torah (the Instruction or Law) was more important than any other.

These are the only laws which the narrative claims were spoken to the entire people by God, the remainder being mediated through Moses. They formed the contents of the two tablets of stone written in the first place by God himself (24:12; 31:18; 32:15–16; Deut. 10:4). The usual pictures of the stone tablets, both in Jewish and in Christian art, ignore the statement that they were written on both sides (32:15). Though deliberately smashed by Moses (32:19), they were renewed by God, though Moses had to cut the tablets himself (34:1, 28). They were put in the Ark (40:20; Deut. 10:1–5). In 40:20 they are called "the testimony", for they served as the virtual charter of Israel becoming God's people.

It is therefore the more striking that when we compare the Exodus version of the Ten Words with that in Deuteronomy (5:6–21), we find both major and minor differences between them. The latter, too small to leave much trace in the English versions, may be ignored here, but that is not the case when we compare Exod. 20:11 with Deut. 5:15, or 20:17 with 5:21. An explanation that appeals to different sources is too facile, for it will hardly explain major differences in quoting the nation's basic charter. It is held by not a few that the Ten Words were originally all positive, which is unlikely, and much briefer, which is likely. In other words, the changes come in commandments which may originally have been simply "Remember the Sabbath day to keep it holy", and "You shall not covet". If that is so, a change in an interpretive clause or in the order of clauses is not so striking; but see commentary on 31:18.

Martin Buber has pointed out that if we were to translate with strict regard for Hebrew grammar, we should render here "You will not have ..., you will not make ..." instead of negative imperatives, i.e. we have a description of the behaviour of a man in covenant relationship with God, instead of a series of prohibitions. In other words the picture is very like that of the New Covenant in Jer. 31:31–34. This, however, does not hold good for the Hebrew of the Deuteronomic version of the Ten Words.

The Ten Words are not "casuistic" or "case" laws such as we get in 21:1–6; 21:7–11, but are what are called "apodictic laws", namely, they are absolute, allowing for no exception, and based on the demands of a man's loyalty to God.

Note that the RSV in dropping the "thou" of the AV in favour of "you", has obscured the fact that the commandments are addressed to the individual. Though the covenant was with the nation as a whole, it was binding on the individual first and foremost.

THE PROCLAMATION OF GOD'S GRACE (20:2)

In a secular suzerainty treaty there would have been at this point a proclamation of the conqueror's triumph (as, e.g. in 19:4). Here it is a proclamation of God's triumph *for* his people, not *over* them. In other words, what follows is an expression of *grace,* not of compulsion. This means that to omit verse 2 in a recitation of the Ten Words is to put them in a false setting, in one of Law and not of grace.

THE TEN COMMANDMENTS TODAY I

Exodus 20:1–17 *(cont'd)*

There is a widespread tendency today, in contrast to the attitude of the Reformers, to deny that the Ten Words have any real applicability to the Christian. It is maintained by many that the New Commandment, "that you love one another, even as I have loved you" (John 13:34), has made the Ten Words an expression of that which has passed away. For that reason the comments that follow will be less concerned with those who first heard them, and more with their applicability today.

1. THE PROHIBITION OF POLYTHEISM (20:3)

Hyatt renders, "You shall not prefer other gods to me". Strict monotheism was a later development in Israel. What is being demanded here is rather "henotheism", a technical word used to express the worship of one God only, without posing the intellectual question of whether other competing powers might exist. Today there are many Christians who attribute undue power to Satan, to the planets and to other influences. We are to give an unqualified 'Amen' to Paul's affirmations in Rom. 8:28, 38–39.

2. THE PROHIBITION OF IDOLATRY (20:4–6)

While the Hebrew word *pesel* is rightly rendered "graven image", Isa. 40:19 and 44:10 show it may be taken in a wider sense. An outstanding peculiarity of Israel's faith was its refusal to make an image of Yahweh. The archaeologist has unearthed many representations of goddesses, but not of male deities, from Israelite sites—for the "golden calf" see the commentary on 32:2–4.

In our understanding of the prohibition we must grasp that the worshipper of images does not, strictly speaking, worship them. He considers that, thanks to a priestly blessing, some element of the deity is present in the image; in addition the form of the image is taken to represent some outstanding quality of the god in question.

The prohibition denies that man can insure the presence of God by any action of his own. It also affirms that God is so wonderful, that no effort of man to depict him is adequate.

God is declared to be "jealous". As the great Lover of men, it matters very much to him how we think of him. That is why the first petition in the Lord's Prayer is, "Hallowed be thy name". Any representation of him, by its very nature inadequate, must reduce the esteem in which he is held.

The modern Christian should seriously ask himself, whether the same does not apply to pictures of Jesus, unless like Holman Hunt's *The Light of the World,* they are entirely and obviously symbolic. Because the artist is forced to concentrate on one aspect of his character, as he sees it, we are not given his full glory, "glory as of the only begotten of the Father". Many an adult has acknowledged that his thinking of Jesus has been shaped by the pictures he saw in his childhood. It is, however, probably far worse to create our concepts of God and Christ on the basis of passing idealisms, than to let the artist, who need not be a Christian, create them for us by his painting or sculpture.

It has been suggested that the typical Englishman is all too ready to attribute to God the standards of the traditional public school. These may be high and noble, but they fall seriously short of those revealed by Jesus Christ. More common is the tendency to ascribe to God or Jesus all those philosophies and ideologies which happen to be in fashion at the moment. All too often the Church has depicted Christ as a conservative or revolutionary, as a socialist or pacifist. The truth is that God's character is so wonderfully rich and wide that any identification of him with our ideologies and ideals gives a completely inadequate picture of his being.

In fact as we study the darkest pages of the Church's history we find that they were almost always due to well-meaning people who isolated and stressed some of the attributes of God. These were doubtless true, but in isolation and overstressed they have led to some of the blackest deeds committed by fallen man.

The force of "the third and fourth generation" has been very widely missed. In early Israelite society the sons, when they married, settled in the immediate vicinity of the parental home. Given the usual age of marriage, the aged head of the family would normally have four generations living in close proximity and being influenced by him. This would be bound to be harmful, if he had an inadequate concept of God as shown by his use of images.

"But showing steadfast [covenant] love to thousands [of generations] of them that love him and keep his command-ments." This rendering (TEV) represents the old rabbinic tradition and is almost certainly correct.

3. THE PROHIBITION OF MISUSING GOD'S NAME (20:7)

The name Yahweh, or for that matter God or Jesus, should not be used for unworthy purposes. This was intended to prohibit three very common practices:

(a) The use of Yahweh for magical purposes. So general was the belief that this was possible, that in the mediaeval *Toledoth Yeshu,* a popular Jewish anti-gospel, the miracles of Jesus are attributed to his possession of the divine name. The same sort of concept lives on today among those who think that by adding "in the name of Jesus" to a prayer, they are guaranteeing a favourable answer, more or less irrespective of its contents. This is sheer magic, which thinks we can force God to do our will.

(b) The use of the name of God to substantiate the truth of a statement. The regular formula found repeatedly in the historical books of the Old Testament is, "May God [Yahweh] do so to me and more also, if . . . ". I have no right to imply that God is at my beck and call. The Christian attitude is that I should be known to be so honest that my word will not be doubted (Matt. 5:33–37).

(c) Thoughtless profanity. This shows both lack of respect to God, and an inability to control one's tongue.

This commandment was applied with unintelligent strictness in the post-Exilic and inter-Testamental periods. The use of Yahweh was replaced by Lord or God and sometimes by "the Name" or "Heaven". The first step in the process may be seen in Books 2 and 3 of the Psalms (42–89), where Yahweh has normally been replaced by *Elohim* (God). The extreme form of this is the modern Jewish hyper-orthodox fad of writing G - d, as may be seen on the "Wayside Pulpit" of some synagogues, i.e. the text or ethical sentiment to be read by the passer-by.

From our modern point of view this commandment involves the control of the tongue, of the language we use. One of the great weaknesses of our time is the readiness of the average person to relieve his feelings by a flood of meaningless expletives. In many cases the name of God is obscured by the use of surrogates, the meaning of which has largely been forgotten. Not so much disrespect to God as misuse of the gift of speech is the important issue here; see Jas. 1:26; 3:2–12; 4:11–16.

THE TEN COMMANDMENTS TODAY II

Exodus 20:1-17 *(cont'd)*

4. THE SANCTIFICATION OF TIME (20:8-11)

None of the Ten Commandments has led to greater controversy than this. The reason for this is obvious enough. The legalist always finds it easier to prohibit completely than to find a spiritual interpretation of a positive command. Though this is generally interpreted as requiring a complete cessation of work one day in seven, in fact it demands that that day should be kept holy, i.e. set aside for God.

Two motivations for keeping the Sabbath are given. In Deut. 5:15 it is linked with the freeing of Israel from slavery in Egypt. Those whom God has set free should not become enslaved by the demands of this life, and that is as valid a motive today as it was for Israel then. Here in Exodus it is linked with the story of creation in Gen. 2:2-3. There it is said that "on the seventh day ... God kept *shabbat* from all his work". Sabbath (Heb. *shabbat*) comes from a verb meaning to desist, not to rest, although the latter is the verb used in Exod. 20:11. This gives the clue to the deeper meaning of this commandment, which is indicated in Heb. 4:9-10; by writing of "ceasing from his labours" he picks up the basic meaning of *shabbat*. The Christian's sabbath-rest is ceasing from his own labours to become a fellow-labourer with God. This should, of course, extend to every day.

By its very nature the Sabbath-command creates an inescapable tension. It presupposes that the preceding six days will have sufficed for the work that had to be done, something implicit in Christ's invitation in Matt. 11:25-30, namely, that anyone accepting it will be able to drop all normal occupations to do Christ's work.

That the Sabbath was, to some extent unwillingly, observed in Israel from an early date is shown by Amos 8:5-6. After the return from the Babylonian Exile, its observance grew steadily stricter, and by the end of the second century A.D. a list of thirty-nine kinds of work had been drawn up, which were prohibited on the Sabbath, a list which can to a great extent be paralleled in Puritan legislation and practice. In spite of all this rigorism and legalism the Sabbath remained until very recently a day of joy and light in Israel, and was largely responsible for the people's preservation down the centuries. Thanks to the rabbinic principle that the Law was given that man might *live* by it, various means were found for relaxing or circumventing the strictness of the rabbinic code.

Outside Christ's controversies with the Jewish religious leaders, we find little interest in Sabbath observance in the New Testament. This can best be explained by the fact that so many of the early Gentile converts were slaves, for whom Sabbath (or Sunday) observance was an impossibility. To have stressed its importance too much would have made second-class church members of them.

Unfortunately, the exaggerated antinomianism of many sections of the Church today has caused many to lose all understanding of the truth of Isa. 58:13–14 and of Christ's statement that "the Sabbath was made for man". This does not mean that we should force Sunday observance on those who have no respect for the Lord of the Sabbath, but we should defend the rights of those who treasure their day of rest and not allow the selfishness of others to rob them of it.

There has long been controversy between those who maintain that the Sabbath commandment is of universal application, one of "the laws of nature", so to speak, and those who maintain that it was a gift to Israel (as in Neh. 9:14). The failure to find a parallel elsewhere in the ancient world supports the latter view. The one apparent exception is Exod. 16:22–30, which seems to suggest that the Sabbath was known before the Sinai lawgiving. A careful reading of the passage, however, will suggest that it was an introduction to the Sabbath concept. After all the meaning of *shabbat* will have been clear to them, even if it had not yet obtained a technical meaning.

5. RESPECT FOR PARENTS (20:12)

This command is far from being, as many think today, a mere reflection of earlier social conditions. We have been unduly influenced today by a cult of youth, springing in part from the guilty conscience of two generations, which involved mankind in two disastrous wars.

For Scripture the family is the keystone of the fabric of society, something modern man is slowly relearning. The Covenant assumed that those in it would seek God's will for their children, something made clear in every service of infant baptism. But even in the family, in which the name of God is not honoured, the child should not forget that his parents were used by God to bring him into the world. In addition, however well or badly it was done, it was normally they who gave him the care in childhood without which he would not have become an adult. Even in these days, when the home often leaves so much to be desired, the thought that there is nothing in one's make-up which has not been derived from one's parents, should make us regard them with a deeper respect. The problem can become bitter for the child in an irreligious home, who has become aware of the love of God and wishes to do his will, often in opposition to his parents' wishes. The best advice that can normally be given is that so long as he is dependent on his parents, he should obey their wishes, provided that they are not positively wrong. Youth workers need to be more aware than they often are of how often they are driving a wedge between the young and their parents.

THE TEN COMMANDMENTS TODAY III

Exodus 20:1–17 *(cont'd)*

6. THE PROHIBITION OF MURDER (20:13)

It is a great pity that the RSV should have followed the AV with "You shall not kill". More correct is "You shall not murder" (RV, NEB, NIV, TEV). The word *ratzach,* with one exception

(Prov. 22:13), is used only of unauthorized killing, though sometimes unintentional. It is not used for killing in war or in carrying out a judicial sentence.

Life is the gift of God, which cannot be replaced by man, if he takes it. Therefore murder stands at the head of the Old Testament's list of iniquities. The prophets extended its meaning to include all that cuts at the roots of life, such as injustice and robbing a man of the means of livelihood. Jesus went further, including every attitude that robbed a man of his self-esteem and that lack of love, which meant the withholding of aid, when it was most needed (Matt. 5:21–26).

There are few biblical insights more alien to the modern mind. It is all too often regarded as "bad luck", if the drunken or impatient driver kills someone on the road. It is considered distasteful, if a vigilant journalist unearths an old scandal and ruins a family in so doing. There is a passing moment of sympathy if someone is robbed of the means of earning his living by the enforcement of a "closed shop" in industry. There is a passing moment of anxiety and little more, when "industrial action", as it is euphemistically called, threatens the sick, the poor, the aged. There is seldom effective church action over the gossip who takes pleasure in tearing members' characters to shreds.

7. THE PROHIBITION OF ADULTERY (20:14)

In few things has modern society departed further from the standards of the Bible than in its attitude towards all aspects of sex. It would be fairer to say that the reaction has been less against the Bible and more against that Puritanical attitude towards anything to do with sex, which tended to regard it as indecent in itself and the worst of sins. So long as sex was not brought into religion in imitation of the Canaanites, sexual promiscuity, though never condoned, was regarded in the Bible as a fact of life, and there is no outspoken condemnation of the harlot. It could hardly be otherwise, for in a male-dominated society, there were few other ways in which a young widow could earn her living, unless she had rich relations.

But there was no tolerance for adultery, for that threatened the stability of the family, the foundation stone of society, as is increasingly being realized today. It is interesting that apart from the sordid story of David and Bathsheba, there is no other story of adulterous love in the Bible, nor is there any attempt to extenuate the unbridled passion that leads to adultery. Jesus corrected the outlook which made adultery principally the woman's sin, and placed both sexes on the same level, making adultery above all a sin of thought.

Our present lowering of standards and a resultant acceptance of divorce with all the tragedy it can bring in its train comes largely from the fact that the concept, "Whom God has joined together . . . " has been so largely displaced by the dominance of romantic love, which is inadequate to create a lifelong bond.

8. THE PROHIBITION OF THEFT (20:15)

Stealing is a double sin. It is a sin against God, for it accuses him of not giving adequately, and it is a sin against love, for it is a denial of loving one's neighbour as oneself. At the same time it is very often a condemnation of the one stolen from, for he has not met the need of another from his abundance. We need to balance this command with, "You shall love your neighbour as yourself" (Lev. 19:18). One form of stealing, which is all too common among Christians, is our failure to give others all the praise and credit they deserve, for they think that if they do it, they in turn may not receive their fair share. They forget that it is the heavenly Father's estimate and not man's that really matters.

9. THE PROHIBITION OF FALSE WITNESS (20:16)

For the West, so strongly influenced by Calvinism, it seems strange that the Ten Words should not simply have forbidden lying, the more so that our lies mostly come from our fearing man more than God. The Old Testament is ambivalent where lying is concerned. It records without comment how some of its leading figures lied, when they feared that their lives were in danger. The simple fact is that it is often very difficult to "tell the truth, the whole truth and nothing but the truth", even when we know it. To do so may cause needless hurt and offence, and jeopardize the well-being of others. Sometimes we are asked questions which should not be answered, but silence is in fact an answer, especially to a skilled interrogator; see comments on 1:15–20.

Here, however, we are concerned with one's being legally interrogated—to bear witness was a public duty (Lev. 5:1). At a time when the death penalty was perforce common, false evidence could be equivalent to murder, so the penalty for it could be death (Deut. 19:18–19). Lev. 19:16 enlarges this law with a prohibition of slander. It is very easy to misjudge another's actions. To make one's misjudgment public, even with the best intentions, can do extreme harm.

10. THE PROHIBITION OF COVETING (20:17)

The word translated "covet" often means no more than "desire" or "lust", as it is rendered by Paul in Rom. 7:7 (AV), but the context shows that coveting is intended.

This is, of course, the outstanding sin of our time, and lies at the root of our social dissatisfaction and economic troubles. He who prays, "Give us this day our daily bread" has no right to be dissatisfied with the Heavenly Father's giving, for he will not withhold any good gift. The commandment, however, looks especially at the selfishness and lovelessness involved. It is not wanting more that is condemned, but wanting it at the expense of others. Jesus, in the parable of the labourers in the vineyard (Matt. 20:1–16), showed up the selfishness behind many a modern demand for equality of reward.

THE PEOPLE'S FEAR

Exodus 20:18–21

18 Now when all the people perceived the thunderings and the light-

nings and the sound of the trumpet and the mountain smoking, the
19 people were afraid and trembled; and they stood afar off, and said to
Moses, "You speak to us, and we will hear; but let not God speak to
20 us, lest we die." And Moses said to the people, "Do not fear; for God
has come to prove you, and that the fear of him may be before your
21 eyes, that you may not sin." And the people stood afar off, while
Moses drew near to the thick darkness where God was.

Other sources make earthquake shock a virtually certain
accompaniment of the theophany (e.g. Judg. 5:5); whether we
are to assume volcanic action as well, or simply a tremendous
thunderstorm must remain an open question. To deny the
former on the basis of a false identification of Jebel Musa as
Mount Sinai shows faulty thinking. The fear of the people was
natural. Moses had seen the fire in the heart of the bush (3:2–3),
leaving it unharmed, so he was unmoved. The trumpet (*sho-
phar*) was the ram's horn, demanding attention. We have a
similar picture in 1 Kgs. 19:11–12. But to Elijah, God an-
nounced his presence by "a gentle whisper" (NIV), "the sound
of a gentle breeze" (JB). For Elijah that was as awe-inspiring as
all the thunders and earthquake shocks of Sinai. Much modern
piety has lost that sense of awe. We need to recapture the vision
of Thomas Binney's hymn:

> Eternal light! Eternal light!
>   How pure the soul must be,
> When, placed within Thy searching sight,
>   It shrinks not, but with calm delight
> Can live and look on Thee.

THE BOOK OF THE COVENANT I

Exodus 20:22–23:33

Basic Cultic Regulations (20:22–26)

22 And the Lord said to Moses, "Thus you shall say to the people of
Israel: 'You have seen for yourselves that I have talked with you
23 from heaven. You shall not make gods of silver to be with me, nor

24 shall you make for yourselves gods of gold. An altar of earth you shall make for me and sacrifice on it your burnt offerings and your peace offerings, your sheep and your oxen; in every place where I cause my name to be remembered I will come to you and bless you.
25 And if you make me an altar of stone, you shall not build it of hewn
26 stones; for if you wield your tool upon it you profane it. And you shall not go up by steps to my altar, that your nakedness be not exposed on it.' "

The Hebrew Slave (21:1–6)

1 "Now these are the ordinances which you shall set before them.
2 When you buy a Hebrew slave, he shall serve six years, and in the
3 seventh he shall go out free, for nothing. If he comes in single, he shall go out single; if he comes in married, then his wife shall go out with
4 him. If his master gives him a wife and she bears him sons or daughters, the wife and her children shall be her master's and he
5 shall go out alone. But if the slave plainly says, 'I love my master, my
6 wife, and my children; I will not go out free,' then his master shall bring him to God, and he shall bring him to the door or the doorpost; and his master shall bore his ear through with an awl; and he shall serve him for life."

The Female Slave (21:7–11)

7 "When a man sells his daughter as a slave, she shall not go out as the
8 male slaves do. If she does not please her master, who has designated her for himself, then he shall let her be redeemed; he shall have no right to sell her to a foreign people, since he has dealt faithlessly with
9 her. If he designates her for his son, he shall deal with her as with a
10 daughter. If he takes another wife to himself, he shall not diminish
11 her food, her clothing, or her marital rights. And if he does not do these three things for her, she shall go out for nothing, without payment of money."

Personal Injuries (21:12–17)

12 13 "Whoever strikes a man so that he dies shall be put to death. But if he did not lie in wait for him, but God let him fall into his hand, then I
14 will appoint for you a place to which he may flee. But if a man wilfully attacks another to kill him treacherously, you shall take him from my altar, that he may die.

15   "Whoever strikes his father or his mother shall be put to death.
16   "Whoever steals a man, whether he sells him or is found in possession of him, shall be put to death.
17   "Whoever curses his father or his mother shall be put to death."

More Personal Injuries (21:18–27)

18   "When men quarrel and one strikes the other with a stone or with his
19   fist and the man does not die but keeps his bed, then if the man rises again and walks abroad with his staff, he that struck him shall be clear; only he shall pay for the loss of his time, and shall have him thoroughly healed.
20   "When a man strikes his slave, male or female, with a rod and the
21   slave dies under his hand, he shall be punished. But if the slave survives a day or two, he is not to be punished; for the slave is his money.
22   "When men strive together, and hurt a woman with child, so that there is a miscarriage, and yet no harm follows, the one who hurt her shall be fined, according as the woman's husband shall lay upon
23   him; and he shall pay as the judges determine. If any harm follows,
24   then you shall give life for life, eye for eye, tooth for tooth, hand for
25   hand, foot for foot, burn for burn, wound for wound, stripe for stripe.
26   "When a man strikes the eye of his slave, male or female, and
27   destroys it, he shall let the slave go free for the eye's sake. If he knocks out the tooth of his slave, male or female, he shall let the slave go free for the tooth's sake."

The Goring Ox (21:28–32)

28   "When an ox gores a man or a woman to death, the ox shall be stoned, and its flesh shall not be eaten; but the owner of the ox shall
29   be clear. But if the ox has been accustomed to gore in the past, and its owner has been warned but has not kept it in, and it kills a man or a woman, the ox shall be stoned, and its owner also shall be put to
30   death. If a ransom is laid on him, then he shall give for the
31   redemption of his life whatever is laid upon him. If it gores a man's
32   son or daughter, he shall be dealt with according to this same rule. If the ox gores a slave, male or female, the owner shall give to their master thirty shekels of silver, and the ox shall be stoned."

Offences against Property (21:33–22:15)

33 "When a man leaves a pit open, or when a man digs a pit and does
34 not cover it, and an ox or an ass falls into it, the owner of the pit shall make it good; he shall give money to its owner, and the dead beast shall be his.

35 "When one man's ox hurts another's, so that it dies, then they shall sell the live ox and divide the price of it; and the dead beast also
36 they shall divide. Or if it is known that the ox has been accustomed to gore in the past, and its owner has not kept it in, he shall pay ox for ox, and the dead beast shall be his.

1 "If a man steals an ox or a sheep, and kills it or sells it, he shall pay five oxen for an ox, and four sheep for a sheep. He shall make
4 restitution; if he has nothing, then he shall be sold for his theft. If the stolen beast is found alive in his possession, whether it is an ox or an ass or a sheep, he shall pay double.

2 "If a thief is found breaking in, and is struck so that he dies, there
3 shall be no bloodguilt for him; but if the sun has risen upon him, there shall be bloodguilt for him.

5 "When a man causes a field or vineyard to be grazed over, or lets his beast loose and it feeds in another man's field, he shall make restitution from the best in his own field and in his own vineyard.

6 "When fire breaks out and catches in thorns so that the stacked grain or the standing grain or the field is consumed, he that kindled the fire shall make full restitution.

7 "If a man delivers to his neighbour money or goods to keep, and it is stolen out of the man's house, then, if the thief is found, he shall
8 pay double. If the thief is not found, the owner of the house shall come near to God, to show whether or not he has put his hand to his neighbour's goods.

9 "For every breach of trust, whether it is for ox, for ass, for sheep, for clothing, or for any kind of lost thing, of which one says, 'This is it,' the case of both parties shall come before God; he whom God shall condemn shall pay double to his neighbour.

10 "If a man delivers to his neighbour an ass or an ox or a sheep or any beast to keep, and it dies or is hurt or is driven away, without any
11 one seeing it, an oath by the Lord shall be between them both to see whether he has not put his hand to his neighbour's property; and the
12 owner shall accept the oath, and he shall not make restitution. But if
13 it is stolen from him, he shall make restitution to its owner. If it is

torn by beasts, let him bring it as evidence; he shall not make restitution for what has been torn.

14 "If a man borrows anything of his neighbour, and it is hurt or dies,
15 the owner not being with it, he shall make full restitution. If the owner was with it, he shall not make restitution; if it was hired, it came for its hire."

Moral Offences (22:16–23:9)

16 "If a man seduces a virgin who is not betrothed, and lies with her, he
17 shall give the marriage present for her, and make her his wife. If her father utterly refuses to give her to him, he shall pay money equivalent to the marriage present for virgins.

18 "You shall not permit a sorceress to live.

19 "Whoever lies with a beast shall be put to death.

20 "Whoever sacrifices to any god, save to the Lord only, shall be utterly destroyed.

21 "You shall not wrong a stranger or oppress him, for you were
22 strangers in the land of Egypt. You shall not afflict any widow or
23 orphan. If you do afflict them, and they cry out to me, I will surely
24 hear their cry; and my wrath will burn, and I will kill you with the sword, and your wives shall become widows and your children fatherless.

25 "If you lend money to any of my people with you who is poor, you shall not be to him as a creditor, and you shall not exact interest
26 from him. If ever you take your neighbour's garment in pledge, you
27 shall restore it to him before the sun goes down; for that is his only covering, it is his mantle for his body; in what else shall he sleep? And if he cries to me, I will hear, for I am compassionate.

28 "You shall not revile God, nor curse a ruler of your people.

29 "You shall not delay to offer from the fulness of your harvest and from the outflow of your presses.

30 "The first-born of your sons you shall give to me. You shall do likewise with your oxen and with your sheep: seven days it shall be with its dam; on the eighth day you shall give it to me.

31 "You shall be men consecrated to me; therefore you shall not eat any flesh that is torn by beasts in the field; you shall cast it to the dogs.

1 "You shall not utter a false report. You shall not join hands with a
2 wicked man, to be a malicious witness. You shall not follow a multitude to do evil; nor shall you bear witness in a suit, turning

3 aside after a multitude, so as to pervert justice; nor shall you be partial to a poor man in his suit.

4 "If you meet your enemy's ox or his ass going astray, you shall
5 bring it back to him. If you see the ass of one who hates you lying under its burden, you shall refrain from leaving him with it, you shall help him to lift it up.

6 "You shall not pervert the justice due to your poor in his suit.
7 Keep far from a false charge, and do not slay the innocent and
8 righteous, for I will not acquit the wicked, And you shall take no bribe, for a bribe blinds the officials, and subverts the cause of those who are in the right.

9 "You shall not oppress a stranger; you know the heart of a stranger, for you were strangers in the land of Egypt."

The Sabbatical Year and the Sabbath (23:10–13)

10 11 "For six years you shall sow your land and gather in its yield; but the seventh year you shall let it rest and lie fallow, that the poor of your people may eat; and what they leave the wild beasts may eat. You shall do likewise with your vineyard, and with your olive orchard.
12 "Six days you shall do your work, but on the seventh day you shall rest; that your ox and your ass may have rest, and the son of your
13 bondmaid, and the alien, may be refreshed. Take heed to all that I have said to you; and make no mention of the names of other gods, nor let such be heard out of your mouth."

The Cultic Calendar (23:14–17)

14 15 "Three times in the year you shall keep a feast to me. You shall keep the feast of unleavened bread; as I commanded you, you shall eat unleavened bread for seven days at the appointed time in the month of Abib, for in it you came out of Egypt. None shall appear before
16 me empty-handed. You shall keep the feast of harvest, of the first fruits of your labour, of what you sow in the field. You shall keep the feast of ingathering at the end of the year, when you gather in from
17 the field the fruit of your labour. Three times in the year shall all your males appear before the Lord God."

Leaven, fat, first fruits, meat and milk (23:18–19)

18 "You shall not offer the blood of my sacrifice with leavened bread, or let the fat of my feast remain until the morning.

19   "The first of the first fruits of your ground you shall bring into the house of the Lord your God.

"You shall not boil a kid in its mother's milk."

Closing Exhortation (23:20–33)

20   "Behold, I send an angel before you, to guard you on the way and to
21   bring you to the place which I have prepared. Give heed to him and hearken to his voice, do not rebel against him, for he will not pardon your transgression; for my name is in him.
22   "But if you hearken attentively to his voice and do all that I say, then I will be an enemy to your enemies and an adversary to your adversaries.
23   "When my angel goes before you, and brings you to the Amorites, and the Hittites, and the Perizzites, and the Canaanites, the Hivites,
24   and the Jebusites, and I blot them out, you shall not bow down to their gods, nor serve them, nor do according to their works, but you
25   shall utterly overthrow them and break their pillars in pieces. You shall serve the Lord your God, and I will bless your bread and your
26   water; and I will take sickness away from the midst of you. None shall cast her young or be barren in your land; I will fulfil the number
27   of your days. I will send my terror before you, and will throw into confusion all the people against whom you shall come, and I will
28   make all your enemies turn their backs to you. And I will send hornets before you, which shall drive out Hivite, Canaanite, and
29   Hittite from before you. I will not drive them out from before you in one year, lest the land become desolate and the wild beasts multiply
30   against you. Little by little I will drive them out from before you,
31   until you are increased and possess the land. And I will set your bounds from the Red Sea to the sea of the Philistines, and from the wilderness to the Euphrates; for I will deliver the inhabitants of the
32   land into your hand, and you shall drive them out before you. You
33   shall make no covenant with them or with their gods. They shall not dwell in your land, lest they make you sin against me; for if you serve their gods, it will surely be a snare to you."

THE BOOK OF THE COVENANT II

Exodus 20:22–23:33 *(cont'd)*

The name, the Book of the Covenant, is today generally applied to this section of Exodus on the basis of 24:7, and need not be questioned. It supplies an application to everyday life of how the "apodictic" demands of the Ten Words should be worked out, even as the Sermon on the Mount does for the Christian.

At one time scholars dated these chapters to the period after the disruption of the kingdom, but today there is a growing awareness that the time of the Judges provides a better setting. There are, however, a number of close similarities between it and the Code of Hammurabi, or Hammurapi of Babylon (1792—1750 B.C.), though the Mosaic laws are consistently more humane. Misunderstanding of the Patriarchs has led to failure to realize that they had brought a tradition of civilization with them from Mesopotamia, which will have been passed on to their descendants in Egypt. This selection of laws—a selection because there are some surprising gaps in it—is best understood as a demonstration of how the Covenant demanded a modification of tradition. Those traditional laws and customs that did not need modification remained unmentioned. Our modern danger is the assumption that the old is of necessity out of date.

BASIC CULTIC REGULATIONS (20:22–26)

Following a reminder that the laws come from God, the prohibition of images, however costly or artistic they might be, is repeated. Need we be surprised that some Jews and Muslims who venture into some Christian church buildings, think that those that worship there are idolaters?

Sacrifice provided the centre round which Old Testament worship revolved, with the altar as its necessary sign. Since God did not want sacrifice, official or unofficial, to create a number of sacred places, he demanded a form of non-permanent altar. An altar of earth acting as a filling for the frame described in 27:1–8, would soon disappear, once the frame was removed. The same was true of one made of rough natural stones. Worship should always maintain sexual decorum ("that your nakedness be not exposed"), something far from obvious in some circles in these days. It is probable that the phrase "in every place" sanctioned sacrificial worship wherever there had been a theophany, and did not restrict it to one central sanctuary.

THE HEBREW SLAVE (21:1–6)

It is probable that the title "Hebrew" is not to be understood merely as a synomym for "Israelite", but is a legacy of the old Mesopotamian term *Habiru,* i.e. we are concerned with someone who had become virtually a second-class citizen after losing his land. He might have sold himself (Lev. 25:39) or have been sold for debt. The basic concept behind this law was that the slave by his work over seven years would have repaid his purchase price many times over. The purchaser had no right to take advantage of a man's passing need; cf. Deut. 15:7–11. The coming round of the Jubilee year (Lev. 25:8ff.) offered the Israelite failure a chance of making a new start, which modern society does not normally afford.

In this essentially humane legislation, the exception of the wife and children is jarring. She will obviously have been a slave of his owner, and for her to go free would have meant financial loss for him—the Hebrew slave was under no obligation to accept her. The rabbinic explanation, based on their interpretation of the slavery laws, was that she would be a non-Israelite, so for her sons to have gone out as free citizens would have "impaired the purity of the race" (Hertz). This is improbable.

Many a Hebrew slave may have decided that a kind master's house offered more security than would freedom. Popular piety has seen in the boring of the ear a typological picture of the Christian's love for Christ, leading to a wish to remain his devoted slave, as expressed in F.R. Havergal's hymn:

> I love, I love my Master,
> I will not go out free,
> For He is my Redeemer;
> He paid the price for me.

But quite apart from the fact that it does not offer an explanation of why it should be the ear, it hardly suits the context. If we must have a fancy explanation, that given by Yohanan ben Zakkai to his students seems more apposite: "The ear that heard the divine utterance, 'For unto me the children of Israel are slaves' (Lev. 25:55) and had yet preferred a human master, let that ear be bored" (Hertz).

"For life" in verse 6 is in Hebrew "for ever". The rabbis and Josephus understood this to mean until the year of Jubilee.

THE FEMALE SLAVE (21:7–11)

The selling of children, especially daughters, to meet debts was not uncommon; see 2 Kgs. 4:1. It was assumed she would become the concubine of her owner, or of one of his sons, i.e. a legal wife. It was felt that a woman had a right to children—and so there was no question of breaking the union, when the seven years were up, unless she had not been given a wife's rights. But she could be redeemed by a kinsman (Lev. 25:48).

THE BOOK OF THE COVENANT III

Exodus 20:22–23:33 *(cont'd)*

PERSONAL INJURIES (21:12–17)

This section is concerned with blows that might kill, whether that result was or was not intended. The "place" appointed by God (verse 13) is presumably the altar mentioned in the next verse. The cities of refuge have not yet been mentioned, and this was legislation for the wilderness.

The death penalty for hitting or cursing parents was not for physical or psychic damage done, but for the breach of a fundamental commandment. It expressed also the feeling that the experience of age was of special value to the community. Kidnapping, in order to sell as a slave, was common at the time, especially among the Phoenicians and Greeks; see Amos 1:6–10; Joel 3:6. The Israelite was God's possession, so the kidnapper was stealing from God.

MORE PERSONAL INJURIES (21:18–27)

The legislation here is essentially down to earth, demanding that the injury done should be, so far as possible, made good. Its actual form reflects the fact that there were no hospitals in which the sick and injured could be taken care of, and there were no insurance societies to provide monetary compensation for the harm done. If we had to care personally for those we injure, we might well be more careful what we do. This section contains the famous *lex talionis* ("life for life" etc.). This has very often been attacked, generally with an avowedly anti-Jewish bias. It is not a demand that there must be retribution, but that the retribution should not exceed the damage done. It is in vain that we quote Matt. 5:38–42. What is wrong with retribution, so long as it is just, where Christ's values are not accepted? At first the law was probably interpreted literally—this would prevent the rich getting off relatively lightly, and the knowledge that such a law existed would have a steadying effect on behaviour—but by the time of Christ the Pharisees were insisting that the punishment must be an equivalent fine.

Poverty and misfortune should not mar a person's dignity in our eyes. The fact of slavery—there is no suggestion that only Israelite slaves are involved—should not deprive a slave of his dignity. He had to be treated with as much consideration as a free person, and if his owner did not, he had no right to keep him as a slave. Had an earlier generation in Britain remembered this, it might not be almost impossible to find a servant maid there today. The critic of the trades' unions should remember that they were created in many cases by the heartlessness of the employers.

THE GORING OX (21:28–32)

In civilized society a man is responsible not merely for his own behaviour, but also for that of animals that are, or should be, under his control. Here the ox, as potentially the most dangerous animal on an Israelite's farm, is chosen to represent all animals that might be involved. The ox was to be "stoned" to death, "in order to implant horror against murder; even the beast, although it had no moral sense, was to be removed from existence" (Hertz); see Gen. 9:5. Its flesh could not be eaten because it "was considered as taboo, because it had blood guilt upon it" (Hyatt). The solemn murder trials against animals that had caused human death, brought from time to time in the Middle Ages, were doubtless based on this law. The warning of the owner was presumably given by the local council of elders. The ransom would have been demanded by and paid to the next of kin. The special rule in the case of a slave (verse 32) will probably have been because there will often have been no next of kin. Thirty shekels of silver was evidently the notional price of a first-class slave—it was adopted to avoid a long legal wrangle in each case. There are grounds for thinking that this was continued even when the purchasing power of silver changed. Hertz suggests that verse 30 ("If a ransom is laid on him . . .") is aimed at a crude and legalistic interpretation of the *lex talionis;* if a son or daughter is gored, not the owner's son or daughter but the owner himself is to suffer.

OFFENCES AGAINST PROPERTY (21:33–22:15)

We start with a fairly common act of carelessness, when a man removed the cover from a cistern for catching rain-water, or for grain-storage, and forgot to replace it. It is remarkable that no mention is made of damage to human life and limb. This presumably came under the *lex talionis,* provided that the injured person could prove that there was no contributary negligence.

The same factor of carelessness plays a part in the law of an ox goring another.

There follow the basic laws for the punishment of theft. Note that the RSV gives a fairly obvious rearrangement of the text (so the NEB and the TEV, but slightly differently in the JB). Burglary, in contrast to housebreaking, may involve the intruder in justifiable homicide. Modern experience shows all too clearly that in the dark one cannot be sure of the burglar's intentions. Double restitution was made standard for theft in later Jewish law. Note that no physical mutilation or branding was to be inflicted.

Jewish tradition understands 22:5 to mean, "When a man burns off a field or a vineyard, and lets the fire spread so that it burns another man's field" (NEB, TEV, mg.). Cattle were not generally turned loose in a vineyard. Modern experience with stubble-burning has shown how easily the flames can spread further than intended. Once again we are dealing with the results of negligence, which never creates a genuine ground for excuse.

Then as now, the doing of a good turn could lead to difficulties for the one doing it; verses 10–13 show how he is to avoid suffering, when it was not his fault. It is not clear what the implications of "come near to God" (verse 8) are. It certainly involved going to the local sanctuary, but whether a solemn oath was to be sworn, or whether the priest by the help of Urim and Thummim should pronounce a verdict is not made clear; verse 9 suggests the latter, verse 11 the former. Amos 3:12 refers to the bringing of evidence that an animal had been killed by wild beasts (verse 13).

THE BOOK OF THE COVENANT IV

Exodus 20:22–23:33 *(cont'd)*

MORAL OFFENCES (22:16–23:9)

Up to this point the legislation has been by modern standards reasonable and acceptable. But much that comes in this section is today rejected out of hand. It must, however, never be forgotten that God was training Israel to reveal his will and character to the world. In addition the fact that the Church has at times misused some of the laws is no argument against their original propriety.

All right-thinking people would agree that if a young man seduces a girl to satisfy his lust he should bear the consequences of his so doing. It is not unreasonable that her father should not agree to the marriage, if he realizes the man's worthlessness.

The terrible use of "You shall not permit a sorceress to live" in the past offers no reason for deleting it from Scripture. The law is applied equally to the man in Lev. 20:27. Behind sorcery in the ancient world lay the avowed turning to evil spirits for the accomplishment of one's purposes, and it was universally condemned. It is not chance that the ancient Greek version translates here "poisoner". In the story of the witch of Endor (1 Sam. 28), it is clear that the woman's speciality was in reality or pretence the consultation of the spirits of the dead to discover the future. Since Saul had been refused this by God's will (1 Sam. 28:6), it was direct rebellion against God's will, when he turned to the woman for the information God had denied him. Whatever the reality behind the modern medium, she is offering information which God has denied to men.

There are, fortunately, few churches that would accept a man or woman into church membership, who openly admitted dabbling in the occult. All attempts to know the future, which do not rely on the Spirit of God, all attempts to control nature by forces which are not subject to God, are by their nature evil, and have as such no place among the people of God. God gave Israel the power of the sword, but has fortunately withheld it from the Church. Hence there can be no excuse for the witch-hunts, which were based more on superstition than on the Bible. In Israel to be known as a sorceress was an implicit denial of God's rule as king over his people.

More and more, sex is today proclaimed as a physical thrill, which may legitimately be heightened by various forms of perversion. For the Bible sex is the supreme gift God has given mankind, that we may imitate the Creator by creating new life. All sexual perversion is therefore a debasing of God's gift and of human dignity. This is particularly true, when an animal is used to provide a sexual "kick" (verse 19). The same is true here as in the previous verse; God has not given the power of the sword to the Church.

It is to be hoped that any Church member, who openly worshipped other gods, would be expelled from membership without delay. That is the modern equivalent of "whoever sacrifices to any god, save to . . .". Rightly understood, however, excommunication is a death sentence (1 Cor. 5:3–5).

We find one of the great central thoughts of the Old Testament in the verses beginning, "You shall not wrong a stranger". We are so accustomed to stress God's love that we are apt to forget that before Hosea could proclaim it Amos had to preach God's righteousness, with its demand, "Let justice roll down like waters, and righteousness like an ever-flowing stream" (5:24). After all injustice is a negation of love.

Israel was warned that the poor must not be favoured in his lawsuit (23:3)—poverty is no proof of righteousness, but then wealth and position are not either. In these verses the demand is that the resident alien and those without family influence and protection should not suffer any disadvantage before the law. Today the media are constantly reminding us what a mockery equality before the law can be for the "submerged tenth" of our population. The excesses that have followed most revolutions have normally been an expression of the bitterness felt by those who have been denied justice. The fact that two harlots could appear before King Solomon appealing for justice (1 Kgs. 3:16–28) shows how seriously the demand for justice was taken in Israel at some periods. Interestingly enough, we have here the threat that God would himself apply the *lex talionis.*

Few questions in the history of Christian ethics have caused greater heart-searching than the question of interest on loans. Apparently the Old Testament prohibition (see also Lev. 25:35–38) of interest applies especially to loans made to the poor, though in Deut. 23:19–20 it is applied to any loan made to an Israelite. The essential difference was that it was a religious duty to lend to the poor, but one had the right to refuse, when the request was made simply for the borrower's convenience. Ideally Jewish communities today have a loan fund for the poor on which no interest is charged. A reasonable attitude would seem to be, that where a person is in real need it is preferable to give than to lend—if repayment is made it can be used for further gifts—but where the request is simply to save trouble or to avoid a high rate of interest, the taking of a reasonable rate of interest would seem to be justified. The mention of the borrower's "cloak" (NIV) indicates how few resources might be left to the one who had been forced to borrow. Comparison may be made with Deut. 24:6. To have to turn to one's neighbour to have one's handful of grain ground would betray one's poverty. A high degree of sensitivity for the feelings of the poor is shown in Deut. 24:10–11.

No motivation is given for commanding no delay in the bringing of the first fruits (verse 29). It was possibly to avoid any damage happening to them, while they were being stored, or to prevent their being mixed with other produce. The regulations for the first-born were considered under 13:11–15; see also 34:20.

One reason why Israelites were not to eat the carcasses of animals killed by wild beasts (verse 31) was that there would be no guarantee that the blood would be fully drained, but the deeper reason is that suggested by Deut. 14:1–2. There should be a certain *noblesse oblige,* where the children of God are concerned. There are things which the average Christian will not do, not because they are wrong, but because they are felt not to be seemly.

In verse 28 God equates the honour that should be shown to his representatives with the respect that should be shown to him. If our legislators were to think of themselves in such a role, it is probable that we would honour them more highly. It is a notorious fact that Rom. 13:1–2 is one of the most difficult New Testament admonitions to carry out, as German Christians were forced to realize in the Nazi period.

The rules beginning "You shall not utter a false report" (23:1–8) are really an expression of Israel's being a family. While they all traced their origin back to Jacob, each tribe felt itself to be a separate entity, as our modern denominations so often do. In verse 2 we are introduced to the vital element, where truth and justice are concerned. These are not necessarily to be found in the majority—a preferable rendering to "multitude" (so JB, NEB, TEV)—indeed they seldom are. This superstition of the rightness of the majority is one of the basic weaknesses of modern democracy, and especially of the Trades' Union movement in Britain. The Christian must always be prepared to stand alone in defence of truth and justice.

The behaviour demanded in this and the following verses is such as would be expected in a family, and it is a sad commentary on life in Ancient Israel that it was necessary to formulate the principle. Unfortunately one cannot assume that all Christians will behave like this.

Driver commented on verse 8, "The prevalence of bribery in the East is notorious." True enough, but though it is less open, it is often far more subtle in the West, and it is very easy to be ensnared by it, before one realizes what is happening. A preferable rendering is, "for bribery makes the discerning man blind and the just man give a crooked answer" (NEB).

THE BOOK OF THE COVENANT V

Exodus 20:22–23:33 *(cont'd)*

THE SABBATICAL YEAR AND THE SABBATH (23:10–13)

One of the great changes in recent years has been the realization of the value of a sabbatical year, but this is regarded as something primarily for intellectuals. In the Old Testament it is prescribed for the manual worker, who is the least likely to get a chance of enjoying it today, and who probably needs it more, especially if he is involved in repetitive work. The Industrial Revolution was largely the result of the Protestant, Puritan work ethic, but its operators failed to humanize it by the application of biblical insights, and we are paying the price for this today. Just as man needs the rhythm of a day's rest in seven, and the woman perhaps even more, so he needs the larger rhythm of a year in seven. It is often claimed that the sabbatical year mirrors the needs of primitive agriculture. This is true, but that does not mean that it was not to serve human needs as well as those of the ground.

THE CULTIC CALENDAR (23:14–17)

Nothing shows the shift in emphasis in the industrial West from those cultures where agriculture predominates more than the fact that its holidays are largely arbitrary. Israel's holy days and feasts were linked to nature, though God deepened their significance by linking them also with outstanding events in Salvation History. The world for feast *(chag)* really means "pilgrim feast". Those celebrating them had to get away from "the daily round and common task".

Passover and Unleavened Bread fell at the beginning of barley harvest and provided a break before the heavy work of summer began. The "feast of harvest" or Pentecost marked the first fruits of the wheat harvest, giving a short break at the height of the summer's work. Tabernacles or Ingathering marked harvest home, the end of the year's work, before the autumn rain started the whole cycle once again. Another sign of the shift from country to town is seen in the fact that we take regular Sunday worship for granted, while God claimed only the three great acts of worship from Israel. The Synagogue was a far later development than we often realize. Apart from the Psalms we are given no clue to Israel's day to day piety and worship. In spite of its later importance and fasting the Day of Atonement is not mentioned here, for attendance at the Sanctuary on that day was not compulsory.

LEAVEN AND FAT (23:18)

For leaven see comment on 12:1–13. The mention of the fat is to the peace offering (Lev. 3:14–16). Since the peace offering was normally eaten the same day (Lev. 7:15), it would have shown deep disrespect to leave the Lord's share to the next day. Closer watch on religious people will show how easily thoughtless acts of disrespect to God can creep in.

FIRST FRUITS (23:19)

The peculiar phrase "the first of the first fruits"—found also in Ezek. 44:30—probably means the best of the first fruits (so

NEB, JB, NIV). The quantity of first fruits is not stated. It was evidently mainly a freewill offering. How often do we show our thanks to God for an increase in our income?

MEAT AND MILK (23:19b)

"You shall not boil a kid in its mother's milk" is a commandment which appears three times, here, at 34:26, and Deut. 14:21. This is the tenuous basis for the rabbinic prohibition of eating meat and milk products at the same meal, a prohibition which among the ultra-orthodox involves the use of separate crockery and cutlery for meat and milk and, where practical, separate refrigerators and kitchens. The rabbis have never agreed on the reason for the law. Some maintained that it was a condemnation of a Canaanite magical rite, a view that seems to be confirmed by archaeological discoveries at Ugarit. Others were of the opinion that humanitarian reasons lay behind it. Certainly it was never intended to keep milk and meat apart.

CLOSING EXHORTATION (23:20–33)

Every major collection of laws has such an exhortation to conclude it; compare Lev. 26:3–45 and Deut. 28:1–68.

There is no reason why we should not take the "angel" literally, but since in Heb. *mal'akh* can equally mean a messenger, Jewish commentators understand it of Moses and Joshua.

Garstang understood the "hornet" (Deut. 7:20; Jos. 24:12) as the symbol of Egypt, which by its campaigns in Canaan had largely broken the power of its kings. The word in Hebrew is singular and is taken by the RSV as a collective. The stress on the gradualness of the conquest ("little by little") is one of the strongest arguments in favour of rejecting the large numbers implied by 12:37; see also Deut. 7:22. The sparing of Rahab and her family (Jos. 6:17) shows that the extermination of the Canaanites had a religious rather than an ethnic motivation. She had accepted the God of Israel.

THE RATIFICATION OF THE COVENANT

Exodus 24:1-11

1 And he said to Moses, "Come up to the Lord, you and Aaron, Nadab, and Abihu, and seventy of the elders of Israel, and worship 2 afar off. Moses alone shall come near to the Lord; but the others shall not come near, and the people shall not come up with him."

3   Moses came and told the people all the words of the Lord and all the ordinances; and all the people answered with one voice, and said, 4 "All the words which the Lord has spoken we will do." And Moses wrote all the words of the Lord. And he rose early in the morning, and built an altar at the foot of the mountain, and twelve pillars, 5 according to the twelve tribes of Israel. And he sent young men of the people of Israel, who offered burnt offerings and sacrificed peace 6 offerings of oxen to the Lord. And Moses took half of the blood and 7 put it in basins, and half of the blood he threw against the altar. Then he took the book of the covenant, and read it in the hearing of the people; and they said, "All that the Lord has spoken we will do, and 8 we will be obedient." And Moses took the blood and threw it upon the people, and said, "Behold the blood of the covenant which the Lord has made with you in accordance with all these words."

9   Then Moses and Aaron, Nadab, and Abihu, and seventy of the 10 elders of Israel went up, and they saw the God of Israel; and there was under his feet as it were a pavement of sapphire stone, like the 11 very heaven for clearness. And he did not lay his hand on the chief men of the people of Israel; they beheld God, and ate and drank.

The sequel to verses 1 and 2 comes in verse 9. In the solemn ratification of the covenant the twelve pillars were intended as a permanent memorial of what had happened; cf. Gen. 31:45; Josh. 4:20; 24:27. There are no grounds for assuming any cultic significance, as such stones often had in Canaanite worship, as symbols of the male god. There has been an uncritical acceptance by many of the ancient Jewish tradition that "the young men" were first-born sons of the elders, because priestly duties in a family devolved on them. For this there does not seem to be any valid evidence. McNeile suggests, "This perhaps reflects a common custom of deputing the duty of slaughtering and manipulating the body of the victim to the young men of the family as being the strongest and most active members of it."

The blood was divided between the altar, representing Yahweh, and the people, thus demonstrating their unity in the covenant. Then the people renewed their acceptance of God's conditions, now known (cf. 19:8). The mention of burnt offerings and peace offerings confirms the impression, gained on other grounds, that the "Levitical sacrifices" were in fact part of Israel's religious tradition even before Sinai, though their ritual will have been modified there.

There remained one act to round off the covenant ceremony, the common fellowship meal (24:1-2; 9-11). No adequate reason has been suggested for the separation of the two sections. Presumably the meal was confined to seventy-four guests, because of the earlier fear shown by the people as a whole (20:18). Nadab and Abihu were the two elder sons of Aaron. From the fact that their children are never mentioned we may conclude that they were quite young. Their premature death is told in Lev. 10.

The story of the divine fellowship meal has no real parallel in Scripture. Hertz comments: they were "vouchsafed a mystic vision of the Divine Glory", which explains nothing but is justified by the use of *chazah* ("they saw", verse 10), which is one of the regular words used for prophetic vision. For "the pavement of sapphire stone", i.e. lapis lazuli, compare Ezek. 1:26; it was symbolic of the sky. Though it was universally accepted in Israel that to see God meant death, these men were spared. There is no suggestion of any supernatural element in the food. It was probably their share of the peace offerings already mentioned.

For the Christian this covenant meal was a prefiguring of the Lord's Supper in which we are privileged to partake of the symbols of the New Covenant. One gains the impression that there is today, in certain circles, such an over-emphasis on the nature of the elements of bread and wine, that the essential nature of the fellowship meal is overlooked.

This is the real end of Exodus. The remaining chapters, with one major exception, belong rather to Leviticus.

MOSES ON MOUNT SINAI

Exodus 24:12–18

12 The Lord said to Moses, "Come up to me on the mountain, and wait there; and I will give you the tables of stone, with the law and the
13 commandment, which I have written for their instruction." So Moses rose with his servant Joshua, and Moses went up into the
14 mountain of God. And he said to the elders, "Tarry here for us, until we come to you again; and, behold, Aaron and Hur are with you; whoever has a cause, let him go to them."
15 Then Moses went up on the mountain, and the cloud covered the
16 mountain. The glory of the Lord settled on Mount Sinai, and the cloud covered it six days; and on the seventh day he called to Moses
17 out of the midst of the cloud. Now the appearance of the glory of the Lord was like a devouring fire on the top of the mountain in the sight
18 of the people of Israel. And Moses entered the cloud, and went up on the mountain. And Moses was on the mountain forty days and forty nights.

The rabbis call the whole complex of Mosaic legislation *Torah,* normally translated "law", but which they render, quite correctly, "instruction". This rendering is the justification for the mass of traditional, for centuries oral, law, which is found primarily in the Talmud, but also in later commentaries on it. The concept is that the divine instruction given to Moses is capable of authoritative application to all conceivable situations in life. More exactly it is claimed that the principles of application were given to Moses on Mount Sinai, and handed down by him to Joshua, and so through him to the prophets until they reached the Pharisaic teachers and modern rabbis. It is claimed that the "oral law" was given to Moses at Sinai, but clearly it is the underlying principles that are meant. This oral tradition was reduced to writing in the Mishnah, about A.D. 200. The other section of the Talmud, the Gemara, contains the rabbinic discussions on and elaborations of the Mishnah. It received its

definitive form about A.D.600. All later developments have had
to be in conformity with Talmudic principles.

Even if we do not accept this view—Jesus obviously by his
criticisms of the "traditions of the elders" did not—it is clear
that God is depicted as using Moses as the mediator of his will.
He was not prepared to overload them with detail to begin with.
Presumably Moses' six days of waiting (verse 16) were spent in
spiritual preparation for his closer approach to God.

Joshua presumably remained on the lower slopes of the
mountain in order to prevent any person from trying to follow
Moses. See 32:17, which shows that Moses was out of touch
with the people.

G. THE SANCTUARY (25:1–31:18)

THE FURNISHINGS I

Exodus 25:1–40

1 2 The Lord said to Moses, "Speak to the people of Israel, that they
take for me an offering; from every man whose heart makes him
3 willing you shall receive the offering for me. And this is the offering
4 which you shall receive from them: gold, silver, and bronze, blue and
5 purple and scarlet stuff and fine twined linen, goats' hair, tanned
6 rams' skins, goatskins, acacia wood, oil for the lamps, spices for the
7 anointing oil and for the fragrant incense, onyx stones, and stones
8 for setting, for the ephod and for the breastpiece. And let them make
9 me a sanctuary, that I may dwell in their midst. According to all that
I show you concerning the pattern of the tabernacle, and of all its
furniture, so you shall make it.

10   "They shall make an ark of acacia wood; two cubits and a half
shall be its length, a cubit and a half its breadth, and a cubit and a
11 half its height. And you shall overlay it with pure gold, within and
without shall you overlay it, and you shall make upon it a moulding
12 of gold round about. And you shall cast four rings of gold for it and
put them on its four feet, two rings on the one side of it, and two
13 rings on the other side of it. You shall make poles of acacia wood,
14 and overlay them with gold. And you shall put the poles into the
15 rings on the sides of the ark, to carry the ark by them. The poles shall

16 remain in the rings of the ark; they shall not be taken from it. And
17 you shall put into the ark the testimony which I shall give you. Then
you shall make a mercy seat of pure gold; two cubits and a half shall
18 be its length, and a cubit and a half its breadth. And you shall make
two cherubim of gold; of hammered work shall you make them, on
19 the two ends of the mercy seat. Make one cherub on the one end, and
one cherub on the other end; of one piece with the mercy seat shall
20 you make the cherubim on its two ends. The cherubim shall spread
out their wings above, overshadowing the mercy seat with their
wings, their faces one to another; toward the mercy seat shall the
21 faces of the cherubim be. And you shall put the mercy seat on the top
of the ark; and in the ark you shall put the testimony that I shall give
22 you. There I will meet with you, and from above the mercy seat,
from between the two cherubim that are upon the ark of the
testimony, I will speak with you of all that I will give you in
commandment for the people of Israel.

23   "And you shall make a table of acacia wood; two cubits shall be its
24 length, a cubit its breadth, and a cubit and a half its height. You shall
overlay it with pure gold, and make a moulding of gold around it.
25 And you shall make around it a frame a handbreadth wide, and a
26 moulding of gold around the frame. And you shall make for it four
rings of gold, and fasten the rings to the four corners at its four legs.
27 Close to the frame the rings shall lie, as holders for the poles to carry
28 the table. You shall make the poles of acacia wood, and overlay
29 them with gold, and the table shall be carried with these. And you
shall make its plates and dishes for incense, and its flagons and
bowls with which to pour libations; of pure gold you shall make
30 them. And you shall set the bread of the Presence on the table before
me always.

31   "And you shall make a lampstand of pure gold. The base and the
shaft of the lampstand shall be made of hammered work; its cups, its
32 capitals, and its flowers shall be of one piece with it; and there shall
be six branches going out of its sides, three branches of the
lampstand out of one side of it and three branches of the lampstand
33 out of the other side of it; three cups made like almonds, each with
capital and flower, on one branch, and three cups made like
almonds, each with capital and flower, on the other branch—so for
34 the six branches going out of the lampstand; and on the lampstand
itself four cups made like almonds, with their capitals and flowers,
35 and a capital of one piece with it under each pair of the six branches
36 going out from the lampstand. Their capitals and their branches

shall be of one piece with it, the whole of it one piece of hammered
37 work of pure gold. And you shall make the seven lamps for it; and
the lamps shall be set up so as to give light upon the space in front of
38 39 it. Its snuffers and their trays shall be of pure gold. Of a talent of pure
40 gold shall it be made, with all these utensils. And see that you make
them after the pattern for them, which is being shown you on the
mountain."

A survey of Christian places of worship will show a very wide
range of architecture. Except where this has been dictated by
poverty, it will normally indicate the type of worship carried
out there. The ancestors of Israel had known the very elaborate
temples of Mesopotamia and Egypt and the simple sanctuaries
of Canaan. For Israel, God commanded a combination of the
complicated and simple, in which the details were intended to
bring a revelation of God to the worshippers.

Some of those lessons can be easily understood, but others
are less clear. We must never forget that many of the details of
materials, etc. were the result of desert conditions, to which no
theological significance may be attached. Over the centuries
there has grown up a body of typology round the Tabernacle,
which finds its theological basis in the Letter to the Hebrews.
Where it has gone further, we should regard it with suspicion,
the more so as there is no evidence that any Jew had grasped it.
No stress should be laid on alleged symbolism, which was not
understood by those most intimately concerned. For some
general principles see the discussion at the end of the commentary on "The Christian and the Tabernacle".

Until recently it was widely held by scholars that the Tabernacle, as here depicted, never existed, but that it was a projection
into the past of the Solomonic temple on a smaller and portable
scale. The arguments to support this theory very largely boil
down to "the presumable absence of the skill and means for
constructing it" (Driver, p.430), but portable pavilions of a
similar type of construction are known from Egypt from long
before the time of Moses. So here the veracity of the text will be
taken for granted, but only a moderate degree of typology will
be suggested.

THE FURNISHINGS II

Exodus 25:1–40 *(cont'd)*

THE MATERIALS FOR THE TENT (25:1–9)

Here we see one of the purposes behind Israel's requests to the Egyptians (12:35–36). In verse 4 render "violet, purple and scarlet yarn" (NIV, NEB mg.) and in verse 5, "hides of sea cows" (NIV, NEB mg.). Stress should not be laid on the colours, until one is sure what colours were normally available. The term "tabernacle" has been so hallowed by usage, that we can easily understand its retention in most recent English versions. The TEV is an exception with "Tent". The Hebrew word in verse 9 is *mishkan*, "dwelling place". It comes from the same root as *Shekhinah*, used in later Hebrew for the abiding glory of God among men. The dream of men was that God should dwell in their midst; John 1:14; Rev. 21:3. The reason for a tent in the wilderness was not merely necessity, but also to teach Israel that a solid temple was *not* a necessity; cf. 2 Sam. 7:6–7. Hebrews ignores the Solomonic and Herodian temples, and deals solely with the Tabernacle. Equally Ezekiel chapters 40–46 seem to look more to the Tabernacle than to the Temple the prophet had known as a young man.

THE ARK OF THE COVENANT (25:10–22)

The Ark, the NEB and the NIV "chest", the TEV "box", is described before the Tent because this was the symbol of God's presence, the Tent being there to protect it. It consisted of two parts, the chest itself approximately $3\frac{3}{4}$ feet by $2\frac{1}{4}$ by $2\frac{1}{4}$. It was made of acacia wood, the only wood available, covered with gold. Many have seen here a picture of Christ's dual nature, God and man, but if this had been intended, one would have expected the wood to be on the outside. The main reason for not having a solid gold chest was presumably the weight involved. There was a separate cover, beautifully but inaccurately called "the Mercy Seat" by Tindale and later translators.

The Hebrew *kapporet* is best rendered "atonement cover" (NIV). The cherubs at either end are to be pictured as spreading their wings horizontally over the cover, thus forming the visible throne of the invisible God; see 2 Sam. 6:2; Pss. 80:1; 90:1. For those who visualized Yahweh as thus enthroned the two tables of stone in the Ark would have been under his feet, the immutability of the Ten Words being thus guaranteed. On the Day of Atonement the High Priest sprinkled blood on the *kapporet* and in front of it (Lev. 16:14–15) thus symbolically making a barrier between the outraged law and God, and between it and the people. Traditionally this was in the shape of a cross.

The cherubim are variously depicted. Here they are not described, but there are variants between Ezek. 1:5–12; 41:18–19; Rev. 4:6–7. They are apparently the guardian spirits of this earthly creation; the description is symbolic, and so variation is unimportant.

When the Ark had to be carried, the *kapporet* was not visible, for it had to be carefully covered (Num. 4:5–6).

We should never forget that Israel's worship centred on a God, who himself moral, made moral demands on his worshippers.

THE TABLE OF SHEWBREAD (25:23–30)

Here only the Table is described; the rules for the Shewbread itself are to be found in Lev. 24:5–9. Neither on the Jewish nor on the Christian side is there general agreement on the meaning of the Shewbread. It would appear that the proximity of the Table to the Ark, even if divided from it by a curtain, was the unspoken plea, "Give us this day our daily bread"; the recognition that man's bread—the staple of life in Israel—depended on God. The symbolism is the more apposite today, when there are so many world-wide, who have to go hungry.

THE LAMPSTAND (25:31–40)

The understanding of its shape in the time of Herod the Great may be seen by its reproduction on the Arch of Titus in Rome. Chapter 27:20 and Lev. 24:2 indicate that its lamps had to kept burning continuously, but that seems to be denied by 27:21; see also 30:7–8; Lev. 24:3; 1 Sam. 3:3; 2 Chron. 13:11. The Mishnah and Josephus explain the apparent contradiction by stating that one, or three, of the lamps burnt by day, but all seven at night. This may well be true, for in the wilderness there was a need to conserve olive oil.

Quite apart from its practical use, the lampstand, standing opposite the Table of Shewbread, signifying God as the Giver of food, witnessed to him as the guide (Ps. 119:105) and the Giver and Preserver of life (Prov. 13:9; 20:20).

Strangely enough, in this enumeration of Tabernacle furniture, the altar of incense is not mentioned; see 30:1–10. No satisfactory explanation for this has been offered. In the inventory of the Temple furniture in 1 Kgs. 7:23–39 the altar of sacrifice similarly finds no mention.

THE TABERNACLE

Exodus 26:1–37

1 "Moreover you shall make the tabernacle with ten curtains of fine twined linen and blue and purple and scarlet stuff; with cherubim
2 skilfully worked shall you make them. The length of each curtain shall be twenty-eight cubits, and the breadth of each curtain four
3 cubits; all the curtains shall have one measure. Five curtains shall be coupled to one another; and the other five curtains shall be coupled
4 to one another. And you shall make loops of blue on the edge of the outmost curtain in the first set; and likewise you shall make loops on
5 the edge of the outmost curtain in the second set. Fifty loops you shall make on the one curtain, and fifty loops you shall make on the edge of the curtain that is in the second set; the loops shall be
6 opposite one another. And you shall make fifty clasps of gold, and couple the curtains one to the other with the clasps, that the tabernacle may be one whole.
7 "You shall also make curtains of goats' hair for a tent over the
8 tabernacle; eleven curtains shall you make. The length of each curtain shall be thirty cubits, and the breadth of each curtain four

9 cubits; the eleven curtains shall have the same measure. And you shall couple five curtains by themselves, and six curtains by themselves, and the sixth curtain you shall double over at the front of the
10 tent. And you shall make fifty loops on the edge of the curtain that is outmost in one set, and fifty loops on the edge of the curtain which is outmost in the second set.

11 "And you shall make fifty clasps of bronze, and put the clasps into the loops, and couple the tent together that it may be one whole.
12 And the part that remains of the curtains of the tent, the half curtain
13 that remains, shall hang over the back of the tabernacle. And the cubit on the one side, and the cubit on the other side, of what remains in the length of the curtains of the tent shall hang over the
14 sides of the tabernacle, on this side and that side, to cover it. And you shall make for the tent a covering of tanned rams' skins and goatskins.

15 "And you shall make upright frames for the tabernacle of acacia
16 wood. Ten cubits shall be the length of a frame, and a cubit and a
17 half the breadth of each frame. There shall be two tenons in each frame, for fitting together; so shall you do for all the frames of the
18 tabernacle. You shall make the frames for the tabernacle: twenty
19 frames for the south side; and forty bases of silver you shall make under the twenty frames, two bases under one frame for its two
20 tenons, and two bases under another frame for its two tenons; and for the second side of the tabernacle, on the north side twenty
21 frames, and their forty bases of silver, two bases under one frame,
22 and two bases under another frame; and for the rear of the
23 tabernacle westward you shall make six frames. And you shall make
24 two frames for corners of the tabernacle in the rear; they shall be separate beneath, but joined at the top, at the first ring; thus shall it
25 be with both of them; they shall form the two corners. And there shall be eight frames, with their bases of silver, sixteen bases; two bases under one frame, and two bases under another frame.

26 "And you shall make bars of acacia wood, five for the frames of
27 the one side of the tabernacle, and five bars for the frames of the other side of the tabernacle, and five bars for the frames of the side of
28 the tabernacle at the rear westward. The middle bar, halfway up the
29 frames, shall pass through from end to end. You shall overlay the frames with gold, and shall make their rings of gold for holders for
30 the bars; and you shall overlay the bars with gold. And you shall erect the tabernacle according to the plan for it which has been shown you on the mountain.

31 "And you shall make a veil of blue and purple and scarlet stuff and
fine twined linen; in skilled work shall it be made, with cherubim;
32 and you shall hang it upon four pillars of acacia overlaid with gold,
33 with hooks of gold, upon four bases of silver. And you shall hang the
veil from the clasps and bring the ark of the testimony in thither
within the veil; and the veil shall separate for you the holy place from
34 the most holy. You shall put the mercy seat upon the ark of the
35 testimony in the most holy place. And you shall set the table outside
the veil, and the lampstand on the south side of the tabernacle
opposite the table; and you shall put the table on the north side.
36 "And you shall make a screen for the door of the tent, of blue and
purple and scarlet stuff and fine twined linen, embroidered with
37 needlework. And you shall make for the screen five pillars of acacia,
and overlay them with gold; their hooks shall be of gold, and you
shall cast five bases of bronze for them."

It would be well to dismiss memories of pictures of the
Tabernacle from Sunday school days. We are dealing not with
one structure, but with two, if not three:

(a) The *mishkan* (dwelling place, verses 1–6), see 25:8.

(b) The *ohel,* a tent erected over the *mishkan* to protect it
(verses 7–13).

(c) The *ohel* was further protected by an extra covering (verse
14).

As is the case with the description of Solomon's temple (1
Kgs. 6) there are details which are far from clear. Those
interested in such matters are referred to the entry on "The
Tabernacle" in Hastings' *Dictionary of the Bible* Vol. IV (by
Kennedy) or in another Bible Dictionary. The main point of
controversy is whether the *ohel* had a ridge-pole, keeping it
clear of the *mishkan.* The view is worthy of far more consideration than given it by Kennedy; see M.L.G. Guillebaud in
Evangelical Quarterly, April-June, 1939.

(a) The *mishkan* was made of best quality linen embroidered
with images of the cherubim. It was given stability by frames of
acacia wood (not boards!) fitted in sockets of silver. It was
thirty cubits long, ten wide and ten high—a cubit was approximately eighteen inches. It was divided into two by a curtain

(verse 31), which made an inner sanctuary for the Ark, a perfect cube of ten cubits a side. The remaining interior was hidden from unauthorized eyes by another curtain acting as a door. The justification of the rendering "frame" rather than "board" is based partly on the enormous weight of a solid board, about one ton each, and partly on the fact that boards would have hidden the beautiful linen tent, which would have been visible through the frames.

(b) The *ohel,* the tent over the *mishkan,* was made of goats' hair, the normal material for Beduin tents.

(c) The covering of the *ohel* was double, tanned rams' skins, and the leather-like hide of sea cows (NIV). This was presumably intended as a protection against rain.

THE TABERNACLE COURT

Exodus 27:1–21

1 "You shall make the altar of acacia wood, five cubits long and five cubits broad; the altar shall be square, and its height shall be three
2 cubits. And you shall make horns for it on its four corners; its horns shall be of one piece with it, and you shall overlay it with bronze.
3 You shall make pots for it to receive its ashes, and shovels and basins
4 and forks and firepans; all its utensils you shall make of bronze. You shall also make for it a grating, a network of bronze; and upon the
5 net you shall make four bronze rings at its four corners. And you shall set it under the ledge of the altar so that the net shall extend
6 halfway down the altar. And you shall make poles for the altar,
7 poles of acacia wood, and overlay them with bronze; and the poles shall be put through the rings, so that the poles shall be upon the two
8 sides of the altar, when it is carried. You shall make it hollow, with boards; as it has been shown you on the mountain, so shall it be made.
9 "You shall make the court of the tabernacle. On the south side the court shall have hangings of fine twined linen a hundred cubits long
10 for one side; their pillars shall be twenty and their bases twenty, of bronze, but the hooks of the pillars and their fillets shall be of silver.
11 And likewise for its length on the north side there shall be hangings a

hundred cubits long, their pillars twenty and their bases twenty, of bronze, but the hooks of the pillars and their fillets shall be of silver.

12 And for the breadth of the court on the west side there shall be
13 hangings for fifty cubits, with ten pillars and ten bases. The breadth
14 of the court on the front to the east shall be fifty cubits. The hangings for the one side of the gate shall be fifteen cubits, with three pillars
15 and three bases. On the other side the hangings shall be fifteen
16 cubits, with three pillars and three bases. For the gate of the court there shall be a screen twenty cubits long, of blue and purple and scarlet stuff and fine twined linen, embroidered with needlework; it
17 shall have four pillars and with them four bases. All the pillars around the court shall be filleted with silver; their hooks shall be of
18 silver, and their bases of bronze. The length of the court shall be a hundred cubits, the breadth fifty, and the height five cubits, with
19 hangings of fine twined linen and bases of bronze. All the utensils of the tabernacle for every use, and all its pegs and all the pegs of the court, shall be of bronze.
20 "And you shall command the people of Israel that they bring to you pure beaten olive oil for the light, that a lamp may be set up to
21 burn continually. In the tent of meeting, outside the veil which is before the testimony, Aaron and his sons shall tend it from evening to morning before the Lord. It shall be a statute for ever to be observed throughout their generations by the people of Israel."

The court round the Tabernacle (verses 9–19) was 150 feet long and 75 feet wide, i.e. a rectangle that could be divided into two squares of 75 feet a side. If we draw a dividing line between them, the front of the Tabernacle would have lain on it. If we draw the diagonals of the two squares, the Ark will have lain at the centre of the western half, and the altar of burnt offering at the centre of the eastern. The laver lay half-way between the altar and the entrance to the Tabernacle.

The curtains shutting in the court were seven and a half feet high (verse 14). So while the top of the Tabernacle could be seen from the camp, what was happening in the court was hidden from inquisitive eyes. There was only one entrance, at the west end.

Plan of the TABERNACLE COURT

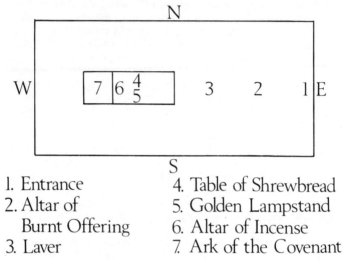

1. Entrance
2. Altar of
   Burnt Offering
3. Laver
4. Table of Shrewbread
5. Golden Lampstand
6. Altar of Incense
7. Ark of the Covenant

THE ALTAR OF BURNT OFFERING (27:1–8)

The altar was made of acacia wood. It was seven and a half feet square and four and a half feet high. This empty frame was probably filled with earth; see 20:24. Obviously the overlaying with bronze had to be on both sides of the boards (verse 2); otherwise they would have charred away very quickly. The bronze censers of Num. 16:38 may have been used only for the outside, and so served as a warning to all who came to sacrifice that only those chosen by God might officiate as his priests. Horned altars were in common use in Canaan. Since horns were a regular symbol of strength and power (Pss. 18:2; 75:10), they presumably symbolized the power of God to meet the needs of the worshipper. The man seeking sanctuary caught hold of them; see 21:14; 1 Kgs. 2:28.

The grating was not inside the altar but was a support for the ledge. That it was outside is shown by the carrying rings being attached to it. The ledge will have been for the officiating priest to stand on, for otherwise the altar would have been too high for convenience. Jewish tradition supports this, affirming that it was 1½ feet wide.

OIL FOR THE LAMPS (27:20–21)

Beaten oil was considered to be the best. The olives were gently pounded in a mortar to produce it. Only our best will allow the glory of God to be seen in us.

THE PRIESTLY GARMENTS I

Exodus 28:1–43

1 "Then bring near to you Aaron your brother, and his sons with him, from among the people of Israel, to serve me as priests—Aaron and
2 Aaron's sons, Nadab and Abihu, Eleazar and Ithamar. And you shall make holy garments for Aaron your brother, for glory and for
3 beauty. And you shall speak to all who have ability, whom I have endowed with an able mind, that they make Aaron's garments to
4 consecrate him for my priesthood. These are the garments which they shall make: a breastpiece, an ephod, a robe, a coat of chequer work, a turban, and a girdle; they shall make holy garments for Aaron your brother and his sons to serve me as priests.

5 "They shall receive gold, blue and purple and scarlet stuff, and
6 fine twined linen. And they shall make the ephod of gold, of blue and
7 purple and scarlet stuff, and of fine twined linen, skilfully worked. It shall have two shoulder-pieces attached to its two edges, that it may
8 be joined together. And the skilfully woven band upon it, to gird it on, shall be of the same workmanship and materials, of gold, blue
9 and purple and scarlet stuff, and fine twined linen. And you shall take two onyx stones, and engrave on them the names of the sons of
10 Israel, six of their names on the one stone, and the names of the
11 remaining six on the other stone, in the order of their birth. As a jeweller engraves signets, so shall you engrave the two stones with the names of the sons of Israel; you shall enclose them in settings of
12 gold filigree. And you shall set the two stones upon the shoulder-pieces of the ephod, as stones of remembrance for the sons of Israel; and Aaron shall bear their names before the Lord upon his two

13 shoulders for remembrance. And you shall make settings of gold
14 filigree, and two chains of pure gold, twisted like cords; and you
shall attach the corded chains to the settings.

15 "And you shall make a breastpiece of judgment, in skilled work;
like the work of the ephod you shall make it; of gold, blue and purple
16 and scarlet stuff, and fine twined linen shall you make it. It shall be
17 square and double, a span its length and a span its breadth. And you
shall set in it four rows of stones. A row of sardius, topaz, and
18 carbuncle shall be the first row; and the second row an emerald, a
19 sapphire, and a diamond; and the third row a jacinth, an agate, and
20 an amethyst; and the fourth row a beryl, an onyx, and a jasper; they
21 shall be set in gold filigree. There shall be twelve stones with their
names according to the names of the sons of Israel; they shall be like
22 signets, each engraved with its name, for the twelve tribes. And you
shall make for the breastpiece twisted chains like cords, of pure gold;
23 and you shall make for the breastpiece two rings of gold, and put the
24 two rings on the two edges of the breastpiece. And you shall put the
25 two cords of gold in the two rings at the edges of the breastpiece; the
two ends of the two cords you shall attach to the two settings of
filigree, and so attach it in front to the shoulder-pieces of the ephod.
26 And you shall make two rings of gold, and put them at the two ends
27 of the breastpiece, on its inside edge next to the ephod. And you
shall make two rings of gold, and attach them in front to the lower
part of the two shoulder-pieces of the ephod, at its joining above the
28 skilfully woven band of the ephod. And they shall bind the breastpiece by its rings to the rings of the ephod with a lace of blue, that it
may lie upon the skilfully woven band of the ephod, and that the
29 breastpiece shall not come loose from the ephod. So Aaron shall
bear the names of the sons of Israel in the breastpiece of judgment
upon his heart, when he goes into the holy place, to bring them to
30 continual remembrance before the Lord. And in the breastpiece of
judgment you shall put the Urim and the Thummim, and they shall
be upon Aaron's heart, when he goes in before the Lord; thus Aaron
shall bear the judgment of the people of Israel upon his heart before
the Lord continually.

31 32 "And you shall make the robe of the ephod all of blue. It shall
have in it an opening for the head, with a woven binding around the
33 opening, like the opening in a garment, that it may not be torn. On
its skirts you shall make pomegranates of blue and purple and
34 scarlet stuff, around its skirts, with bells of gold between them, a

golden bell and a pomegranate, a golden bell and a pomegranate,
35 round about on the skirts of the robe. And it shall be upon Aaron
when he ministers, and its sound shall be heard when he goes into the
holy place before the Lord, and when he comes out, lest he die.

36 "And you shall make a plate of pure gold, and engrave on it, like
37 the engraving of a signet, 'Holy to the Lord.' And you shall fasten it
on the turban by a lace of blue; it shall be on the front of the turban.
38 It shall be upon Aaron's forehead, and Aaron shall take upon
himself any guilt incurred in the holy offering which the people of
Israel hallow as their holy gifts; it shall always be upon his forehead,
that they may be accepted before the Lord.

39 "And you shall weave the coat in chequer work of fine linen, and
you shall make a turban of fine linen, and you shall make a girdle
embroidered with needlework.

40 "And for Aaron's sons you shall make coats and girdles and caps;
41 you shall make them for glory and beauty. And you shall put them
upon Aaron your brother, and upon his sons with him, and shall
anoint them and ordain them and consecrate them, that they may
42 serve me as priests. And you shall make for them linen breeches to
cover their naked flesh; from the loins to the thighs they shall reach;
43 and they shall be upon Aaron, and upon his sons, when they go into
the tent of meeting, or when they come near the altar to minister in
the holy place; lest they bring guilt upon themselves and die. This
shall be a perpetual statute for him and for his descendants after
him."

The disparity in detail between the description of Aaron's robes
and those of his sons (verses 40–43) brings out, what would in
any case be clear from other passages, that there was really only
one priest in Israel. His sons were little more than his deputies.
That is why Hebrews can ignore the other priests, and confine
itself to a comparison of Aaron the High Priest and Jesus.
Aaron was not only Israel's representative before God, but also
God's representative to Israel. He had on official occasions to
be suitably dressed, according to the standards of the time, but
once God sent his perfect representative in the guise of a poor
Galilean villager, one may reasonably question the justification
for ornate ecclesiastical robes.

THE PRIESTLY GARMENTS II

Exodus 28:1-43 *(cont'd)*

THE EPHOD (28:5-14)

We have no means of giving a definitive meaning to "ephod", the English being simply a transliteration of the Hebrew. As Cole says, "The extent of our puzzlement is shown by the fact that we do not know whether the ephod was a waistcoat or a kilt, to use modern terms." The real difficulty is the result of the word being used with apparently different meanings.

The "linen ephod", of which this was a superior example, was a priestly, or at least a sanctuary garment; see 1 Sam. 2:18; 22:18; 2 Sam. 6:14. It is connected with the discovery of God's will in 1 Sam. 23:9, and it had been carried, not worn, when Abiathar fled to David (1 Sam. 23:6). It is not likely to mean an article of dress in Judg. 8:27; 17:5; Hos. 3:4. The most likely explanation of the divergence in use is that the high-priestly ephod is clearly closely connected with the "breastpiece of judgment", which contained the Urim and Thummim (verse 30), used by the High Priest to ascertain God's will. Those who did not have access to the breastpiece, or did not know how to use the Urim and Thummim, probably made their own substitutes. At all times there has been the temptation to use human substitutes for the methods appointed by God.

THE BREASTPIECE AND THE URIM AND THUMMIM (28:15-30)

The breastpiece was made of the same material as the ephod, i.e. it was a square cloth bag having the emblems of the twelve tribes on the front. Just as it is impossible to identify the precious stones on the breastpiece with any certainty—compare the variant renderings in the NEB and the NIV—so it is impossible to attribute any spiritual meaning to them, beyond the fact that the names coming in such a setting, also on the onyx stones of the ephod (verse 12), indicated the preciousness of the tribes to God. The Urim and Thummim seem to have disappeared at a relatively early date, and as a result there is no reliable Jewish tradition about their nature or the manner of their use. Their names mean "the Lights and the Perfections", i.e. "perfect lights", and they were a method by which God could give guidance where it was needed. 1 Sam. 28:6 shows that one could fail to get an answer, though the reasonable suggestion has been made that Saul had a series of questions to which he received contradictory answers. Many Christians have found that when they have tried to get unduly explicit guidance all at one time, instead of being satisfied with the first step, they have been disappointed.

If we follow the Septuagint in 1 Sam. 14:41, as do most modern versions, we may infer that the Urim and Thummim were two similar (precious?) stones. According to which was drawn out by the priest, so was the answer. Others, taking "casting lots" literally, have thought of two virtually identical stones, one side of each marked Urim and the other Thummim. If these were thrown out of the oracular bag, and the two Urim sides showed, it meant "Yes"; the two Thummim sides meant "No"; if they were different, there was no answer.

Reference to older commentaries and handbooks will show that all sorts of fanciful suggestions have been made, none of which have any probability, and so may be ignored.

Though we can have no certainty how the Urim and Thummim were used, we can easily understand how they came to be displaced by the sanctuary prophets. Yet a longing for their replacement never really died out; see Ezra 2:63.

We need find no difficulty in the institution of the Urim and Thummim. I had the privilege of friendship with a semi-literate but spiritual Christian. Because he was a very slow reader, he was accustomed to using a "promise box", which was the source of much blessing to him, though he remained surprised that it always yielded a comfortable word. Even so we may see in the Urim and Thummim God's gracious way of meeting the needs of his people at the beginning of their long walk with him.

There are Christians to whom the gift has been given of knowing God's will for others, though without the use of mechanical means. Those who would use a gift like this to the glory of God and for the good of others must be prepared like Aaron "to bear the judgment of the people of Israel upon his heart before the Lord" (verse 30), i.e. to know that God's will for others involves an understanding of the way God is looking at them. The knowledge of God's will is never a merely mechanical or intellectual matter.

THE ROBE OF THE EPHOD (28:31–35)

The robe was presumably the long undergarment over which the ephod and the breastpiece of judgment were worn. The unusual order in which the garments are mentioned can be best explained by the fact that the more important are mentioned first.

There is no obvious significance in the colour of the robe, for the blue should be rendered "violet". The ornaments along the bottom hem, pomegranates made of coloured stuff and golden bells, seem to have had a double purpose, though the pomegranates seem to have had no symbolic purpose, but will have acted as weights to prevent the robe riding up. Aaron was waiting on the King of kings in his priestly duties, and as representative of the people he had to be duly ushered into the divine presence; when he came out he had to be treated and regarded with due respect. The bells were not essential but had a real symbolic purpose.

HOLY TO THE LORD (28:36–38)

In John's vision of life in heaven we find "his name shall be on their foreheads" (Rev. 22:4). Aaron symbolized the millions, since his day, who have humbly entered the presence of God through Jesus Christ and been transformed into his image; 2 Cor. 3:18. Aaron was in addition the representative of his people, which as God's people was holy, i.e. set apart for God's purposes.

OTHER GARMENTS (28:39)

The linen coat was a tunic (NEB) worn under the robe of the ephod. It was made of linen for the sake of coolness, as was the turban. Marks of courtesy tend to depend on climatic circumstances. The bared head was a sign of equality. Respect was shown by the removal of the shoes; cf. 3:5. While travelling through the wilderness Aaron doubtless wore sandals, but they are not mentioned among the high-priestly garments, for he will have served barefooted.

GARMENTS FOR ASSISTANT PRIESTS (28:40-43)

The garments for Aaron's sons were coats (i.e. tunics), girdles (i.e. woven girdles) and turbans. We know from other sources that they also wore linen ephods. The linen breeches applied equally to Aaron.

It is worth noting that in 29:5 and Lev. 8:7-9 the more logical order of Aaron's garments is followed.

THE CONSECRATION OF THE PRIESTS I

Exodus 29:1-37

1 "Now this is what you shall do to them to consecrate them, that they may serve me as priests. Take one young bull and two rams without
2 blemish, and unleavened bread, unleavened cakes mixed with oil, and unleavened wafers spread with oil. You shall make them of fine
3 wheat flour. And you shall put them in one basket and bring them in
4 the basket, and bring the bull and the two rams. You shall bring Aaron and his sons to the door of the tent of meeting, and wash them
5 with water. And you shall take the garments, and put on Aaron the coat and the robe of the ephod, and the ephod, and the breastpiece,
6 and gird him with the skilfully woven band of the ephod; and you shall set the turban on his head, and put the holy crown upon the
7 turban. And you shall take the anointing oil, and pour it on his head
8 and anoint him. Then you shall bring his sons, and put coats on
9 them, and you shall gird them with girdles and bind caps on them; and the priesthood shall be theirs by a perpetual statute. Thus you shall ordain Aaron and his sons.

10   "Then you shall bring the bull before the tent of meeting. Aaron
11 and his sons shall lay their hands upon the head of the bull, and you
shall kill the bull before the Lord, at the door of the tent of meeting,
12 and shall take part of the blood of the bull and put it upon the horns
of the altar with your finger, and the rest of the blood you shall pour
13 out at the base of the altar. And you shall take all the fat that covers
the entrails, and the appendage of the liver, and the two kidneys with
14 the fat that is on them, and burn them upon the altar. But the flesh of
the bull, and its skin, and its dung, you shall burn with fire outside
the camp; it is a sin offering.

15   "Then you shall take one of the rams, and Aaron and his sons shall
16 lay their hands upon the head of the ram, and you shall slaughter the
ram, and shall take its blood and throw it against the altar round
17 about. Then you shall cut the ram into pieces, and wash its entrails
18 and its legs, and put them with its pieces and its head, and burn the
whole ram upon the altar; it is a pleasing odour, an offering by fire to
the Lord.

19   "You shall take the other ram; and Aaron and his sons shall lay
20 their hands upon the head of the ram, and you shall kill the ram, and
take part of its blood and put it upon the tip of the right ear of Aaron
and upon the tips of the right ears of his sons, and upon the thumbs
of their right hands, and upon the great toes of their right feet, and
21 throw the rest of the blood against the altar round about. Then you
shall take part of the blood that is on the altar, and of the anointing
oil, and sprinkle it upon Aaron and his garments, and upon his sons
and his sons' garments with him; and he and his garments shall be
holy, and his sons and his sons' garments with him.

22   "You shall also take the fat of the ram, and the fat tail, and the fat
that covers the entrails, and the appendage of the liver, and the two
kidneys with the fat that is on them, and the right thigh (for it is a
23 ram of ordination), and one loaf of bread, and one cake of bread
with oil, and one wafer, out of the basket of unleavened bread that is
24 before the Lord; and you shall put all these in the hands of Aaron
and in the hands of his sons, and wave them for a wave offering
25 before the Lord. Then you shall take them from their hands, and
burn them on the altar in addition to the burnt offering, as a pleasing
odour before the Lord; it is an offering by fire to the Lord.

26   "And you shall take the breast of the ram of Aaron's ordination
and wave it for a wave offering before the Lord; and it shall be your
27 portion. And you shall consecrate the breast of the wave offering,

and the thigh of the priests' portion, which is waved, and which is offered from the ram of ordination, since it is for Aaron and for his
28 sons. It shall be for Aaron and his sons as a perpetual due from the people of Israel, for it is the priests' portion to be offered by the people of Israel from their peace offerings; it is their offering to the Lord.

29 "The holy garments of Aaron shall be for his sons after him, to be
30 anointed in them and ordained in them. The son who is priest in his place shall wear them seven days, when he comes into the tent of meeting to minister in the holy place.

31 "You shall take the ram of ordination, and boil its flesh in a holy
32 place; and Aaron and his sons shall eat the flesh of the ram and the
33 bread that is in the basket, at the door of the tent of meeting. They shall eat those things with which atonement was made, to ordain and consecrate them, but an outsider shall not eat of them, because
34 they are holy. And if any of the flesh for the ordination, or of the bread, remain until the morning, then you shall burn the remainder with fire; it shall not be eaten, because it is holy.

35 "Thus you shall do to Aaron and to his sons, according to all that I have commanded you; through seven days shall you ordain them,
36 and every day you shall offer a bull as a sin offering for atonement. Also you shall offer a sin offering for the altar, when you make
37 atonement for it, and shall anoint it, to consecrate it. Seven days you shall make atonement for the altar, and consecrate it, and the altar shall be most holy; whatever touches the altar shall become holy."

Obviously, as Israel was starting from scratch, someone had to act as consecrating pirest, and for that no one was more suitable than Moses. If the idea that Moses had learnt of Yahweh from Jethro was correct, one would have expected him to serve. Moses' actions in Lev. 9:23; 10:16 show that he considered himself to have a unique place in the religion of his people. He was in fact the first High Priest in Israel, a position he voluntarily abandoned in favour of his brother.

There is always a temptation for an outstanding man to gather all the positions of authority into his own hands. We see Moses' true greatness in his willingness to share both civil and religious authority with others.

In certain denominations there has been an undue tendency

to think that the ordination of a man as minister has made him omnicompetent. Acts 6:2–4 should be a warning against such an attitude.

THE CONSECRATION OF THE PRIESTS II

Exodus 29:1–37 *(cont'd)*

In consecrating, literally making holy, a priest, he was being set apart entirely for God's service. The completeness of the act was indicated by its sevenfold repetition (verse 35). Ultimately, however, whatever the local church and its officers may do and whatever the individual may intend, it must be God who sets a person apart for his service (verse 44). The concept of human ordination, conferring perpetual validity, has done much harm in the Church.

The ceremony began with ritual cleansing (verse 4) as had the Covenant ceremony (19:10,14). The symbolism behind baptism is one that hardly needs explaining. Those who lay special stress on Rom. 6:4 forget that the obvious is normally likely to be true, though there may be a further and deeper explanation.

Then followed a sin offering (verses 10–14). Sin is no external matter that can be remedied by soap and water, even though we may find the clean sinner socially more acceptable, nor can anyone stand as mediator between man and God without being compelled to acknowledge that he too is in need of a mediator. As the writer to the Hebrews insists, the uniqueness of Jesus Christ as our great High Priest lies in the fact that he is "holy, blameless, pure, set apart from sinners, exalted above the heavens" (7:26).

Then followed a burnt offering (verses 15–17), the symbol of the new priest's complete dedication to God. The next sacrifice with the other ram (verses 19–28) was one unique to this ceremony. In verse 22 the ram is called "a ram of ordination"; far better is the NEB "installation"; perhaps "induction" would be still better. The symbolism of the application of the sacrificial blood to Aaron's right ear, thumb and toe is too obvious to need much development. "The ear was touched with the blood, that it may hear the word of God; the hand, to perform the duties connected with the priesthood; and the foot, to walk in the path of righteousness" (Hertz).

As is made clear by verses 31–34 the sacrifice of "ordination" was a peace offering, the flesh of the ram being divided between the altar for God (verses 22–25) and the priests being inducted (verses 26ff.). The underlying concept—not confined to Israel—is that the priests were inducted by doing the work of priests. They had participated in the three main groups of offerings, namely sin, burnt and peace offerings.

The composition of the anointing oil (verse 7) will be found in 30:22–33. It is dangerous to argue from silence, but the apparent significance of verses 35 and 36 ("Thus shall you do to Aaron . . .") is that it was only the sin offering that had to be repeated for a week before the consecration ceremony was complete. This is quite understandable. God takes no special pleasure in repeated acts of self-dedication (the burnt offering), for he knows the genuineness, or otherwise, of such an act. Nor did the priests require to be inducted more than once, but they, like us, needed to be reminded how far short they fell of God's standards. As Canon Twells' hymn so perfectly expresses it:

Not for our sins alone
Thy mercy, Lord, we sue;
Let fall Thy pitying glance
On our devotions too,
What we have done for Thee
And what we think to do.

The holiest hours we spend
In prayer upon our knees,
The times when most we deem
Our songs of praise will please;
Thou searcher of all hearts
Forgiveness pour on these.

In verse 37 we are introduced to a far-reaching concept in Hebrew theology. There had to be a seven days' consecration of the altar, making atonement for it—a similar act had to take place on the Day of Atonement (Lev. 16:18). Sin is contagious. The very bringing of parts of the sin offering onto the altar in itself defiled it. But equally holiness is contagious; see also 30:29 and the comments on 19:12–13.

In this modern age the average Christian has largely forgotten what the impact of the world means. Never has the pressure to conform to this world been stronger or more subtle, never has the need for the transformation of our minds been more necessary. The Holy Spirit still produces saints, as the term is popularly understood, but they are all too few and far between, but when we meet them we find their lives contagious. The contagion of holiness in the Tabernacle had, as its effect, extreme care with holy things, for anything touching them was automatically lost to its owner and became God's property. In Zech. 14:20–21 the division of sacred and profane has vanished.

THE DAILY SACRIFICES AND THE ALTAR OF INCENSE

Exodus 29:38–30:10

38 "Now this is what you shall offer upon the altar: two lambs a year
39 old day by day continually. One lamb you shall offer in the morning,
40 and the other lamb you shall offer in the evening; and with the first
   lamb a tenth measure of fine flour mingled with a fourth of a hin of
41 beaten oil, and a fourth of a hin of wine for a libation. And the other
   lamb you shall offer in the evening, and shall offer with it a cereal
   offering and its libation, as in the morning, for a pleasing odour, an
42 offering by fire to the Lord. It shall be a continual burnt offering
   throughout your generations at the door of the tent of meeting
   before the Lord, where I will meet with you, to speak there to you.
43 There I will meet with the people of Israel, and it shall be sanctified
44 by my glory; I will consecrate the tent of meeting and the altar;
45 Aaron also and his sons I will consecrate, to serve me as priests. And
46 I will dwell among the people of Israel, and will be their God. And
   they shall know that I am the Lord their God, who brought them

forth out of the land of Egypt that I might dwell among them; I am the Lord their God.

1 "You shall make an altar to burn incense upon; of acacia wood
2 shall you make it. A cubit shall be its length, and a cubit its breadth; it shall be square, and two cubits shall be its height; its horns shall be
3 of one piece with it. And you shall overlay it with pure gold, its top and its sides round about and its horns; and you shall make for it a
4 moulding of gold round about. And two golden rings shall you make for it; under its moulding on two opposite sides of it shall you make them, and they shall be holders for poles with which to carry it.
5 You shall make the poles of acacia wood, and overlay them with
6 gold. And you shall put it before the veil that is by the ark of the testimony, before the mercy seat that is over the testimony, where I
7 will meet with you. And Aaron shall burn fragrant incense on it;
8 every morning when he dresses the lamps he shall burn it, and when Aaron sets up the lamps in the evening, he shall burn it, a perpetual
9 incense before the Lord throughout your generations. You shall offer no unholy incense thereon, nor burnt offering, nor cereal
10 offering; and you shall pour no libation thereon. Aaron shall make atonement upon its horns once a year; with the blood of the sin offering of atonement he shall make atonement for it once in the year throughout your generations; it is most holy to the Lord."

(i)

The daily ritual of the Sanctuary was a public recognition that Israel was God's people, and so it consisted of the burnt offering, of which the cereal offering formed part. For the first time the use of wine in the ritual is mentioned. Later passages make it clear that the burnt offering was preceded by a sin offering.

One of the greatest difficulties in theology is the reconciliation of the transcendence of God, his existence outside his creation, with his immanence, his presence within it. It is probable that a true reconciliation can be found only in a Trinitarian theology. In verse 46 ("... who brought them forth ... that I might dwell ... I am the Lord ...") we have an attempt to bring the two together. The Tent was the symbol and place of God's meeting Israel; a tent, because there could be no guaranteed permanence; cf. Jer. 7:1–15. Man could not use

God's condescension to force him to remain among them. Note the increasing depth of revelation as we contrast these verses with Jer. 3:16–17, and the Jeremiah verses with Rev. 21:22–26.

(ii)

We saw earlier that there was no mention of the altar of incense in chapter 25, which dealt with the furniture of the Tent. That its omission there need have no special significance is shown by the omission of any reference to the laver (verses 18–21) in chapter 27, which deals with the court of the Tabernacle.

Heb. 9:4 reckoned the incense altar as belonging to the Holiest. Symbolically it did, for the incense symbolized the prayers of the people going up to the throne of God in their midst (Rev. 5:8). For practical reasons, it had to be placed outside the curtain separating off the Holiest, since the High Priest entered it only on the Day of Atonement. The rules for the incense are found in verses 34–38.

Incense disappears from the New Testament, except in a symbolic sense, for we have the certainty that our prayers are heard through Jesus Christ.

There is a danger of believing that God must be approached in a special, sacred language, but it is perhaps even more dangerous to think that the everyday language of street, market and workshop is adequate. Our reaction to the Highest should be the highest of which we are capable. Obviously the cry of utter need should come in the most natural words. Even if someone overhearing them might think them disrespectful, God will not think so.

THE CENSUS TAX AND OTHER MATTERS

Exodus 30:11–38

11 12 The Lord said to Moses, "When you take the census of the people of Israel, then each shall give a ransom for himself to the Lord when you number them, that there be no plague among them when you 13 number them. Each who is numbered in the census shall give this:

half a shekel according to the shekel of the sanctuary (the shekel is
14 twenty gerahs), half a shekel as an offering to the Lord. Every one
who is numbered in the census, from twenty years old and upward,
15 shall give the Lord's offering. The rich shall not give more, and the
poor shall not give less, than the half shekel, when you give the
16 Lord's offering to make atonement for yourselves. And you shall
take the atonement money from the people of Israel, and shall
appoint it for the service of the tent of meeting; that it may bring the
people of Israel to remembrance before the Lord, so as to make
atonement for themselves."

17 18 The Lord said to Moses, "You shall also make a laver of bronze,
with its base of bronze, for washing. And you shall put it between the
19 tent of meeting and the altar, and you shall put water in it, with
which Aaron and his sons shall wash their hands and their feet.
20 When they go into the tent of meeting, or when they come near the
altar to minister, to burn an offering by fire to the Lord, they shall
21 wash with water, lest they die. They shall wash their hands and their
feet, lest they die: it shall be a statute for ever to them, even to him
and his descendants throughout their generations."

22 23 Moreover, the Lord said to Moses, "Take the finest spices: of
liquid myrrh five hundred shekels, and of sweet-smelling cinnamon
half as much, that is, two hundred and fifty, and of aromatic cane
24 two hundred and fifty, and of cassia five hundred, according to the
25 shekel of the sanctuary, and of olive oil a hin; and you shall make of
these a sacred anointing oil blended as by the perfumer; a holy
26 anointing oil it shall be. And you shall anoint with it the tent of
27 meeting and the ark of the testimony, and the table and all its
utensils, and the lampstand and its utensils, and the altar of incense,
28 and the altar of burnt offering with all its utensils and the laver and
29 its base; you shall consecrate them, that they may be most holy;
30 whatever touches them will become holy. And you shall anoint
Aaron and his sons, and consecrate them, that they may serve me as
31 priests. And you shall say to the people of Israel, 'This shall be my
32 holy anointing oil throughout your generations. It shall not be
poured upon the bodies of ordinary men, and you shall make no
other like it in composition; it is holy, and it shall be holy to you.
33 Whoever compounds any like it or whoever puts any of it on an
outsider shall be cut off from his people.' "
34 And the Lord said to Moses, "Take sweet spices, stacte, and
onycha, and galbanum, sweet spices with pure frankincense (of each

35 there shall be an equal part), and make an incense blended as by the
36 perfumer, seasoned with salt, pure and holy; and you shall beat
some of it very small, and put part of it before the testimony in the
tent of meeting where I shall meet with you; it shall be for you most
37 holy. And the incense which you shall make according to its
composition, you shall not make for yourselves; it shall be for you
38 holy to the Lord. Whoever makes any like it to use as perfume shall
be cut off from his people."

THE CENSUS TAX (30:11–16)

The idea has been and still is widespread that the taking of a
census is fraught with danger; see 2 Sam. 24. While this is
clearly mirrored in the Old Testament, it is never explained. In
all probability it was linked with the motives behind it, which
were normally military service. While there are not a few today
who have strong objections to census taking, it is questionable
whether they can really be justified. The census lists of Num. 1
makes it clear that they were concerned with those able to fight,
and this is repeated in Num. 26:2. War, even a holy war, was
bound to cause death, and so those numbered paid a ransom
(kopher), a word used for the penalty paid by the one guilty of
manslaughter (not murder). The plague mentioned in verse 12
probably means defeat in battle. The fixed sum of the poll tax
was due to the fact that the guilt involved in manslaughter was
the same, irrespective of a man's income and social standing.

While there is much warfare in the Old Testament, it is not
glorified, but rather the reverse; see 1 Chron. 28:3. Presumably
the silver was used for the sockets, into which the boards of the
Tabernacle were fixed (26:19).

Some time after the time of Nehemiah (10:32) the half-shekel
became a compulsory annual tax on all Jews; see Matt. 17:24.
After the destruction of the Temple in A.D. 70, it was continued
as a special tax by the Romans under the name of *Fiscus
Judaicus.* To add insult to injury it was paid into the treasury of
Jupiter Capitolinus in Rome.

THE LAVER (30:17–21)

There is a recollection of this legislation in John 13:10. The laver was not for major ablutions but for the cleansing of the unshod feet and soiled hands of those ministering in the Tabernacle. To have ministered with soiled hands and feet would have been an insult to the majesty of God, which would have deserved death. This should serve as a serious warning to those called to God's service today. To represent him, when conscious of unforgiven sin, carries great danger with it.

THE ANOINTING OIL (30-22–33)

A reasonable question would be, How could Israel in the wilderness make such an oil, the more so as some of the ingredients came from distant lands? The embalming customs of the Egyptians for their dead caused a widespread import trade in such aromatic herbs, so they may well have figured among the valuables pressed on the departing Israelites. The combination will have made a fragrant fluid with an olive oil base.

At a time when after-shave lotions and the like are commended for their perfumes even more than for their effectiveness, we find a recognition that sweet-smelling is attractive. The incidents related in Luke 7:37–38 and Mark 14:3–6 gain in depth in the light of this passage.

THE HOLY INCENSE (30:34–38)

The use of incense was widespread in the ancient world, including Canaan, where a number of old incense altars have been found by the archaeologists. Mal. 1:11 treats its use as a recognition of Yahweh's deity. Ps. 141:2 shows that it was symbolic of prayer; cf. Rev. 8:3–4. While some today dislike it, others find it stimulating to their senses. In Israel it was used partly to veil the glory of God (Lev. 16:12–13).

BEZALEL AND OHOLIAB

Exodus 31:1–18

1 2 The Lord said to Moses, "See, I have called by name Bezalel the son

3 of Uri, son of Hur, of the tribe of Judah: and I have filled him with
  the Spirit of God, with ability and intelligence, with knowledge and
4 all craftsmanship, to devise artistic designs, to work in gold, silver,
5 and bronze, in cutting stones for setting, and in carving wood, for
6 work in every craft. And behold, I have appointed with him
  Oholiab, the son of Ahisamach, of the tribe of Dan; and I have given
  to all able men ability, that they may make all that I have com-
7 manded you: the tent of meeting, and the ark of the testimony, and
8 the mercy seat that is thereon, and all the furnishings of the tent, the
  table and its utensils, and the pure lampstand with all its utensils,
9 and the altar of incense, and the altar of burnt offering with all its
10 utensils, and the laver and its base, and the finely worked garments,
  the holy garments for Aaron the priest and the garments of his sons,
11 for their service as priests, and the anointing oil and the fragrant
  incense for the holy place. According to all that I have commanded
  you they shall do."
12 13   And the Lord said to Moses, "Say to the people of Israel, 'You
  shall keep my sabbaths, for this is a sign between me and you
  throughout your generations, that you may know that I, the Lord,
14 sanctify you. You shall keep the sabbath, because it is holy for you;
  every one who profanes it shall be put to death; whoever does any
15 work on it, that soul shall be cut off from among his people. Six days
  shall work be done, but the seventh day is a sabbath of solemn rest,
  holy to the Lord; whoever does any work on the sabbath day shall be
16 put to death. Therefore the people of Israel shall keep the sabbath,
  observing the sabbath throughout their generations, as a perpetual
17 covenant. It is a sign for ever between me and the people of Israel
  that in six days the Lord made heaven and earth, and on the seventh
  day he rested, and was refreshed.' "
18   And he gave to Moses, when he had made an end of speaking with
  him upon Mount Sinai, the two tables of the testimony, tables of
  stone, written with the finger of God.

The section on the two craftsmen is virtually identical with
35:30–36:2. It is the answer to the frequently heard objection
that the Israelites would not have had the knowledge to create
the Tabernacle and its furnishings. "I have called by name"
(verse 2) is reminiscent of 33:12 and Isa. 45:4, which show that
the term virtually implies predestination. Inborn artistic genius
and skill is something that defies all logical explanation. It is

worth pondering that Bezalel belonged to Judah, the largest tribe (Num. 1:27), while Oholiab belonged to Dan, one of the smaller tribes (Num. 1:39). God has a habit of spreading his gifts around.

There is no need to question that Bezalel's grandfather was the Hur of 17:10 and 24:14.

THE SABBATH (31:12–17)

It could come as a surprise, especially in view of what was happening in the camp at the time, that the keeping of the Sabbath should have been re-emphasized. But it was to be expected that the people would use their best endeavours to hurry forward the building of the Tabernacle, seeing in it a possibility of regaining Yahweh's favour. But God was saying by implication that the making of the Tabernacle should not take precedence over the Sabbath; cf. 35:1–3.

There are many Christians who lose the benefit of a weekly day of rest by over-using Sunday in religious activity. If they were more careful of their activities on other days, they would have more time to devote to God—not necessarily to work for him—on the Sunday.

THE DECALOGUE (31:18)

Rabbinic fancy has allowed itself to run riot on how God wrote the Ten Words. But leaving fancies to one side as irrelevant— Christian preachers are sometimes too highly esteemed for flights of fancy in the pulpit—we should not pass by the statement as being of no importance, the more so as we are explicitly told that the two tables in their final form were made by Moses himself (34:1), but that the commandments were once again written by God (34:1).

In the first place it reinforces the opinion that the Ten Words were the real basis of the Covenant, the Book of the Covenant being little more than authoritative commentary. Secondly it stresses their unchangeable and unchanging nature. Quite consistent with this, there is no suggestion in Jer. 31:31–34 that the New Covenant will involve a new Torah, but simply that it will find its expression in changed natures (Ezek. 36:26–27; Jer. 31:33).

We may legitimately ask ourselves whether the author of Job was thinking of this verse when he made the anguished man break out in his expression of certainty, when the first rays of light illumined the dark night of his soul:

Oh, that my words were written!
  Oh that they were inscribed in a book!
Oh that with an iron pen and lead
  They were graven in the rock for ever! (19:23–24)

No man has the right to claim that he knows all that is to be known about God, but there are certainties he can and should share as he sings with Charles Wesley:

No condemnation now I dread;
  Jesus, and all in Him is mine!
Alive in Him, my living Head,
  And clothed in righteousness divine,
Bold I approach the eternal throne,
  And claim the crown, through Christ, my own.

H. THE GOLDEN CALF (32:1–34:35)

THE MAKING OF THE CALF

Exodus 32:1–6

1 When the people saw that Moses delayed to come down from the mountain, the people gathered themselves together to Aaron, and said to him, "Up, make us gods, who shall go before us; as for this Moses, the man who brought us up out of the land of Egypt, we do
2 not know what has become of him." And Aaron said to them, "Take off the rings of gold which are in the ears of your wives, your sons,
3 and your daughters, and bring them to me." So all the people took off the rings of gold which were in their ears, and brought them to
4 Aaron. And he received the gold at their hand, and fashioned it with

a graving tool, and made a molten calf; and they said, "These are your gods, O Israel, who brought you up out of the land of Egypt!"
5 When Aaron saw this, he built an altar before it; and Aaron made proclamation and said, "Tomorrow shall be a feast to the Lord."
6 And they rose up early on the morrow, and offered burnt offerings and brought peace offerings; and the people sat down to eat and drink, and rose up to play.

For a full understanding of the story, we should realize that "calf" is an unintelligent translation of *'egel,* which means "a young bull in its first strength" (Cole). In Gen. 15:9 the feminine is used for a three-year-old heifer and in Ps. 106:20 it is called an ox. The TEV rightly renders "bull". A calf, as we picture the term, would not be a normal image in ancient idolatry.

Moses had spent forty days on Mount Sinai (24:18), an indefinite period of more than a month. In that period there had been no specific activity for the people, and after the terrifying natural accompaniments of the covenant ceremony, it was quite natural to assume that Moses had perished.

Moses had served as a visible sign of Yahweh in their midst. It was to be expected, in spite of the Second Commandment, that they should want a visible replacement for him. It is probable that we should render in verse 1—similarly in verses 4 and 8— "Make us a god" (JB, NIV, mg.). In Gen. 35:4 we find Jacob's company wearing ear-rings. If they disappear from Israelite history after this event, it was probably out of a sense of shame. We gain the impression from the story that Aaron, unwilling to take a firm stand against the people, was playing for time, hoping that his problem would solve itself. It could be that he hoped that the sacrifice of the gold would be too great and so the demand would die down. The NEB is probably correct with "cast the metal in a mould" (verse 4; so JB, TEV).

Unless we assume that there was genuine misunderstanding between Aaron and the people, for which there are no grounds, there was no wish to abandon the worship of Yahweh. The bull was to serve as a sign of his presence. Albright has insisted, on the basis of archaeological evidence, that the bull was the throne of Yahweh and that he was conceived of as standing or sitting on it. So to be able to control the bull showed his strength and power. It has often been suggested that the choice of a bull was due to the people's familiarity with bull worship in Egypt, but it is hardly credible that they would have attributed their deliverance from Egypt to an Egyptian god. Far rather it will have been a hangover from the distant past, for among the Canaanites the bull was a regular symbol of divine power.

Although no image had been made of Yahweh, he had been linked not with cherubim, heavenly beings, but with the beasts of the field, and thus put on a level with the nature gods of the heathen. This tendency was to plague Israel until after the Babylonian Exile.

THE BREAKING OF THE STONE TABLES

Exodus 32:7–20

7 And the Lord said to Moses, "Go down; for your people, whom you brought up out of the land of Egypt, have corrupted themselves;
8 they have turned aside quickly out of the way which I commanded them; they have made for themselves a molten calf, and have worshipped it and sacrificed to it, and said, 'These are your gods, O
9 Israel, who brought you up out of the land of Egypt!'" And the Lord said to Moses, "I have seen this people, and behold, it is a stiff-
10 necked people; now therefore let me alone, that my wrath may burn hot against them and I may consume them; but of you I will make a great nation."
11 But Moses besought the Lord his God, and said, "O Lord, why does thy wrath burn hot against thy people, whom thou has brought forth out of the land of Egypt with great power and with a mighty
12 hand? Why should the Egyptians say, 'With evil intent did he bring them forth, to slay them in the mountains, and to consume them from the face of the earth'? Turn from thy fierce wrath, and repent of
13 this evil against thy people. Remember Abraham, Isaac, and Israel, thy servants, to whom thou didst swear by thine own self, and didst say to them, 'I will multiply your descendants as the stars of heaven, and all this land that I have promised I will give to your descendants,

14 and they shall inherit it for ever.'" And the Lord repented of the evil which he thought to do to his people.

15   And Moses turned, and went down from the mountain with the two tables of the testimony in his hands, tables that were written on
16 both sides; on the one side and on the other were they written. And the tables were the work of God, and the writing was the writing of
17 God, graven upon the tables. When Joshua heard the noise of the people as they shouted, he said to Moses, "There is a noise of war in
18 the camp." But he said, "It is not the sound of shouting for victory, or the sound of the cry of defeat, but the sound of singing that I
19 hear." And as soon as he came near the camp and saw the calf and the dancing, Moses' anger burned hot, and he threw the tables out of
20 his hands and broke them at the foot of the mountain. And he took the calf which they had made, and burnt it with fire, and ground it to powder, and scattered it upon the water, and made the people of Israel drink it.

(i)

As God broke the news to Moses of what was happening at the foot of the mountain, he also tested him by offering to fulfil his promise to the Patriarchs through him.

It would have been easy for him to accept. He had already learnt something of the difficulties that faced him, of how few thanks he would receive, of how little recognition there was of his "instruction in all the wisdom of the Egyptians" (Acts 7:22). Now here was the offer that he might become a second Abraham. But the forty years in Midian seem to have burnt all ambition out of him.

Though ambition is as much a reality among church leaders as among others, we might have acted as did Moses, but would we have prayed as he did? We, in tune with so much modern sentimentality, would probably have started to make excuses for the sinners. Moses accepted God's verdict on them and did not challenge it. Rather he pleaded God's honour and promises, and he prevailed.

(ii)

The sight of the reality was something far worse than God's warning had prepared him for. It seems clear that the shock did not so unman him, that he let the tables of the law fall and so break. The language clearly implies that he broke them deliberately.

For over a month he had been more intimately in contact with God than we can really imagine (34:33–35). After his experience of the "Beatific Vision" suddenly to be faced with the reality of the crude bull image was overwhelming. He felt that a great gulf had opened between Yahweh and Israel, and that the bringing of God's gift across it could only cause disaster. We are not called on to judge whether he was right in his action, but only to understand it.

Some of us may well have felt as did Moses, when after a more than normally affecting Good Friday experience, we have been faced by an inept and sentimental portrayal of Golgotha in picture or in words.

Making the people drink the gold dust was intended to impress on them the powerlessness of any sacred image. We tend to be so influenced by the alleged power of the demonic that we fail sometimes to realize that the overwhelming power of God All-Sovereign can empty it of all influence and might.

THE PUNISHMENT OF REBELLION

Exodus 32:21–35

21 And Moses said to Aaron, "What did this people do to you that you
22 have brought a great sin upon them?" And Aaron said, "Let not the anger of my lord burn hot; you know the people, that they are set on
23 evil. For they said to me, 'Make us gods, who shall go before us; as for this Moses, the man who brought us up out of the land of Egypt,
24 we do not know what has become of him.' And I said to them, 'Let any who have gold take it off'; so they gave it to me, and I threw it into the fire, and there came out this calf."
25 And when Moses saw that the people had broken loose (for Aaron had let them break loose, to their shame among their
26 enemies), then Moses stood in the gate of the camp, and said, "Who is on the Lord's side? Come to me." And all the sons of Levi gathered
27 themselves together to him. And he said to them, "Thus says the

Lord God of Israel, 'Put every man his sword on his side, and go to and fro from gate to gate throughout the camp, and slay every man his brother, and every man his companion, and every man his
28 neighbour.'" And the sons of Levi did according to the word of Moses; and there fell of the people that day about three thousand
29 men. And Moses said, "Today you have ordained yourselves for the service of the Lord, each one at the cost of his son and of his brother, that he may bestow a blessing upon you this day."
30 On the morrow Moses said to the people, "You have sinned a great sin. And now I will go up to the Lord; perhaps I can make
31 atonement for your sin." So Moses returned to the Lord and said, "Alas, this people have sinned a great sin; they have made for
32 themselves gods of gold. But now, if thou wilt forgive their sin—and if not, blot me, I pray thee, out of thy book which thou hast written."
33 But the Lord said to Moses, "Whoever has sinned against me, him
34 will I blot out of my book. But now go, lead the people to the place of which I have spoken to you; behold my angel shall go before you. Nevertheless, in the day when I visit, I will visit their sin upon them."
35 And the Lord sent a plague upon the people, because they made the calf which Aaron made.

(i)

One look at his brother's face had told Moses where the blame lay. His question to him implied that he was willing to believe that Aaron had acted under severe pressure, even the threat of death. To Aaron's credit, let it be said that he did not avail himself of this loophole, though he did put the blame, fairly enough, on the people, hinting at compulsion, without detailing it, and then pitiably he blamed an accident. "How was I to know that the molten gold would come out in the shape of a bull?" For the one who loves God, chance does not exist, (Rom. 8:28). But how often do we hear the plea, "I've been so unlucky!"?

In Deut. 9:20 we find that it was only Moses' intercession which saved the life of the High Priest designate.

(ii)

The people had rebelled ("broken loose") against their covenant Lord, and so there had to be punishment. Moses applied the law of 22:20, and called for volunteers to carry it out. We are not to infer that the tribe of Levi had not been involved in the worship of the golden bull, for verse 29 ("at the cost of his son and of his brother") seems to show that they executed members of their own tribe. "All" the sons of Levi in verse 26 is to be understood as meaning all who were not implicated. Clearly the guilty looked upon the Levites as God's executioners and apparently offered no resistance. Obviously there could be no certainty as to who had participated, and so God completed man's justice with a plague (verse 35). No indication is given how many died in the plague.

Just as the priests were later inducted by carrying out priestly functions (chapter 29), so the Levites by their judicial action were inducted into their later functions.

(iii)

When Moses approached God the second time, he did not try to extenuate the people's sin either to them or to God. In the light of 1 Cor. 13:7 love will be very loath to sit in the judge's chair, but it is lack of love so to judge sin that the sinner will gain false confidence before God. Joseph in Gen. 50:20 made it clear that he bore no grudge against his brothers, but he did not try to minimize their sin. Even Jesus, when he prayed, "Father forgive them, for they know not what they do" (Luke 23:34) did not suggest that forgiveness was not needed.

Now the one-time shepherd's heart was breaking over his new flock. If a price had to be paid for the rebellion and the insult done to his God, let him pay the penalty and be blotted out of God's book.

Moses' words remind us of Paul's willingness to be accursed for his people's sake (Rom. 9:3). But while their prayers were heard, neither he nor Paul could be the expiation for their people's sin. For as Mrs Alexander sang of her Lord:

> There was no other good enough
>   To pay the price of sin;
> He only could unlock the gate
>   of heaven, and let us in.

It is not clear whether the threat of punishment ("Whoever has sinned . . . will I blot out") found its fulfilment in the plague of verse 35, or in the débâcle of Kadesh Barnea. One consequence the sin would have; God would not guarantee his presence with the people, but simply promised an angel as the guide to Canaan.

PENALTIES AND PROMISE

Exodus 33:1–23

1 The Lord said to Moses, "Depart, go up hence, you and the people whom you have brought up out of the land of Egypt, to the land of which I swore to Abraham, Isaac, and Jacob, saying, 'To your 2 descendants I will give it.' And I will send an angel before you, and I will drive out the Canaanites, the Amorites, the Hittites, the 3 Perizzites, the Hivites, and the Jebusites. Go up to a land flowing with milk and honey; but I will not go up among you, lest I consume you in the way, for you are a stiff-necked people."

4 When the people heard these evil tidings, they mourned; and no 5 man put on his ornaments. For the Lord had said to Moses, "Say to the people of Israel, 'You are a stiff-necked people; if for a single moment I should go up among you, I would consume you. So now put off your ornaments from you, that I may know what to do with 6 you.'" Therefore the people of Israel stripped themselves of their ornaments, from Mount Horeb onward.

7 Now Moses used to take the tent and pitch it outside the camp, far off from the camp; and he called it the tent of meeting. And every one who sought the Lord would go to the tent of meeting, which was 8 outside the camp. Whenever Moses went out to the tent, all the people rose up, and every man stood at his tent door, and looked 9 after Moses, until he had gone into the tent. When Moses entered the tent, the pillar of cloud would descend and stand at the door of 10 the tent, and the Lord would speak with Moses. And when all the people saw the pillar of cloud standing at the door of the tent, all the 11 people would rise up and worship, every man at his tent door. Thus the Lord used to speak to Moses face to face, as a man speaks to his friend. When Moses turned again into the camp, his servant Joshua the son of Nun, a young man, did not depart from the tent.

12 Moses said the Lord, "See, thou sayest to me, 'Bring up this people'; but thou hast not let me know whom thou wilt send with me. Yet thou hast said, 'I know you by name, and you have also
13 found favour in my sight.' Now therefore, I pray thee, if I have found favour in thy sight, show me now thy ways, that I may know thee and find favour in thy sight. Consider too that this nation is thy
14 people." And he said, "My presence will go with you, and I will give
15 you rest." And he said to him, "If thy presence will not go with me,
16 do not carry us up from here. For how shall it be known that I have found favour in thy sight, I and thy people? Is it not in thy going with us, so that we are distinct, I and thy people, from all other people that are upon the face of the earth?"

17 And the Lord said to Moses, "This very thing that you have spoken I will do; for you have found favour in my sight, and I know
18 19 you by name." Moses said, "I pray thee, show me thy glory." And he said, "I will make all my goodness pass before you, and will proclaim before you my name 'The Lord'; and I will be gracious to whom I will be gracious, and will show mercy on whom I will show mercy.
20 But," he said, "you cannot see my face; for man shall not see me and
21 live." And the Lord said, "Behold, there is a place by me where you
22 shall stand upon the rock; and while my glory passes by I will put you in a cleft of the rock, and I will cover you with my hand until I
23 have passed by; then I will take away my hand, and you shall see my back; but my face shall not be seen."

(i)

God confirmed his intention of handing over the leadership and care of Israel to an angel. It is not easy for us, after the Cross, to put ourselves into the feelings of ancient Israel. There can be very few church attenders, who are not familiar with Christ's saying, "Where two or three are gathered in my name, there am I in the midst of them" (Matt. 18:20). The fact is often mentioned as a source of encouragement and joy, yet it is clear that the average congregation would feel most uncomfortable, if it were really conscious of the fact. In Israel a consciousness of Yahweh's proximity created fear (20:18–19), yet an outward sign of his presence—through the pillar of cloud and fire—was welcomed. Hence the outward signs of mourning (verse 4).

The position was given visible reality and expression by the "tent of meeting". In most modern works it is suggested that here we have the earliest and truest picture of the Tabernacle, a simple and not elaborate tent, at a distance from the camp, not in its centre, served by Moses and Joshua, not by Aaron and the Levites.

Basically this claim is, of course, correct. But there is no necessary contradiction between the two views. According to the story as it stands, the Tabernacle had not yet been made nor the Aaronic priesthood instituted. In addition the camp had been so defiled by the incident of the golden bull, that it was necessary to have the meeting place with God well outside it. The statement that the people worshipped, when Moses went to the tent and the cloud descended on it (verse 10) would be better rendered "prostrated themselves"; it was the product of a guilty conscience, now that God had come visibly into their midst.

"The Lord used to speak to Moses face to face." Compare Num. 12:6–8. It is impossible to fix the exact implications. The most important is presumably intimacy, causing perfect understanding.

(ii)

God had offered to fulfil his purposes in Moses (32:10). Whatever may have been his first reaction, Moses had now realized that without God he could achieve nothing. He claimed that God had said, under circumstances unknown to us, "I know you by name", cf. 31:18, i.e. he knew him personally, and therefore knew that his prayer was genuine. He asked to know God's "ways", i.e. the principles behind God's dealings with men, so that he, as God's representative, might act accordingly. God's answer was the promise that he would fulfil Moses' unspoken prayer; his presence, literally his "Face", would go with the people. Moses' immediate reaction was to ask to see God's glory. Glory *(kavod)*, literally "weight", was the inner reality that made God's character what it is.

God assured Moses that this was more than mortal man could bear. It has, however, been mediated to men through Jesus Christ, but veiled by his human flesh. We may well ask ourselves whether even eternity will grant us more than we can find in him.

It seems imperative that we take God's promise metaphorically. "Passing by" need not be understood to mean that God adopted a human form—there is no suggestion of this in the sequel, where the fulfilment is purely verbal. He was to see God's "back", i.e. understand him in retrospect, in the light of what he had done.

THE GLORY OF GOD

Exodus 34:1-9

1 The Lord said to Moses, "Cut two tables of stone like the first; and I will write upon the tables the words that were on the first tables,
2 which you broke. Be ready in the morning, and come up in the morning to Mount Sinai, and present yourself there to me on the top
3 of the mountain. No man shall come up with you, and let no man be seen throughout all the mountain; let no flocks or herds feed before
4 that mountain." So Moses cut two tables of stone like the first; and he rose early in the morning and went up on Mount Sinai, as the Lord had commanded him, and took in his hand two tables of stone.
5 And the Lord descended in the cloud and stood with him there, and
6 proclaimed the name of the Lord. The Lord passed before him, and proclaimed, "The Lord, the Lord, a God merciful and gracious, slow
7 to anger, and abounding in steadfast love and faithfulness, keeping steadfast love for thousands, forgiving iniquity and transgression and sin, but who will by no means clear the guilty, visiting the iniquity of the fathers upon the children and the children's children,
8 to the third and the fourth generation." And Moses made haste to
9 bow his head toward the earth, and worshipped. And he said, "If now I have found favour in thy sight, O Lord, let the Lord, I pray thee, go in the midst of us, although it is a stiff-necked people; and pardon our iniquity and our sin, and take us for thy inheritance."

The new tables of stone were for the renewed covenant (verse 10). This time they were man-made to stress that though the past was forgiven, its effects continued. We should note that beyond the cloud (verse 5) we are not told that Moses saw anything; we are told only what he heard (verses 6-7). There are eight statements, which the rabbis list as the thirteen attributes of God.

(1) *Yahweh, Yahweh:* the two-fold pronouncing of the divine name implies what is conveyed by the Alpha and Omega of Rev. 1:8; 22:13. The whole history of Israel had begun, continued and existed until then because of the power of Yahweh, and its future would also depend on him. The Church in its long history has repeatedly been plagued by those who have wanted to go beyond the Scriptures instead of plumbing their depths. We know how the philosopher faces us with problems, which seem to be ignored by the revelation of God in Christ. Equally there is the mystic, who suggests that there are depths and heights in the knowledge of God, which can be reached only on the mystic path. Eternity will clarify our understanding of the wonder of God in Christ, but it is not likely to teach us anything new. The repetition of the divine name has much the same force as Heb. 13:8.

(2) *El rachum ve-channun,* "a God merciful and gracious". The word *rachum* comes from the same root as *rechem,* the mother's "womb", and means the type of understanding and feeling for men's weaknesses a mother shows towards her child; see also Ps. 103:13. The word *channun* is adequately rendered "gracious". It comes from the same root as *chen,* which expresses the behaviour of the Good Samaritan, kindness to one who has no claim on us, as Paul expressed it in Rom. 5:8, "God shows his love for us in that while we were yet sinners Christ died for us".

(3) *erekh appaim,* "slow to anger". Salvation history shows that God's anger is a reality; it is worth remembering that it plays a special role in the book of Revelation. It has been the slowness of God's reaction to human sin in history that has made many not take it seriously.

(4) *ve-rav chesed ve-emet,* "abounding in covenant love and faithfulness". *Chesed,* the RSV "steadfast love", is essentially a matter of grace. It expresses the behaviour we expect from one who is in covenant relationship with us. In a purely human

situation "loyalty" is often an adequate rendering, but when it is applied to God, it includes the love with which he loves his own, unchanging, utterly reliable and understanding. In the New Testament it is expressed by "grace". *Emet* is not "truth", as in the AV, but rather "faithfulness, trustworthiness". The Bible lays less stress on an abstract concept of truth and far more on reliability and trustworthiness. The trustworthy man can be relied on to tell the truth in the measure that it is known to him.

(5) *notzer chesed la-alaphim,* "keeping covenant love for thousands (of generations)". This is the rabbinic interpretation as in 20:6, and is almost certainly correct. We can have little idea how the influence of godly ancestors can reach down the generations.

(6) *nose 'avon ve-pesha' ve-chatta'ah,* "bearing crookedness and rebellion and failure". The verb is usually translated "forgiving", which is correct, but does not bring out the cost to God himself. The three aspects of sin are generally rendered "iniquity and transgression and sin", but the rendering offered here tries to bring out the particular shade of meaning in each word more clearly. 'avon is what Christian theology calls "original sin", an inbred crookedness.

(7) *ve-naqqeh lo yenaqqeh,* "and that will by no means clear (the guilty)". However loving God may be, there is something in man, made in the image of God, which demands that he should be just.

(8) "visiting the sins of the fathers upon the children . . . unto the third and fourth generation"; see comments on 20:5.

Unlike the New Testament the Old is not given to quoting older scriptures, but the importance of this revelation of God's character is indicated by its being quoted in whole or in part ten times, namely, Num. 14:18; 2 Chron. 30:9; Neh. 9:17; Pss. 86:15; 103:8; 108:4; 111:4; 116:5; 145:8; Joel 2:13. It also plays a big part in the worship of the Synagogue.

Before anyone joins in the popular criticism of "the God of the Old Testament", he ought to read and reread this expression of Yahweh's "glory" and ask himself what is missing except that which could be revealed only in God incarnate, Jesus Christ.

With a God like this, Moses argued, Israel's obstinacy and sin were no real bar to God's presence going with them.

THE RENEWAL OF THE COVENANT

Exodus 34:10–28

10 And he said, "Behold, I make a covenant. Before all your people I will do marvels, such as have not been wrought in all the earth or in any nation; and all the people among whom you are shall see the work of the Lord; for it is a terrible thing that I will do with you.
11 "Observe what I command you this day. Behold, I will drive out before you the Amorites, the Canaanites, the Hittites, the Perizzites,
12 the Hivites, and the Jebusites. Take heed to yourself, lest you make a covenant with the inhabitants of the land whither you go, lest it
13 become a snare in the midst of you. You shall tear down their altars,
14 and break their pillars, and cut down their Asherim (for you shall worship no other god, for the Lord, whose name is Jealous, is a
15 jealous God), lest you make a covenant with the inhabitants of the land, and when they play the harlot after their gods and sacrifice to
16 their gods and one invites you, you eat of his sacrifice, and you take of their daughters for your sons, and their daughters play the harlot after their gods and make your sons play the harlot after their gods.
17 "You shall make for yourself no molten gods.
18 "The feast of unleavened bread you shall keep. Seven days you shall eat unleavened bread, as I commanded you, at the time appointed in the month Abib; for in the month Abib you came out
19 from Egypt. All that opens the womb is mine, all your male cattle,
20 the firstlings of cow and sheep. The firstling of an ass you shall redeem with a lamb, or if you will not redeem it you shall break its neck. All the first-born of your sons you shall redeem. And none shall appear before me empty.
21 "Six days you shall work, but on the seventh day you shall rest; in
22 ploughing time and in harvest you shall rest. And you shall observe the feast of weeks, the first fruits of wheat harvest, and the feast of
23 ingathering at the year's end. Three times in the year shall all your
24 males appear before the Lord God, the God of Israel. For I will cast out nations before you, and enlarge your borders; neither shall any man desire your land, when you go up to appear before the Lord your God three times in the year.

25 "You shall not offer the blood of my sacrifice with leaven; neither shall the sacrifice of the feast of the passover be left until the
26 morning. The first of the first fruits of your ground you shall bring to the house of the Lord your God. You shall not boil a kid in its mother's milk."
27 And the Lord said to Moses, "Write these words; in accordance with these words I have made a covenant with you and with Israel."
28 And he was there with the Lord forty days and forty nights; he neither ate bread nor drank water. And he wrote upon the tables the words of the covenant, the ten commandments.

God renewed the Sinai covenant. That it was not a new covenant but a renewal is shown by the fact that the Ten Words retained their pride of place (verses 1, 28). The same is true of the New Covenant (Jer. 31:31–34) for there too no new covenant conditions are mentioned. It is new because it contains a new power.

The confirmation of the fact of renewal would be seen in the conquest of Canaan (verse 11). The use of "terrible" in verse 10 is linguistically inept. A better rendering is the NEB, "for fearful is that which I will do for you".

The collection of laws which follows has never found a satisfactory explanation from scholars. It is a sort of parallel to the Book of the Covenant, but it is difficult to explain why they have been chosen and others omitted; none are new. With verse 12 compare 23:32–33. The worship of the golden bull had been a harking back to what they had learnt in Canaan in the time of the Patriarchs, which had lain dormant in their racial memory. With verse 13 compare 23:24. Critics of modern television constantly remind us that what we see has a much deeper effect on us than what we hear. With verse 14 compare 20:5. The special stress on Canaanite women (verse 16) is true to experience, which has repeatedly shown that old religious concepts have been normally preserved by the women of the family, sometimes for good.

With verse 17 compare 20:4,23; with verse 18 compare 23:14–15; verses 19–20 repeat 13:2, 11–16. In verse 21 we have a repetition of the Sabbath commandment, but without any motivation offered. 23:14–17 is repeated in verses 22–24. For verse 25 see 12:10, 23:18; for verse 26 see 23:19. This conjunction of apparently disparate passages shows that we are dealing with a summary of the Book of the Covenant, but that is no explanation of the choice of items.

THE GLORIFICATION OF MOSES

Exodus 34:29–35

29 When Moses came down from Mount Sinai, with the two tables of the testimony in his hand as he came down from the mountain, Moses did not know that the skin of his face shone because he had 30 been talking with God. And when Aaron and all the people of Israel saw Moses, behold, the skin of his face shone, and they were afraid 31 to come near him. But Moses called to them; and Aaron and all the leaders of the congregation returned to him, and Moses talked with 32 them. And afterward all the people of Israel came near, and he gave them in commandment all that the Lord had spoken with him in 33 Mount Sinai. And when Moses had finished speaking with them, he 34 put a veil on his face; but whenever Moses went in before the Lord to speak with him, he took the veil off, until he came out; and when he 35 came out, and told the people of Israel what he was commanded, the people of Israel saw the face of Moses, that the skin of Moses' face shone; and Moses would put the veil upon his face again, until he went in to speak with him.

In traditional pictures of Moses he is often depicted with rays of light coming from his temples, which occasionally look like horns. These all go back to this section. It had been granted to Moses to have a vision of the glory of God. It was only fitting that Israel should have a fleeting glimpse of that glory in his face.

At first sight one might infer that Moses veiled his face because of the glory that shone from it, which caused fear among those that saw it. Paul, however, in 2 Cor. 3:7–18 explains that it was to prevent their seeing the fading of the glory.

The Christian should have a similar experience (2 Cor. 3:18), and like Moses he will not know that he has had it, but he need not fear its outward passing, for it comes not from an external vision but from the indwelling Spirit. After all, Christ's glory had waned before he descended from the Mount of Transfiguration. It is given us for our sakes, not for that of others. In taking on "the likeness of sinful flesh" Christ had to veil his glory, which he had with the Father, and as John reminds us, "it does not yet appear what we shall be" (1 John 3:2).

I. THE MAKING OF THE TABERNACLE (Chs. 35–40)

These chapters are a repetition, sometimes virtually verbatim, of what has gone before—only, of course, the work is now being carried out—until we reach the triumphant conclusion where the Tabernacle of God is with man. They call for little additional exposition. We have contented ourselves with showing the breakdown of the chapters, referring to the sections where they have been dealt with in detail, and adding, where necessary, a few extra remarks.

The Priority of the Sabbath (35:1–3)

1 Moses assembled all the congregation of the people of Israel, and said to them, "These are the things which the Lord has commanded
2 you to do. Six days shall work be done, but on the seventh day you shall have a holy sabbath of solemn rest to the Lord; whoever does
3 any work on it shall be put to death; you shall kindle no fire in all your habitations on the sabbath day."

See comments on 31:12–17. There would have been a real danger of the ignoring of the Sabbath law, as the people showed their zeal in trying to undo the sin they had committed.

The Materials for the Tabernacle (35:4–9)

4 Moses said to all the congregation of the people of Israel, "This is the
5 thing which the Lord has commanded. Take from among you an offering to the Lord; whoever is of a generous heart, let him bring

6 the Lord's offering: gold, silver, and bronze; blue and purple and
7 scarlet stuff and fine twined linen; goats' hair, tanned rams' skins,
8 and goatskins; acacia wood, oil for the light, spices for the anointing
9 oil and for the fragrant incense, and onyx stones and stones for
setting, for the ephod and for the breastpiece."

See comments on 25:1–9. No one individual could have
contributed all that was needed, so an opportunity was offered
for each to decide what contribution he could best make.
Equally it is impossible for any one of us to provide all that is
needed for the building up of the local church.

The Work and Work-People (35:10–29)

10 "And let every able man among you come and make all that the
11 Lord has commanded: the tabernacle, its tent and its covering, its
12 hooks and its frames, its bars, its pillars, and its bases; the ark with
13 its poles, the mercy seat, and the veil of the screen; the table with its
14 poles and all its utensils, and the bread of the Presence; the
lampstand also for the light, with its utensils and its lamps, and the
15 oil for the light; and the altar of incense, with its poles, and the
anointing oil and the fragrant incense, and the screen for the door, at
16 the door of the tabernacle; the altar of burnt offering, with its
grating of bronze, its poles, and all its utensils, the laver and its base;
17 the hangings of the court, its pillars and its bases, and the screen for
18 the gate of the court; the pegs of the tabernacle and the pegs of the
19 court, and their cords; the finely wrought garments for ministering
in the holy place, the holy garments for Aaron the priest, and the
garments of his sons, for their service as priests."
20   Then all the congregation of the people of Israel departed from
21 the presence of Moses. And they came, every one whose heart stirred
him, and every one whose spirit moved him, and brought the Lord's
offering to be used for the tent of meeting, and for all its service, and
22 for the holy garments. So they came, both men and women; all who
were of a willing heart brought brooches and earrings and signet
rings and armlets, all sorts of gold objects, every man dedicating an
23 offering of gold to the Lord. And every man with whom was found
blue or purple or scarlet stuff or fine linen or goats' hair or tanned
24 rams' skins or goatskins, brought them. Every one who could make
an offering of silver or bronze brought it as the Lord's offering; and

every man with whom was found acacia wood of any use in the
25 work, brought it. And all women who had ability spun with their
hands, and brought what they had spun in blue and purple and
26 scarlet stuff and fine twined linen; all the women whose hearts were
27 moved with ability spun the goats' hair. And the leaders brought
onyx stones and stones to be set, for the ephod and for the
28 breastpiece, and spices and oil for the light, and for the anointing oil,
29 and for the fragrant incense. All the men and women, the people of
Israel, whose heart moved them to bring anything for the work
which the Lord had commanded by Moses to be done, brought it as
their freewill offering to the Lord.

As important as the materials were the workers. There was a
call not merely for materials but also for time and talents. The
stress here is on willingness (verse 22). Sometimes there is an
over-emphasis on duty in our preaching, when it should be on
asking the Spirit to make us willing. Since he will normally give
the ability, there would be fewer round pegs in square holes, if
we did that.

The Recognition of Gifts (35:30–36:1)

30 And Moses said to the people of Israel, "See, the Lord has called by
31 name Bezalel the son of Uri, son of Hur, of the tribe of Judah; and he
has filled him with the Spirit of God, with ability, with intelligence,
32 with knowledge, and with all craftsmanship, to devise artistic
33 designs, to work in gold and silver and bronze, in cutting stones for
34 setting, and in carving wood, for work in every skilled craft. And he
has inspired him to teach, both him and Oholiab the son of
35 Ahisamach of the tribe of Dan. He has filled them with ability to do
every sort of work done by a craftsman or by a designer or by an
embroiderer in blue and purple and scarlet stuff and fine twined
linen, or by a weaver—by any sort of workman or skilled designer.
1 "Bezalel and Oholiab and every able man in whom the Lord has
put ability and intelligence to know how to do any work in the
construction of the sanctuary shall work in accordance with all that
the Lord has commanded."

See comments on 31:1–11. If the Holy Spirit raises up someone
for a task, we must not let our willingness to work usurp the
position of those uniquely called to the task.

The Provision of the Materials (36:2–7)

2 And Moses called Bezalel and Oholiab and every able man in whose
mind the Lord had put ability, every one whose heart stirred him up
3 to come to do the work; and they received from Moses all the
freewill offering which the people of Israel had brought for doing the
work on the sanctuary. They still kept bringing him freewill offer-
4 ings every morning, so that all the able men who were doing every
sort of task on the sanctuary came, each from the task that he was
5 doing, and said to Moses, "The people bring much more than
enough for doing the work which the Lord has commanded us to
6 do." So Moses gave command, and word was proclaimed throughout the camp, "Let neither man nor woman do anything more for
the offering for the sanctuary." So the people were restrained from
7 bringing; for the stuff they had was sufficient to do all the work, and
more.

One of the glories of the Tabernacle, frequently overlooked, is
that, to use modern terms, it opened free of debt. It is a sad
thing, when any form of work for God starts in debt. This may
be due to failure to grasp God's will, or the seeking of a
magnificence intended to glorify man rather than God. All too
often it is due to a lack of willingness, partially motivated by the
failure to count the cost beforehand; compare the man who
built a tower (Luke 14:28–30).

The Making of the Tabernacle (36:8–38)

8 And all the able men among the workmen made the tabernacle with
ten curtains; they were made of fine twined linen and blue and
9 purple and scarlet stuff, with cherubim skilfully worked. The length
of each curtain was twenty-eight cubits, and the breadth of each
curtain four cubits; all the curtains had the same measure.
10 And he coupled five curtains to one another, and the other five
11 curtains he coupled to one another. And he made loops of blue on
the edge of the outmost curtain of the first set; likewise he made
12 them on the edge of the outmost curtain of the second set; he made
fifty loops on the one curtain, and he made fifty loops on the edge of
the curtain that was in the second set; the loops were opposite one
13 another. And he made fifty clasps of gold, and coupled the curtains
one to the other with clasps; so the tabernacle was one whole.

14 He also made curtains of goats' hair for a tent over the tabernacle;
15 he made eleven curtains. The length of each curtain was thirty cubits, and the breadth of each curtain four cubits; the eleven
16 curtains had the same measure. He coupled five curtains by them-
17 selves, and six curtains by themselves. And he made fifty loops on the edge of the outmost curtain of the one set, and fifty loops on the
18 edge of the other connecting curtain. And he made fifty clasps of
19 bronze to couple the tent together that it might be one whole. And he made for the tent a covering of tanned rams' skins and goatskins.
20 Then he made the upright frames for the tabernacle of acacia
21 wood. Ten cubits was the length of a frame, and a cubit and a half
22 the breadth of each frame. Each frame had two tenons, for fitting
23 together; he did this for all the frames of the tabernacle. The frames for the tabernacle he made thus: twenty frames for the south side;
24 and he made forty bases of silver under the twenty frames, two bases under one frame for its two tenons, and two bases under another
25 frame for its two tenons. And for the second side of the tabernacle,
26 on the north side, he made twenty frames and their forty bases of silver, two bases under one frame and two bases under another
27 frame. And for the rear of the tabernacle westward he made six
28 frames. And he made two frames for corners of the tabernacle in the
29 rear. And they were separate beneath, but joined at the top, at the
30 first ring; he made two of them thus, for the two corners. There were eight frames with their bases of silver: sixteen bases, under every frame two bases.
31 And he made bars of acacia wood, five for the frames of the one
32 side of the tabernacle, and five bars for the frames of the other side of the tabernacle, and five bars for the frames of the tabernacle at the
33 rear westward. And he made the middle bar to pass through from
34 end to end halfway up the frames. And he overlaid the frames with gold, and made their rings of gold for holders for the bars, and overlaid the bars with gold.
35 And he made the veil of blue and purple and scarlet stuff and fine
36 twined linen; with cherubim skilfully worked he made it. And for it he made four pillars of acacia, and overlaid them with gold; their
37 hooks were of gold, and he cast for them four bases of silver. He also made a screen for the door of the tent, of blue and purple and scarlet
38 stuff and fine twined linen, embroidered with needlework; and its five pillars with their hooks. He overlaid their capitals, and their fillets were of gold, but their five bases were of bronze.

For comments see 26:1–37. The Tabernacle had to be made first, so that its furnishings, especially the Ark, might find a home as soon as they were ready.

The Making of the Tabernacle Furnishings (37:1–29)

1 Bezalel made the ark of acacia wood; two cubits and a half was its length, a cubit and a half its breadth, and a cubit and a half its height.
2 And he overlaid it with pure gold within and without, and made a
3 moulding of gold around it. And he cast for it four rings of gold for its four corners, two rings on its one side and two rings on its other
4 side. And he made poles of acacia wood, and overlaid them with
5 gold, and put the poles into the rings on the sides of the ark, to carry
6 the ark. And he made a mercy seat of pure gold; two cubits and a half
7 was its length, and a cubit and a half its breadth. And he made two cherubim of hammered gold; on the two ends of the mercy seat he
8 made them, one cherub on the one end, and one cherub on the other end; of one piece with the mercy seat he made the cherubim on its
9 two ends. The cherubim spread out their wings above, overshadowing the mercy seat with their wings, with their faces one to another; toward the mercy seat were the faces of the cherubim.
10 He also made the table of acacia wood; two cubits was its length, a
11 cubit its breadth, and a cubit and a half its height; and he overlaid it
12 with pure gold, and made a moulding of gold around it. And he made around it a frame a handbreadth wide, and made a moulding
13 of gold around the frame. He cast for it four rings of gold, and
14 fastened the rings to the four corners at its four legs. Close to the
15 frame were the rings, as holders for the poles to carry the table. He made the poles of acacia wood to carry the table, and overlaid them
16 with gold. And he made the vessels of pure gold which were to be upon the table, its plates and dishes for incense, and its bowls and flagons with which to pour libations.
17 He also made the lampstand of pure gold. The base and the shaft of the lampstand were made of hammered work; its cups, its
18 capitals, and its flowers were of one piece with it. And there were six branches going out of its sides, three branches of the lampstand out of one side of it and three branches of the lampstand out of the other
19 side of it; three cups made like almonds, each with capital and flower, on one branch, and three cups made like almonds, each with capital and flower, on the other branch—so for the six branches

20 going out of the lampstand. And on the lampstand itself were four
21 cups made like almonds, with their capitals and flowers, and a
capital of one piece with it under each pair of the six branches going
22 out of it. Their capitals and their branches were of one piece with it;
23 the whole of it was one piece of hammered work of pure gold. And
he made its seven lamps and its snuffers and its trays of pure gold.
24 He made it and all its utensils of a talent of pure gold.
25 He made the altar of incense of acacia wood; its length was a
cubit, and its breadth was a cubit; it was square, and two cubits was
26 its height; its horns were of one piece with it. He overlaid it with pure
gold, its top, and its sides round about, and its horns; and he made a
27 moulding of gold round about it, and made two rings of gold on it
under its moulding, on two opposite sides of it, as holders for the
28 poles with which to carry it. And he made the poles of acacia wood,
and overlaid them with gold.
29 He made the holy anointing oil also, and the pure fragrant
incense, blended as by the perfumer.

For comments see 25:10–22; 25:23–29; 25:31–39; 30:1–5;
30:23–35. The repetition of the details, less natural in ancient
writing than in modern print, is meant to imply that the
instructions were followed to the letter.

The Making of the Furnishings for the Court (38:1–20)

1 He made the altar of burnt offering also of acacia wood; five cubits
was its length, and five cubits its breadth; it was square, and three
2 cubits was its height. He made horns for it on its four corners; its
3 horns were of one piece with it, and he overlaid it with bronze. And
he made all the utensils of the altar, the pots, the shovels, the basins,
4 the forks, and the firepans: all its utensils he made of bronze. And he
made for the altar a grating, a network of bronze, under its ledge,
5 extending halfway down. He cast four rings on the four corners of
6 the bronze grating as holders for the poles; he made the poles of
7 acacia wood, and overlaid them with bronze. And he put the poles
through the rings on the sides of the altar, to carry it with them; he
made it hollow, with boards.
8 And he made the laver of bronze and its base of bronze, from the
mirrors of the ministering women who ministered at the door of the
tent of meeting.

9   And he made the court; for the south side the hangings of the
10   court were of fine twined linen, a hundred cubits; their pillars were
     twenty and their bases twenty, of bronze, but the hooks of the pillars
11   and their fillets were of silver. And for the north side a hundred
     cubits, their pillars twenty, their bases twenty, of bronze, but the
12   hooks of the pillars and their fillets were of silver. And for the west
     side were hangings of fifty cubits, their pillars ten, and their sockets
13   ten; the hooks of the pillars and their fillets were of silver. And for
14   the front to the east, fifty cubits. The hangings for one side of the
15   gate were fifteen cubits, with three pillars and three bases. And so for
     the other side; on this hand and that hand by the gate of the court
16   were hangings of fifteen cubits, with three pillars and three bases. All
17   the hangings round about the court were of fine twined linen. And
     the bases for the pillars were of bronze, but the hooks of the pillars
     and their fillets were of silver; the overlaying of their capitals was
     also of silver, and all the pillars of the court were filleted with silver.
18   And the screen for the gate of the court was embroidered with
     needlework in blue and purple and scarlet stuff and fine twined
     linen; it was twenty cubits long and five cubits high in its breadth,
19   corresponding to the hangings of the court. And their pillars were
     four; their four bases were of bronze, their hooks of silver, and the
20   overlaying of their capitals and their fillets of silver. And all the pegs
     for the tabernacle and for the court round about were of bronze.

For comments see 27:1–8; 27:9–19; 30:18.

The Cost of the Sanctuary (38:21–31)

21   This is the sum of the things for the tabernacle, the tabernacle of the
     testimony, as they were counted at the commandment of Moses, for
     the work of the Levites under the direction of Ithamar the son of
22   Aaron the priest. Bezalel the son of Uri, son of Hur, of the tribe of
23   Judah, made all that the Lord commanded Moses; and with him was
     Oholiab the son of Ahisamach, of the tribe of Dan, a craftsman and
     designer and embroiderer in blue and purple and scarlet stuff and
     fine twined linen.
24   All the gold that was used for the work, in all the construction of
     the sanctuary, the gold from the offering, was twenty-nine talents
     and seven hundred and thirty shekels, by the shekel of the sanctuary.
25   And the silver from those of the congregation who were numbered
     was a hundred talents and a thousand seven hundred and seventy-

26 five shekels, by the shekel of the sanctuary: a beka a head (that is, half a shekel, by the shekel of the sanctuary), for every one who was numbered in the census, from twenty years old and upward, for six
27 hundred and three thousand, five hundred and fifty men. The hundred talents of silver were for casting the bases of the sanctuary, and the bases of the veil; a hundred bases for the hundred talents, a
28 talent for a base. And of the thousand seven hundred and seventy-five shekels he made hooks for the pillars, and overlaid their capitals and
29 made fillets for them. And the bronze that was contributed was
30 seventy talents, and two thousand and four hundred shekels; with it he made the bases for the door of the tent of meeting, the bronze
31 altar and the bronze grating for it and all the utensils of the altar, the bases round about the court, and the bases of the gate of the court, all the pegs of the tabernacle, and all the pegs round about the court.

After a due recognition of the leaders of the work—however much a person has been endowed by God, we should always be ready to give him due credit—there follows a reckoning of all the metal used in the work. In our ignorance of the exact value of the shekel of the sanctuary we are unable to translate the weights into their modern equivalents. Hyatt suggests gold 1,900 lbs., silver 6,437 lbs., bronze 4,522 lbs.

In the modern world it is sometimes legitimate to ask whether the immense value in church plate, etc., could not be put to better use, as did the Communists, when they came to power in Russia, but in the wilderness and even after the Conquest the riches involved in the building and equipping of the Tabernacle had no other use or value, so that the problems that so often face the wealthier Christian today did not affect the Israelites.

The Making of Aaron's Robes (39:1–31)

1 And of the blue and purple and scarlet stuff they made finely wrought garments, for ministering in the holy place; they made the holy garments for Aaron; as the Lord had commanded Moses.
2 And he made the ephod of gold, blue and purple and scarlet stuff,
3 and fine twined linen. And gold leaf was hammered out and cut into threads to work into the blue and purple and the scarlet stuff, and
4 into the fine twined linen, in skilled design. They made for the ephod

5 shoulder-pieces, joined to it at its two edges. And the skilfully woven band upon it, to gird it on, was of the same materials and workmanship, of gold, blue and purple and scarlet stuff, and fine twined linen; as the Lord had commanded Moses.

6 The onyx stones were prepared, enclosed in settings of gold filigree and engraved like the engravings of a signet, according to the
7 names of the sons of Israel. And he set them on the shoulder-pieces of the ephod, to be stones of remembrance for the sons of Israel; as the Lord had commanded Moses.

8 He made the breastpiece, in skilled work, like the work of the ephod, of gold, blue and purple and scarlet stuff, and fine twined
9 linen. It was square; the breastpiece was made double, a span its
10 length and a span its breadth when doubled. And they set in it four rows of stones. A row of sardius, topaz, and carbuncle was the first
11 row; and the second row, an emerald, a sapphire, and a diamond;
12 13 and the third row, a jacinth, an agate, and an amethyst; and the fourth row, a beryl, an onyx, and a jasper; they were enclosed in
14 settings of gold filigree. There were twelve stones with their names according to the names of the sons of Israel; they were like signets,
15 each engraved with its name, for the twelve tribes. And they made on
16 the breastpiece twisted chains like cords, of pure gold; and they made two settings of gold filigree and two gold rings, and put the two rings
17 on the two edges of the breastpiece; and they put the two cords of
18 gold in the two rings at the edges of the breastpiece. Two ends of the two cords they had attached to the two settings of filigree; thus they
19 attached it in front to the shoulder-pieces of the ephod. Then they made two rings of gold, and put them at the two ends of the
20 breastpiece, on its inside edge next to the ephod. And they made two rings of gold, and attached them in front to the lower part of the two shoulder-pieces of the ephod, at its joining above the skilfully woven
21 band of the ephod. And they bound the breastpiece by its rings to the rings of the ephod with a lace of blue, so that it should lie upon the skilfully woven band of the ephod, and that the breastpiece should not come loose from the ephod; as the Lord had commanded Moses.

22 23 He also made the robe of the ephod woven all of blue; and the opening of the robe in it was like the opening in a garment, with a
24 binding around the opening, that it might not be torn. On the skirts of the robe they made pomegranates of blue and purple and scarlet
25 stuff and fine twined linen. They also made bells of pure gold, and put the bells between the pomegranates upon the skirts of the robe

26 round about, between the pomegranates; a bell and a pomegranate, a bell and a pomegranate round about upon the skirts of the robe for ministering; as the Lord had commanded Moses.

27 They also made the coats, woven of fine linen, for Aaron and his
28 sons, and the turban of fine linen, and the caps of fine linen, and the
29 linen breeches of fine twined linen, and the girdle of fine twined linen and of blue and purple and scarlet stuff, embroidered with needlework; as the Lord had commanded Moses.

30 And they made the plate of the holy crown of pure gold, and wrote upon it an inscription, like the engraving of a signet, "Holy to the
31 Lord." And they tied to it a lace of blue, to fasten it on the turban above; as the Lord had commanded Moses.

See comments on chapter 28. In several verses there is a special mention that the God-given instructions had been followed, presumably because in the making of clothes deviations from the pattern would be easier than with the larger objects.

The Erection of the Tabernacle (39:32–40:33)

32 Thus all the work of the tabernacle of the tent of meeting was finished; and the people of Israel had done according to all that the
33 Lord had commanded Moses; so had they done. And they brought the tabernacle to Moses, the tent and all its utensils, its hooks, its
34 frames, its bars, its pillars, and its bases; the covering of tanned
35 rams' skins and goatskins, and the veil of the screen; the ark of the
36 testimony with its poles and the mercy seat; the table with all its
37 utensils, and the bread of the Presence; the lampstand of pure gold and its lamps with the lamps set and all its utensils, and the oil for the
38 light; the golden altar, the anointing oil and the fragrant incense,
39 and the screen for the door of the tent; the bronze altar, and its grating of bronze, its poles, and all its utensils; the laver and its base;
40 the hangings of the court, its pillars, and its bases, and the screen for the gate of the court, its cords, and its pegs; and all the utensils for
41 the service of the tabernacle, for the tent of meeting; the finely worked garments for ministering in the holy place, the holy garments for Aaron the priest, and the garments of his sons to serve as
42 priests. According to all that the Lord had commanded Moses, so
43 the people of Israel had done all the work. And Moses saw all the work, and behold, they had done it; as the Lord had commanded, so had they done it. And Moses blessed them.

1 2   The Lord said to Moses, "On the first day of the first month you
3 shall erect the tabernacle of the tent of meeting. And you shall put in
it the ark of the testimony, and you shall screen the ark with the veil.
4 And you shall bring in the table, and set its arrangements in order;
5 and you shall bring in the lampstand, and set up its lamps. And you
shall put the golden altar for incense before the ark of the testimony,
6 and set up the screen for the door of the tabernacle. You shall set the
altar of burnt offering before the door of the tabernacle of the tent of
7 meeting, and place the laver between the tent of meeting and the
8 altar, and put water in it. And you shall set up the court round
9 about, and hang up the screen for the gate of the court. Then you
shall take the anointing oil, and anoint the tabernacle and all that is
in it, and consecrate it and all its furniture; and it shall become holy.
10 You shall also anoint the altar of burnt offering and all its utensils,
11 and consecrate the altar; and the altar shall be most holy. You shall
12 also anoint the laver and its base, and consecrate it. Then you shall
bring Aaron and his sons to the door of the tent of meeting, and shall
13 wash them with water, and put upon Aaron the holy garments, and
you shall anoint him and consecrate him, that he may serve me as
14 priest. You shall bring his sons also and put coats on them, and
15 anoint them, as you anointed their father, that they may serve me as
priests: and their anointing shall admit them to a perpetual priesthood throughout their generations."

16   Thus did Moses; according to all that the Lord commanded him,
17 so he did. And in the first month in the second year, on the first day
18 of the month, the tabernacle was erected. Moses erected the tabernacle; he laid its bases, and set up its frames, and put in its poles, and
19 raised up its pillars; and he spread the tent over the tabernacle, and
put the covering of the tent over it, as the Lord had commanded
20 Moses. And he took the testimony and put it into the ark, and put
21 the poles on the ark, and set the mercy seat above on the ark; and he
brought the ark into the tabernacle, and set up the veil of the screen,
and screened the ark of the testimony; as the Lord had commanded
22 Moses. And he put the table in the tent of meeting, on the north side
23 of the tabernacle, outside the veil, and set the bread in order on it
24 before the Lord; as the Lord had commanded Moses. And he put the
lampstand in the tent of meeting, opposite the table on the south side
25 of the tabernacle, and set up the lamps before the Lord; as the Lord
26 had commanded Moses. And he put the golden altar in the tent of
27 meeting before the veil, and burnt fragrant incense upon it; as the
28 Lord had commanded Moses. And he put in place the screen for the

29 door of the tabernacle. And he set the altar of burnt offering at the
door of the tabernacle of the tent of meeting, and offered upon it the
burnt offering and the cereal offering; as the Lord had commanded
30 Moses. And he set the laver between the tent of meeting and the
31 altar, and put water in it for washing, with which Moses and Aaron
32 and his sons washed their hands and their feet; when they went into
the tent of meeting, and when they approached the altar, they
33 washed; as the Lord commanded Moses. And he erected the court
round the tabernacle and the altar, and set up the screen of the gate
of the court. So Moses finished the work.

To Moses had been given a vision of the Tabernacle while he
was on Mount Sinai (25:9, 40; 26:30), and so he had to check each
individual part of the work to see whether it matched the master
plan. There will be a blessing for us also, if our work fits into
Christ's master plan for the Church.

Nearly a year after the Exodus the work was finished, for
there was little else for the people to do and they worked whole-
heartedly. Not Aaron and his sons, as would be the case later,
but Moses himself had the satisfaction of erecting the finished
Tabernacle and seeing to it that everything accorded with the
vision engraved on his memory. He it was that also offered the
first burnt offering (40:29). Aaron was not consecrated until
after this.

"So Moses finished the work" (verse 33). In so far as man
could do God's work, Moses had done it, but it was one greater
than he, who with virtually his last breath could truly say "It is
finished!" (John 19:30).

God's Amen (40:34–38)

34 Then the cloud covered the tent of meeting, and the glory of the
35 Lord filled the tabernacle. And Moses was not able to enter the tent
of meeting, because the cloud abode upon it, and the glory of the
36 Lord filled the tabernacle. Throughout all their journeys, whenever
the cloud was taken up from over the tabernacle, the people of Israel
37 would go onward; but if the cloud was not taken up, then they did
38 not go onward till the day that it was taken up. For throughout all
their journeys the cloud of the Lord was upon the tabernacle by day,
and fire was in it by night, in the sight of all the house of Israel.

By God's grace a man may complete the work to which he has been called, but it needs God's seal before it can be of use to his fellow men. All the symbolism of God's presence was there, but the symbolism without the reality was of no use. So God's glory filled the Tabernacle (compare 1 Kgs. 8:10–11) to guarantee that the effectiveness of what would be done there would not depend on the priests but on God himself. Even so, when the Servant of Yahweh prayed on the Mount of Transfiguration, and the "Majestic Glory" (2 Pet. 1:17) bore witness to him, it was the guarantee that, as the Lamb of God went on to Jerusalem, God in Christ was reconciling the world to himself (2 Cor. 5:19).

THE CHRISTIAN AND THE TABERNACLE

It should need very little argument to convince the reader, that if the details of the Tabernacle are given so fully, and such stress is laid on their having been faithfully carried out, those who made it and used it for worship were intended to draw spiritual lessons from it. The Epistle to the Hebrews takes this for granted and encourages us to believe that these lessons are not without value for the Christian, even if, for the most part, unlike his spiritual ancestors, he tends to lay decreasing value on the symbolic in worship. When he does, it is apt to be negative, i.e. he often stresses what he does not do, rather than what he does. But since the positive is always likely to be more spiritually enriching, we will do well to look at some of its positive lessons before we end our daily readings in the book of Exodus. These thoughts must be inadequate since the actual ritual of worship is dealt with in Leviticus.

THE CENTRALITY OF WORSHIP

In the ancient Near-Eastern world it was axiomatic that a town's main temple and the royal palace should be in a central and dominant position. This was obvious to the Israelite, where the Tabernacle and later the Temple were concerned, for they contained the Ark of the Covenant, the visible throne of Yahweh, the king of Israel. At a much later date the rabbis laid down that whenever it was possible a synagogue should be built in a dominant position in a Jewish community. So while there is in all probability an idealistic element in the rules laid down in a passage like Numbers chapter 2—natural features and the lie of the land would frequently have made a literal implementation impossible—they certainly express the Israelite ideal.

It is a very ancient British and indeed European tradition, increasingly being forgotten in our secularized age, that the village should be dominated by its church, the city by its cathedral. Indeed the status of "city" used to depend less in Britain on the size of a community and more on its possession of a cathedral.

We desperately need to recapture today the age-old concept of the centrality of God both for the individual and for community life.

THE CONCEPT OF THE HOLY

There are few visitors to Jerusalem who are not deeply impressed by the spaciousness of the *Haram esh-Sherif* (the Temple Area), which so markedly sets off the beauty of the Dome of the Rock. Such spaciousness was King Herod's intention, when he enlarged the Temple Area to its present size, but he did not merely wish the beauty of his rebuilt temple to be clearly seen; he wanted to stress the holiness of the site. The spaciousness was intended to stress the separation, i.e. the holiness of God.

Though on a much smaller scale, the same effect was created by the Tabernacle. The worshipper entering the Tabernacle court was faced by an almost empty space, seventy-five feet each way (27:9-19) in front of the Tent itself. The only objects breaking the emptiness were the altar of burnt offering and the laver.

The basic concept behind "holy" (*qadosh*) was that God, or the gods, were separated from man, being essentially different.

The bringing of man into contact with God creates that sense of awe we so often meet in the Old Testament (3:6; 20:18–20; 34:8), which has been called the "numinous". Perhaps the best examples in the Bible are the fear of the disciples on the Mount of Transfiguration (Mark 9:6) and of John at the vision of the glorified Christ (Rev. 1:17).

In many cases this fear expressed itself by an effort to place distance between the worshipper and the deity. In the Tabernacle this was done by the virtually empty court with its two symbols of cleansing, the altar and the laver, and the outer section of the Tent, which none but the priests might enter.

The classic expression of this aspect of God's holiness is found in God's words to Moses, "You cannot see my face, for man shall not see my face and live" (33:20).

It seems that it was not until Isaiah that the realization really came that the separation between man and God was caused essentially by man's sinful nature, and so "holy" acquired an essentially moral connotation, as it has with us today.

The position for the Christian was in its turn radically changed, when God "veiled in flesh" dwelt among men, and so we are urged to "draw near with a true heart in full assurance of faith" (Heb. 10:22).

Nevertheless, there are grave dangers in forgetting the older meaning of "holy". In wide circles today few signs are shown that there is any consciousness of God's holiness, and hence of the respect that should be shown him. The lack of respect is shown in the language, music and dress used, and not seldom in the architecture of the building. There seems in these circles to be little understanding for the hymn:

Yes, we know that Thou rejoicest
  O'er each work of Thine,
Thou didst ears and hands and voices
  For Thy praise design-
Craftsman's art and music's measure
  For Thy pleasure
    All combine.

It is true that the justification urged is that we can thus best attract the illiterate, the poor, the deprived, but such surely existed in Israel, and there is no evidence that compromise was made in the Tabernacle on their behalf. Lack of respect may attract some, but probably repels more.

THE CONCEPT OF ATONEMENT

Most modern Westerners would be thoroughly disgusted and repelled could they be transported back in time to a session of worship in the Tabernacle, or the Temple that followed it. It was not until the rise of the Synagogue during the Inter-Testamental period that the worship of Israel ceased to be dominated by sacrifice. Sacrificial worship was concerned mainly with the propitiation (AV, RV) of God, or with expiation (RSV) before God. However little many modern Christians may like this, they cannot deny that the New Testament, especially in its evaluation of the death of Christ, is dominated by these concepts. To seek to eliminate this element from the New Testament would reduce it to rags.

Our modern dislike of the worship of Israel does not at all mean that we have nothing to learn from it.

Meaningful ritual seeks to act out a reality difficult to express in words. For the outsider, who happened to learn the details of the Tabernacle, it would have appeared absurd that the Ark of the Covenant, the only visible sign of Yahweh's presence among the people—for there was no image—should be hidden away in the darkness of the innermost tent, unseen by any except the officiating priest on the Day of Atonement. However we may explain them, the golden bulls of Jeroboam were obviously visible to the worshippers (1 Kgs. 12:26–29).

For the Israelites, however, this apparent absurdity was, or should have been, deeply significant. The Ark, containing the tables of the Covenant, was the positive, concrete sign that Yahweh had come among them, delivered them from bondage and made them his people, but as Solomon said at the dedication of the Temple, "Yahweh has set the sun in the heavens, but has said he would dwell in thick darkness" (1 Kgs. 8:12). This was in essence repeated many years later by "Isaiah", "Truly, thou art a God who hidest thyself, O God of Israel, the Saviour" (Isa. 45:15).

Though God revealed himself to Israel and intervened in history on their behalf, there was a point beyond which he did not go, even as it is said of his supreme revelation in Jesus Christ, that he did not "trust himself" to those who believed in his name, when they saw the signs which he did (John 2:24).

The whole ritual of the Tabernacle revolves around the concept that communion with this half-revealed, half-hidden God depends on sacrifice. The blood, which has played an exaggerated role in some of our hymns, stood simply as a symbol of life laid down. The attitude of many of the prophets towards sacrifice makes it clear that they had realized the truth of the New Testament statement, "It is impossible that the blood of bulls and goats should take away sins" (Heb. 10:4). On the highest and deepest level the New Testament teaching is that the death of Christ makes it possible for a man to begin a new life, to die to the past; cf. John 3:3,5; Gal. 2:20; Rom. 12:1–2.

The purpose of the ritual was atonement, not in its modern sense, but in its original meaning at-one-ment, i.e. reconciliation. The wider usage of the Hebrew word employed suggests that this was achieved by "covering" the wrongdoing. Later writers, however, realized that more was involved than this, e.g. "I have swept away your transgressions like a cloud, and your sins like mist" (Isa. 44:22) and "Thou wilt cast all our sins into the depth of the sea" (Mic. 7:19). But, however we interpret the ritual of the Tabernacle, it stresses that the initiative in the forgiving of man's sin has been taken by God. Similarly the New Testament assures us that "God was in Christ reconciling the world to himself" (2 Cor. 5:19). The history of Christian theology shows that man cannot fathom the mystery of God's love and working, but just as the cross stands as the assurance of God's forgiveness going out to all men today, so the Tabernacle with its ritual served God's first people Israel in past centuries.

APPENDICES

Appendix I. JETHRO

Moses' father-in-law is called Jethro in 3:1, 4:18 and repeatedly in chapter 18. But in 2:18 he is Reuel. In Num. 10:29 he is apparently Hobab, while Reuel is his father, and this agrees with Judg. 4:11, but in these passages the NEB renders brother-in-law as against the RSV, JB, and the NIV, father-in-law. However we explain this, Moses' father-in-law had two names, Jethro and either Reuel or Hobab. If it was Reuel, which could mean "Shepherd of God", it could be a title for "the priest of Midian". McNeile cut the knot by assuming that Reuel was father of Jethro-Hobab, and that its appearance in 2:18 is due to an early scribal error.

Appendix II. THE NAME YAHWEH

Out of respect the Massoretes, the scribes to whom we owe the Hebrew Bible in its definitive form, gave no indication how this name or title of the God of Israel should be pronounced. The form Jehovah is due to a misunderstanding by Christians at the time of the Reformation; it is indubitably wrong. Though there is no absolute proof that Yahweh is correct, it may be regarded as virtually certain.

On the basis of certain phenomena in Genesis and especially on the apparently obvious interpretation of Exod. 6:1–3—but see comment on the passage—it has been widely held for nearly two centuries that the use of Yahweh for Israel's God began in the time of Moses, even though this theory is in contradiction to Gen. 4:26 and much of the usage of Genesis. This has in turn led to a variety of theories as to the origin of the name.

One of the more interesting is the one put forward by the Jewish scholar Martin Buber, who sought to reconcile conflicting views and to do justice to all the facts. He pointed out that beside Yahweh we find Yah (AV Jah), and in proper names Yah- and Ye-; also -iah, -iahu, etc. He maintained that it was most improbable that the divine name should have been abbreviated, so he suggested Yaho or Yahu as its original form, a call on God in worship with no definite meaning. The change of spelling at the bush linked it with the verb "to be"; see the comment on 3:14.

Appendix III. THE HARDENING OF PHARAOH'S HEART

In Hebrew anthropology the heart represents the whole inner man. In our terminology it represents the intellect, the will and the emotions. Which aspect is chiefly intended can be deduced only from the context, though when special emphasis is being laid on the emotions, the kidneys (AV reins) or liver may be used.

This means that when we find that Pharaoh's heart has been hardened, it does not necessarily mean that he was what we call a hard-hearted man.

Three different words are used in Exodus. Most commonly his heart is said to be or to be made strong. In about half the number of cases it is said to be or to be made heavy. These two uses are distinguished in the RV margin. Once, only, is it said to be hardened (7:3).

Pharaoh's heart is said to be hard in 7:13,14,22; 8:19; 9:17, 35. He is said to harden it himself in 8:15,32; 9:34. The hardening is attributed to God in 4:21; 7:3; 9:12; 10:1,20,27; 11:10; 14:4,8. Only in 7:3 is the translation "to harden" fully justified.

It seems clear that the very common fault of obstinacy, deliberate and unjustifiable obstinacy, is intended. In Pharaoh this was to be expected when we consider his upbringing and conviction that he was divine.

With this type of obstinacy a certain amount of diplomacy in approach can often work marvels. We may well understand God's hardening as meaning that he did not employ an approach through Moses that might have had such a diplomatic effect.

FURTHER READING

COMMENTARIES

B.S. Childs, *Exodus, A Commentary* (Old Testament Library), 1974

R.E. Clements, *Exodus* (The Cambridge Bible Commentary on the New English Bible), 1972

R.A. Cole, *Exodus* (Tyndale Old Testament Commentaries), 1973

G. Henton Davies, *Exodus* (Torch Bible Commentaries), 1967

S.R. Driver, *The Book of Exodus in the Revised Version* (Cambridge Bible for Schools and Colleges), 1918

J.H. Hertz, *The Pentateuch and Haftorahs,* 1938

J.P. Hyatt, *Exodus* (New Century Bible), revised ed., 1980

A.H. McNeile, *The Book of Exodus* (Westminster Commentaries), 3rd ed., 1931

STUDIES

W.F. Albright, *Archaeology and the Religion of Israel,* 1942

W.F. Albright, *From the Stone Age to Christianity,* 2nd ed., 1957

John Bright, *A History of Israel,* 2nd ed., 1972

Martin Buber, *Moses,* 1946

R.S. Cansdale, *Animals of Bible Lands,* 1970

J. Garstang, *Joshua: Judges,* 1931

C.S. Jarvis, *Yesterday and Today in Sinai,* 1931

R. de Vaux, *Studies in Old Testament Sacrifice,* 1964